Edith Stein

Edith Stein

A Philosophical Prologue, 1913–1922

Alasdair MacIntyre

A SHEED & WARD BOOK

ROWMAN & LITTLEFIELD PUBLISHERS, INC.
Lanham • Boulder • New York • Toronto • Plymouth, UK

A Sheed & Ward Book

ROWMAN & LITTLEFIELD PUBLISHERS, INC.

Published in the United States of America
by Rowman & Littlefield Publishers, Inc.
A wholly owned subsidiary of The Rowman & Littlefield Publishing Group, Inc.
4501 Forbes Boulevard, Suite 200, Lanham, Maryland 20706
www.rowmanlittlefield.com

Estover Road
Plymouth PL6 7PY
United Kingdom

British Library Cataloguing in Publication Information Available

Library of Congress Cataloging-in-Publication Data

The hardback edition of this book was previously cataloged by the Library of
Congress as follows:

MacIntyre, Alasdair C.
   Edith Stein : a philosophical prologue, 1913–1922 / Alasdair MacIntyre.
      p. cm.
   1. Stein, Edith, Saint, 1891–1942. 2. Philosophy, Modern—20th century. I. Title.
BX4705.S814M33 2005
193—dc22

2005011093

   ISBN-13: 978-0-7425-4995-1 (cloth : alk. paper)
   ISBN-10: 0-7425-4995-X (cloth : alk. paper)
   ISBN-13: 978-0-7425-5953-0 (pbk. : alk. paper)
   ISBN-10: 0-7425-5953-X (pbk. : alk. paper)

Printed in the United States of America

Contents

Contents

To the Reader

This book is an attempt both to give some account of Edith Stein's beginnings as a philosopher and to understand her life—or at least the part of it treated in this book—as one kind of philosophical life possible in the twentieth century. The need for the first of these tasks arises from the general neglect of her philosophical work in the English-speaking world. There is no entry for Edith Stein in the *Oxford Dictionary of Philosophy*, the *Cambridge Dictionary of Philosophy*, the *Oxford Companion to Philosophy*, or the *Routledge Encyclopedia of Philosophy*. In the *Blackwell Companion to Continental Philosophy* her name is nowhere mentioned. So is her work as devoid of philosophical interest as this would suggest?

One reason why her work has been undervalued may be that its significance can only be adequately understood, when it is viewed in its philosophical contexts, first as a set of contributions first to phenomenological enquiry and later to Thomistic and other Neoscholastic enquiries, and secondly as one particular kind of response to the condition of German philosophy in the first four decades of the twentieth century. But to view it in this light it is necessary also to understand something of the course of German philosophy from the late nineteenth century onwards and the responses to its condition by Edith Stein's predecessors and contemporaries. So in order to explain and situate her work I have had to tell a somewhat larger and longer tale. This narrative serves an additional purpose. It enables us, I hope, to acquire some sense of the relationship of Edith Stein's philosophy to her life, by considering not only the philosophical context of her own and her contemporaries' work, but also the social context within which she worked.

Where contemporary American and European academic philosophers are concerned, Edith Stein suffers from another marked disadvantage. She has been canonized. And among the prejudices of most such philosophers is a belief not only that what makes a philosopher a good philosopher is one thing and what makes someone a saint in the judgment of the Catholic church quite another—which is true—but also that saintliness, unless you have been dead for a very, very long time, precludes philosophical merit. It would have been difficult enough to convince such philosophers to take an interest in Edith Stein. But to convince them to take an interest in St. Teresa Benedicta a Cruce, Discalced Carmelite, will be a good deal more difficult.

Yet there are of course also readers, not professional philosophers, some but not all of them Catholics, who will be interested in the philosophy just because it was *her* philosophy. And I have therefore tried, so far as possible, to make my narrative intelligible to them. The result may have been to fall between two stools, to have written in too simple and introductory a way for those with established philosophical interests, while at the same time making matters too complex and inaccessible for lay readers. Yet it seems worthwhile to make this attempt to address the educated common reader.

What I have written is not a scholarly work. My references are almost all to texts available to English readers, not to the German originals, and I have relied on the translations of others, rather than making my own. My account of Edith Stein's life is drawn from standard biographical sources and those who are primarily or exclusively interested in having a full and detailed account of that life will do well to go to those sources rather than to read this book. I am deeply indebted to a number of previous writers about Edith Stein, including Dr. Waltraut Stein, Sister Waltraud Herbstrith, O.C.D., Sister Teresia de Spirito Sanctu, O.C.D., and Sister Maria Amata Neyer, O.C.D. I am especially grateful to Dr. Marianne Sawicki whose remarkable work of scholarship and translation has become an indispensable aid for anyone writing about Edith Stein. To her I have a more particular debt, since she read an earlier version of this book and saved me from a number of errors. Her generosity is all the greater, in that she and I disagree on some key matters. I am similarly grateful to my colleague, Karl Ameriks, for correction and commentary, once again from a different perspective from my own. And I am also very much in debt to Robert Sokolowski, who read this book in typescript for my publisher and whose comments and criticisms were quite unusually valuable. My greatest debt of all is to the late Sister Mary Catharine Baseheart of the Sisters of Charity of Nazareth, Professor of Philosophy at Spalding University, and founder of its Edith Stein Center for Study and Research.

Finally, let me put on record some large debts of a different kind. This book would not exist but for the patient, unflagging and generous help of Claire Shely and, during her absence, of Rosalee Hamlin. I was able to complete it only because of the support afforded by my colleagues at the Center for Ethics and Culture of the University of Notre Dame, where I have been a fellow since 2000, and especially that best of all colleagues, its director, David Solomon. I must also give special mention to Tracy Westlake, who restores order to chaos over and over again. To all of them my thanks and my admiration.

Alasdair MacIntyre

discalced carmelite
└ order fm 13th century
└ shoeless / barefoot / or w/ sandals

Acknowledgments

I wish to thank ICS Publications and Brother Bryan Paquette O.C.D. for permission to quote from the following works published by ICS Publications:

from *On the Problem of Empathy* by Edith Stein translated by Waltraut Stein, Ph.D. Copyright © 1989 by Washington Province of Discalced Carmelites ICS Publications 2131 Lincoln Road, N.E. Washington, DC 20002-1199 U.S.A. www.icspublications.org;

from *Self-Portrait in Letters* by Edith Stein translated by Josephine Koeppel, O.C.D. Copyright © 1993 by Washington Province of Discalced Carmelites ICS Publications 2131 Lincoln Road, N.E. Washington, DC 20002-1199 U.S.A. www.icspublications.org;

from *Life in a Jewish Family* by Edith Stein translated by Josephine Koeppel, O.C.D. Copyright © 1986 by Washington Province of Discalced Carmelites ICS Publications 2131 Lincoln Road, N.E. Washington, DC 20002-1199 U.S.A. www.icspublications.org;

from *Philosophy of Psychology and the Humanities* by Edith Stein translated by Mary Catharine Baseheart and Marianne Sawicki. Copyright © by Washington Province of Discalced Carmelites ICS Publications 2131 Lincoln Road, N.E. Washington, DC 20002-1199 U.S.A. www.icspublications.org;

from *Knowledge and Faith* by Edith Stein translated by Walter Redmond. Copyright © by Washington Province of Discalced Carmelites ICS Publications 2131 Lincoln Road, N.E. Washington, DC 20002-1199 U.S.A. www.icspublications.org.

For his kindness in identifying and enabling me to correct a number and variety of small errors in the text as originally published I am grateful to Professor Reinhard Hütter.

1

Why Take an Interest in Edith Stein as a Philosopher?

When in the third century of the Christian era Diogenes Laertius wrote his ten books on the lives of famous philosophers, beginning with Thales and ending with Epicurus, he did so from a conviction, shared with his intended readers, that the salient facts about philosophical enquiry and philosophical conclusions concern the difference that philosophy makes to the lives of those engaged in its practice. What is important about philosophy is the way in which a life informed by the activities of philosophical enquiry and guided by its conclusions will be significantly different from the life of someone in other respects like the philosopher, but untouched by philosophy. The disagreements between rival philosophies are in this view, commonly held in the ancient Greco-Roman world, differences not only in theoretical, but in practical commitment, concerning the nature of the human good. So that the lives of philosophers are of philosophical interest.

Modern readers by contrast are apt to see in much—although certainly not all—that Diogenes Laertius wrote little more than gossip tangential to philosophy, perhaps because their own dominant assumption, unlike his, is that, generally speaking, the lives of philosophers are one thing, philosophy itself quite another, and that the incidental and accidental connections between the two are of little importance. So, for example, in Bertrand Russell's *History of Western Philosophy*, each chapter begins with a brisk account of some particular philosopher's life and times, an account which is almost always irrelevant to the exposition and critique of that philosopher's enquiries and conclusions, which follows it. Excise the biography and the history from Russell's book and little or nothing of what he took to be philosophical substance would have been lost.

1

It is scarcely surprising that the vast majority of contemporary European and North American readers should share the attitudes of Russell rather than those of Diogenes Laertius. For 'philosophy' in our culture has become the name of a specialized, professionalized, academic discipline, and the role of the professional philosopher is socially defined and circumscribed, so that almost, even if not quite universally it is not the highly specific activities of philosophical enquiry or the particular philosophical conclusions which some philosopher defends, but rather the status-bearing and role-playing that are characteristic of *any* professionalized academic which determine the overall shape of a professional philosopher's life. Philosophers, like other professionalized academics, become licensed, through competing success-fully in those tests that lead to the *Agrégation* and its sequels, or to the doc-torate and the *Habilitationsschrift*, or to the Ph.D., and that success is achieved by performing a series of demanding tasks designed to render one obedient and conformable to the specializations and compartmentalizations of the professional life. Moreover, the evident expectations of one's senior colleagues are that one will respectfully conform in private life to the general norms of the professional classes, in a way that makes one's particular aca-demic discipline, let alone one's own particular enquiries, irrelevant to one's everyday life. Correspondingly, one's students will generally have learned that the tasks required of them in philosophy courses are something soon to be left behind, part of an educational routine leading towards the achieve-ment of career goals, already determined for them and by them, very likely before they had ever entered upon the study of philosophy, and not liable to be changed by that study. The norms of both teachers and students are well designed for the purpose of defending everyday social life from inva-sion by philosophy.

There are of course exceptions: contemporary or recent philosophers who are notable for violating these socially constraining norms, philosophers whose conclusions and modes of argument inform their activities in areas outside philosophy. Lukács in his earlier life provided one type of example, Sartre and de Beauvoir another. But notice how the work of these excep-tional cases is usually treated within academic philosophy. Characteristically and generally, in a manner reminiscent of Russell's *History*, their philosoph-ical thought, insofar as it enters the curriculum, is abstracted from its context in their lives and presented as matter for purely academic examination, as thought which can be appropriated by us without any question of the con-sequences of that thought for their lives and therefore for ours ever arising.

Yet at the same time contemporary philosophy, even when most con-strained by its academic, professionalized, specialized norms, nonetheless also sustains within itself a very different conception of its relationship to the actions of those who engage in it in any systematic way, and it does so just because it is philosophy. For philosophy, if it is to be recognizable as philosophy, must always be understood as a continuation of Plato's enterprise. And Plato's conclusion that engagement in the life of philosophy necessarily involves a radical critique of the everyday social life of political societies, and a consequent withdrawal from that life into a particular type of philosophical community, remains one with which, explicitly or implicitly, everyone who engages in philosophy has somehow or other to come to terms. One way of coming to terms with it is of course to endorse by making explicit the dominant contemporary view and so denying the relevance of philosophy to everyday practical activity. But this has a clear initial implausibility. How so?

That implausibility derives from the fact that our everyday activities, including our political activities, often presuppose and give expression to beliefs which already have an evidently philosophical character. Characteristically and generally the rules which tacitly or explicitly guide each of us in inferring from past experience to the legitimacy of future expectations, the grounds upon which we rely in ascribing to others those thoughts and feelings to which we respond in our own cooperative or uncooperative actions, the frameworks in terms of which we order our experiences, the type and degree of authority which we concede or deny to particular moral standpoints, the patterns of the reasoning which supports our evaluations of a variety of religious and political claims, and the relationships between all of these are such as either to accord with or to be at odds with theses and arguments debated within philosophy. Partly this is because the very language that we cannot avoid speaking, our everyday vocabulary and idiom, is itself not philosophically innocent, but to a significant degree inherited from and still informed by past philosophical theories whose presence in our modes of speech, belief and action is no longer recognized. What, for example, are taken to be prosaic maxims of mere common sense are often enough fragments of past philosophies, still carrying with them some of the presuppositions of the contexts from which they were abstracted. But it is also because our everyday idioms, beliefs and assumptions, even when not informed by past philosophies, are, to an extent that is not always remarked, theory-laden, committing us thereby to unrecognized philosophical allegiances. So that someone who avails her or himself of some opportunity to participate in systematic institutionalized philosophical enquiry is always apt to find some degree of tension and incoherence between the beliefs and modes of reasoning which she or he has brought with her or him to that participation and those conclusions and arguments to which she or he has come to give her or his allegiance in the course of philosophical enquiry. Such tensions and incoherencies can of course always be disregarded by resolutely turning away from philosophical enquiry.

Yet even without the initial stimulus afforded by engagement with philosophical enquiry, tensions and incoherencies within our own beliefs or radical disagreements between others and us may prompt reflections about our everyday judgments and activities that in time become philosophical. For we may well discover that, when incoherences identified in our own beliefs or issues uncovered through disagreement with others compel us to ask whether we do indeed have sufficiently good reasons for asserting what we have hitherto asserted, we may not be able to respond adequately except without posing such questions as 'What in relation to this subject matter is a good rather than a bad reason?' and 'How are we to evaluate rival arguments?' If we do pose such questions persistently, we will already have begun, even if tentatively, to engage in philosophical enquiry, enquiry which may in the end require of us conclusions mandating more or less drastic changes in our everyday beliefs and activities. So that whether the problems of the relationship of our everyday beliefs and activities to philosophical enquiry initially arise from encounter with some form of already ongoing philosophical activity—as for some in fourth-century Athens, second-century Nalanda, ninth-century Baghdad and nineteenth-century Berlin—or instead is generated from within reflections occasioned by everyday life, it may be that such problems cannot be rationally resolved without some degree of transformation of our previously held beliefs, activities and relationships.

That philosophy may have this transforming and perhaps disruptive effect receives its most signal recognition in the sentences of death or exile occasionally imposed on philosophers and the condemnations of philosophical books sometimes issued by those with a responsibility for sustaining the established order of belief and action in this or that society. What is thereby acknowledged is that philosophy may put in question not only the beliefs of individuals, but also those shared beliefs, embodied in or presupposed by a variety of institutions and practices, a high degree of assent to which is required if the established social and political order is to be sustained. Those beliefs too may be vulnerable to philosophical enquiry, with the result that from time to time it may seem necessary to the guardians of order to resort to drastic measures. Such sentences and condemnations are of course not the only or even the most effective ways of preventing philosophy from having a transforming and disruptive influence. Imprisoning philosophy within the professionalizations and specializations of an institutionalized curriculum, after the manner of our own contemporary European and North American culture, is arguably a good deal more effective in neutralizing its effects than either religious censorship or political terror. But because in our case the outcome thus contrived, the neutralization of the influence of philosophy, is largely unintended, it involves no explicit tribute to the social power of philosophy of the kind offered by such very different regimes as that of the Athenian *polis* in its treatment of Anaxagoras and Socrates, of the members of the English Parliament who condemned *Leviathan*, and that of the authorities who used to enforce the *Index Librorum Prohibitorum*.

Modern totalitarian rulers who prescribe ideological conformity and punish dissent savagely, such as those of the Soviet Union under Stalin, Khrushchev and Brezhnev, or those of Nazi Germany, or those of the contemporary regimes of China and Saudi Arabia, may seem to provide equally clear examples of conflicts between established power and philosophy. But it can be and has been argued that in fact what they exemplify is something rather different. For such regimes consider themselves threatened by free enquiry of any kind, so that their dealings with philosophy may have little or nothing to do with the specific character of philosophical enquiry, but are rather a matter of the nature of intellectual life in general. Such tyrannies have the effect of encouraging in some individuals a rigid separation between their public, official utterances and their private thoughts, so that a philosopher, like any other intellectual, may in public pay the minimum deference required to whatever happens to be the official ideological standpoint, while in her or his private reflections pursuing lines of thought free from this ideological contamination. Such self-imposed compartmentalization, although importantly different from the curricular compartmentalization of North American academic life, resembles it in encouraging the belief that philosophical thought and enquiry are one thing, the vicissitudes of everyday activity quite another and that any connections between them are incidental and accidental. And it is on the basis of such a belief that some intellectuals later constructed a narrative of their lives during the Nazi period in Germany: how they acted in public was one thing, so they tell us, how they reflected in private quite another.

Just this has been claimed on behalf of Martin Heidegger by others. The history of Heidegger's philosophical development is one thing, so these apologists say, the history of his political commitments and activities quite another. This suggests a deep rift within Heidegger himself, a bifurcation of the personality, so that one set of character traits was exhibited in that part of his life given over to philosophy, but a very different set in his public and political life. Such a rift, such a bifurcation would itself have been a remarkable phenomenon, one inviting close psychological scrutiny. But in fact the story of this division within Heidegger is a piece of mythology, mythology that enables those who teach Heidegger's philosophy in the classrooms of today to domesticate it and render it innocuous, while at the same time projecting onto Heidegger the type of compartmentalization that they take for granted in their own academic lives.

Heidegger himself in the later part of his life cooperated generously with those who were laying the basis for this later myth. But even Heidegger's role as coauthor of the myth is something for which the myth itself can find no place. For Heidegger's postwar activities in constructing a mythological screen behind which much of the truth about his earlier activities could be concealed was itself a continuation of those activities, activities in which questions about the relationship of everyday life to philosophy recurrently arose and were answered both in theory and in practice.

Heidegger's is an extreme case, both in the degree of his political involvement and in the complexity of his attempt to appear to have distanced himself from that involvement. As such, it poses the question: what would it have been in that period of German history in which Heidegger grew up, served his philosophical apprenticeship, and became the most influential of twentieth century German philosophers to have lived quite otherwise as a philosopher, to have consistently taken seriously both the implications for one's life outside philosophy of one's philosophical enquiries and the implications for one's philosophy of one's other activities? One answer to that question is supplied by the life of Edith Stein, a phenomenologist who, unlike Heidegger, moved towards rather than away from the ontology characteristic of Thomism.

Yet it is not just that the history of Stein's philosophical development from her earliest studies to the work on which she was engaged in her years as a Carmelite nun cannot be intelligibly narrated, if it is abstracted from the history of her life as a whole, and that much that is crucial to her life outside philosophy can only be adequately understood in the light of her philosophical development. It is also that she deliberately and intentionally brought her philosophical thinking to bear on the practices of her everyday life and drew upon the experiences afforded by those practices in formulating philosophical problems and arriving at philosophical conclusions. In the years 1913–1922 with which this book is mostly concerned this is perhaps less immediately evident and less striking than it is in Stein's later life. But even in that earlier period the direction of Stein's life beyond a certain point becomes intelligible only in the light of her philosophy, and even before this her philosophical stances are in significant ways informed by her life experiences. So that even at this stage the contrast between her history and Heidegger's is philosophically instructive.

The interest of Edith Stein's philosophical thought is not of course exhausted by considering its relationship to the rest of her life. For, so I shall argue, her enquiries raised crucial and still inadequately answered questions for what were then or were to become influential philosophical movements and positions both in Germany and elsewhere: Husserl's phenomenology, the positions taken by Heidegger in *Sein und Zeit*, and the Thomism of the 1920s and 1930s. Stein was certainly not the only philosopher to pose such questions and the significance of her work perhaps only becomes clear when both her enquiries and her life are compared with those of some of her philosophical contemporaries, including thinkers as different as Franz Rosenzweig, Gyorgy Lukács, Roman Ingarden and Hans Lipps. Stein's philosophical progress can be partially mapped by contrasting the conclusions that she reached at each stage of her enquiries with the often very different conclusions of such contemporaries. This is a task too ambitious to be undertaken here. But a necessary first step towards understanding it is to write the history of the stages through which her thought and her life passed. What emerged in the end from her life as a philosopher was an incomplete project, incomplete not only because of her murder at the age of fifty in Auschwitz-Birkenau, but more importantly because what she left us was not so much a set of answers as a set of philosophical and theological questions. Her questions of course, like all such questions, presuppose positions taken, conclusions at which she had arrived. But the point of those conclusions is to make us aware of the inescapable character of the questions.

ontology what exists what true/real , like Q Does God Exist
Do emotions exist

epistemology - how we can know about the existence of
such a thing principles of what can be know & how u can
know it

ontology: seeks the classefication & explanation of entities
L3 types realism   realism   Assump of nature reality
          idealism   empuricist   Parmenides
          materialism   positivism
                              post modernism

epis: study k & how people know what they know

2

Stein and Reinach

Soon after Stein arrived in Göttingen on April 17, 1913, she called on Adolf Reinach. A friend had told her: "When you get to Göttingen, the first place to go is to Reinach. He arranges everything else." Stein had been a student in Breslau, the city where she had grown up, from 1911–1913. In Breslau it had been her classes in psychology that had elicited her first philosophical questioning, while her classes in philosophy provided nothing that seemed relevant to answering her questions. Finally, the same friend who was to send her to Reinach gave her a copy of the second volume of Husserl's *Logical Investigations*, but even before she had been able to read it through she had arrived at a decision. She needed to go to Göttingen to study with Husserl. She was twenty-one years old.

Reinach was twenty-nine. He had been among the ablest of the remarkable set of students whom Husserl had attracted and he had the rare gift of being able to explain Husserl to Husserl. "It was really Reinach," said Husserl, "who introduced me to my *Logical Investigations*." Reinach was a gifted teacher, one who understood that no philosophical position has been adequately stated until it has become teachable. And, even in teaching Husserl's texts, he was always a contributor to as well as an expositor of Husserl's enterprise. So it is to the point to ask: what were the questions that Stein had brought with her to Göttingen? And what was it in Husserl's system of thought, as Reinach had understood it, that might provide answers to those questions? But first it will be useful to say something about the very different histories that had made Stein and Reinach what they were, when they met in 1913.

Stein brought with her a character formed by her successive experiences as a child in a loving and devoted Jewish home, as an outstanding pupil in a

Prussian *Gymnasium* for girls, and as a student at Breslau with an extraordinary capacity for hard work, one without which she would have been unable to pursue so many different intellectual and aesthetic interests so passionately. The first and most important influence upon her had been that of her mother, Auguste Stein née Courant (1849–1938), a woman of extraordinary resource, warm and loving towards her seven children, energetic and enterprising in the timber trade. Less than two years after Edith was born her husband had died, leaving her a debt-ridden lumberyard. Refusing any assistance from her brothers—the Courants were a close-knit family—she transformed it into a profitable business and gave all of her not always very easy children a splendid upbringing.

It was central to Auguste Stein's life that she was a devout and observant Jew, herself brought up in one of those small Jewish communities that had flourished on both sides of the Silesian border, communities that had been able to provide their members with only the bare elements of instruction in their religion, but that had been sustained by their observance of the Sabbath and the High Holy Days, especially Rosh Hashanah—the New Year and Yom Kippur—the Day of Atonement, Edith Stein had been born on Yom Kippur in 1891—and Sukkoth, Chanukah, Purim, and Passover, both in their synagogues and in their homes. So Edith Stein had a distinctively Jewish childhood in which, while she was the youngest of those present at her family's Passover feast, it fell to her to ask the questions whose answers narrate God's deliverance of Israel. Yet this she was for quite a number of years to put behind her, in part as a result of the openness of her mother to the possibilities of a new and different life for educated Jews.

The vast majority of Jews in Auguste Stein's parents' generation had lived a severely restricted social existence, one that continued the segregation imposed upon Jews since the Middle Ages. But during their lifetime new educational opportunities opened up and beyond these new career possibilities. For most of German history Jews had been excluded from the ownership of land and from membership in craft guilds. So theirs had for the most part been the trades of peddlers, dealers, storekeepers, sometimes merchants, and in a few cases bankers. Now increasingly they were to become physicians, lawyers and journalists, to engage in a wider range of business activities, and to distinguish themselves in academic life. In this respect the younger members of the Courant and Stein families were typical of the time.

Moreover, many of these new opportunities had been opened up for women as well as for men and Auguste Stein encouraged all her children, but especially her two youngest daughters, Erna and Edith, to set their career goals as high as they wished. Erna, who was a year and eight months older than Edith, and who was to qualify as a physician, was at each stage the pathbreaker, making it easier for Edith to follow her in moving onwards, first in the *Viktoriaschule*, then at the *Gymnasium,* and finally at the University of Breslau. But the way ahead was not always clear.

In 1906, when she was not yet fifteen, Edith, dissatisfied with her grades, decided to leave school. Happily she was to reverse this decision and to follow Erna to the *Gymnasium.* But it was in the intervening period, during an extended visit to her eldest sister and brother-in-law in Hamburg, that, as she put it in her autobiography, "Deliberately and aware of what I was doing I gave up praying" (*Life in a Jewish Family, 1891–1916,* tr. J. Koeppel, O.C.D., Washington, DC: ICS Publications, 1986, p. 148). Else and Max Gordon were altogether without religious belief and there was no one else at hand to exert any influence that might have counteracted the effects of her private reading. She seems at this time to have talked to no one about her skepticism about Judaism and, when she returned home, she continued to attend the synagogue with her mother, but now as a silent unbeliever. In later life she would refer sardonically to this stage of her upbringing as "my enlightened period."

What she had rejected was of course not Judaism as such, but only the Judaism of her childhood, and the rejection of *that* Judaism seems to have been part and parcel of her rejection of childhood, an adolescent assertion of adult independence that allowed her to make for herself the decision that all along her mother had wanted her to make, to enter the *Gymnasium*. It was the humane and conservative teachers there who both reinforced the German patriotism that she had already learned from her family, although she was critical of the archconservatism of her principal and history teacher, and imbued her with a love of literature. How she first became interested in philosophy is not clear, but she seems to have been one of those—and I suspect that they are numerous—who decide that they need to study philosophy before they know, except in a vague and general way, what philosophy is. While still at the *Gymnasium* she was asked by her cousin Richard Courant, a remarkable mathematician—the Courant Institute at New York University is named after him—and already assistant to David Hilbert at Göttingen, how she explained her decision to study philosophy. When she replied by asking him how he had come to study mathematics, he asked her if she had as yet done any work in the subject. "No," she replied, "not really, so far. But I do want to. Of course I've read a little of Haeckel. But that doesn't deserve to be called philosophy" (*Life in a Jewish Family, 1891–1916,* p. 173).

It does not seem to have occurred to her that her being a Jew and her being a woman might not at some point be obstacles to her realizing her ambitions. As a student she became a member of the Prussian Society for Women's Right to Vote, most of whose members were social democrats, but she said of herself that "I now came to hold a positive, nearly conservative view of the state, though this was never tainted by the peculiar stamp of Prussian conservatism. Added to purely theoretical considerations was a personal motive of deep gratitude to the state which had granted me academic citizenship with its free access to the wisdom of humanity" (*Life in a Jewish Family*, p. 191). The state and the culture alike were, so it seemed to her, hers to identify with and her Jewish origins and familial ties appeared as no kind of obstacle to this identification.

It is of course important that the members of Edith Stein's family had little or no contact with the wider German Jewish culture beyond the home and the local synagogue, a culture expressed in numerous Jewish books and journals, both Zionist and anti-Zionist, and by a variety of Jewish institutions and societies, ranging from theaters to gymnastic associations. So they were never drawn into and indeed seem never to have become aware of the debates about the relationship between being a Jew and being a German that were characteristic of that larger culture, debates informed by varying degrees of awareness of the dangers of anti-Semitism. There is a remarkable contrast in this respect between Gershom Scholem's memoir of his early life in Berlin (in the first two chapters of *From Berlin to Jerusalem*, tr. H. Zohn, New York: Schocken Books, 1980) and Edith Stein's memories of her early life in Breslau. Scholem was nearly six years younger than Stein, but the age difference is not significant. And it is not that the strains and stresses between a Jewish inheritance and the assimilation of German high culture were unknown in Breslau.

Breslau was after all the home of the Jüdisch-Theologisches Seminar, founded by Zacharias Frankel in 1854, one of the most influential institutions of German Judaism, until its destruction by the Nazis in 1938. The central aim of the Seminar had been to educate Jewish rabbis and teachers in the methods of scholarly enquiry developed with German classical and historical studies and so to regenerate the inheritance of orthodox learning. Among its earliest teachers were Heinrich Graetz, whose eleven-volume *Geschichte der Juden* was requested as a bar mitzvah present by the young Scholem (together with the four volumes of Theodor Mommsen's *Römische Geschichte*), and Jacob Bernays, a classical scholar of extraordinary talent and insights, who had been denied a position in any Prussian university because of his refusal to convert to Christianity.

Bernays had taught both classics and Jewish philosophy at the Seminar, until in the late 1860s he accepted a position as university librarian and *extraordinarius* at Bonn, although still denied a full chair. (The Prussian ministry had earlier refused to sanction the offer of chairs to him at Breslau and at Heidelberg.) Mommsen had been Bernays' friend and Graetz, Mommsen and Bernays were all in different degrees involved in the controversies generated by the anti-Semitic utterances of the Prussian historian, Heinrich von Treitschke, in 1879 and thereafter. So that the educated Jews of Breslau, more especially those with connections to the Seminar, could not have been unaware not only of continuing old-fashioned anti-Semitism, but also of the double character of most German and especially Prussian cultural responses to the recent emancipation of the Jews, of the terrible inability of late nineteenth-century Germans to allow Jews to be Jews and yet to be Germans too, of the all too common German insistence that the Jew who remained faithful to Judaism thereby made her or himself less of a German.

Edith Stein however grew up among Jews for whom the anti-Semitism of the present was not a central fact of consciousness. That it existed, that it was painful and deplorable, that it needed to be exposed and combated, none of this would they have denied. When Stein enrolled as a student at Breslau, the attitudes that had excluded Bernays from that university were still influential. Her earliest teachers in philosophy and in psychology, Richard Hönigswald and Louis William Stern, had both been denied academic advancement because of their Jewish ancestry. And Edith Stein knew this. But—and it is important to remember that she was only twenty years old—this did not seem at that stage to raise questions for her about her own future relationships, on the one hand to the academic culture and milieu of which she was so anxious to become a part, and on the other to the Jewish community, from which she had already separated herself in spirit.

To the first philosophy teaching that she encountered she had mixed reactions. The teacher was Richard Hönigswald (1875–1947), who had been a student of Alois Riehl at Halle. From Riehl he took his Neo-Kantianism, but developed his own version of it, one whose central project was to find a place within the Kantian scheme for the subjectivity of the individual. He had begun teaching at Breslau in 1906 and continued teaching there until 1930, when, relatively late in life, he became *Ordinarius* at Munich. The delay was certainly due to his being a Jew. Three years later, when the Nazis took power, he was expelled from the university, and, after *Kristallnacht* in 1938, was sent to Dachau. (He was among the fortunate few released from Dachau, emigrated to New York, and continued his philosophical writing until his death in 1947.)

Stein praised Hönigswald's lectures on the history of philosophy and she was impressed by his insight and his dialectical skill. But his introductory course on natural philosophy seems to have been devoted exclusively to the exposition of his own Neo-Kantian positions, expositions that produced a striking lack of conviction in his student audience. That audience he expected to be already familiar with the Kantian framework in terms of which his arguments were framed and for which they were an apologia. "The young persons in his seminar were enticed into engaging in dialectical skirmishes against such finely-honed weapons. Anyone who tried to introduce the fruit of an idea which had not ripened on Hönigwsald's acre was reduced to silence by his superior dialectic and biting irony, but, at heart, was rarely vanquished." And Stein quoted an older student as saying, "There are things which one dares not even think during Hönigswald's seminar. Yet outside of class I cannot ignore them" (*Life in a Jewish Family, 1891–1916*, p. 186).

Stein's own response to Hönigswald's teaching was more complex. But when she found herself asking for the first time her own philosophical questions, they were questions to which Hönigswald's Neo-Kantianism offered no answers. What questions were these? They arose from her studies in psychology. Stein very much enjoyed the classes in which Stern introduced his students to the recent findings of empirical psychology. She developed her interest in psychology further by attending the weekly meeting of the Pedagogical Group, a society founded by students who intended to become school teachers. It was through these meetings that Stein first encountered George Moskiewicz—the friend who was later to recommend a visit to Reinach—who had adopted the experimental methods of the Würzburg School for the studies on which he intended to report in his dissertation. Stein not only became one of his experimental subjects, but developed an independent interest in the psychology of that school, especially in the work of Külpe, Bühler and Messer, an interest that she was able to pursue in the summer of 1912 and the winter of 1912–1913 in Stern's seminar, which was devoted to examining the positions on the psychology of thinking taken by the members of the Würzburg school.

The founder and presiding genius of that school was Oswald Külpe, although its experimental work had been done almost entirely by others. Külpe had been a student of Wilhelm Wundt at Leipzig, where Wundt had set up the very first laboratory of experimental psychology in 1875. There one of his major concerns had been to devise experiments that would enable him to study the contents of consciousness by controlled introspection. It was this attempt to use introspective methods to study consciousness empirically that Külpe carried further, focusing not, as Wundt had done, on sensations, images, volitions and feelings, but on thought. And members of the Würzburg school had shown both that apparently random associations can be partly determined by underlying purposes, unrecognized by the conscious subject, and that thought can be imageless. But some of Stern's students recognized that the reports of their observations by members of the Würzburg school raised philosophical as well as psychological questions, questions about how thoughts are to be individuated, about how the content of some particular act of thinking is to be determined, about how thinking is to be distinguished from and related to other types of mental activity.

In her reading of the literature by and about the Würzburg school Stein kept coming across references to Husserl's *Logical Investigations,* while in Breslau there seemed to be no one who could help her to formulate, let alone to answer her philosophical questions. And she had read in a magazine about Hedwig Martius, later Conrad-Martius, to whom the philosophy faculty at Göttingen had awarded a prize for her essay on *Die erkenntnistheoretischen Grundlagen des Positivismus.* (What she did not then know was that Conrad-Martius had had to accept the fact that no women could as yet expect to teach philosophy in a German university. After she had received her doctorate from Munich in 1912—she had studied there before moving to Göttingen—she and her husband, Theodor Conrad, bought land at Bergzabern in the Palatinate, where their fruit farm provided them with both an income and time for Conrad-Martius to pursue her philosophical work. They divided their time between Munich, where Theodor Conrad taught, and Bergzabern, which became a meeting place for the younger Göttingen and Munich phenomenologists. See H. Spiegelberg, *The Phenomenological Movement: A Historical Introduction*, Third Edition, The Hague: Martinus Nijhoff, 1982, pp. 212–13.) So for these large and small reasons Stein decided to move to Göttingen, in order to study with Husserl. She had an additional reason for her decision. Her mother had received a letter from Richard Courant's wife, saying how much the Courants would like it, if Erna and Edith were to move to Göttingen, where Courant had recently become *Privatdozent*. Erna remained in Breslau, however, with her fiancée, when Edith left for Göttingen.

Husserl had been at Göttingen since 1901, when he had been appointed Professor Extraordinarius against the wishes of the philosophers, who also opposed his promotion in 1906. The appointment and the promotion were both due to the excellent judgment of Friedrich Althoff, who from the Ministry of Culture in Berlin was often able to recognize what German universities needed far better than the professors themselves did. It had been Althoff who had furthered Hilbert's efforts to recruit the very best mathematicians to Göttingen. And it was Althoff who rescued philosophy at Göttingen from the philosophers.

Husserl had since then attracted to Göttingen an extraordinary group of gifted younger philosophers. Some came from Munich, where the influence of the *Logical Investigations* had resulted in the genesis of a set of independent philosophical enquiries and debates, the most important participant in which was Max Scheler. It was here that Adolf Reinach (1883–1917) had first encountered phenomenology, before in 1905 he left for Göttingen in order to write his *Habilitationsschrift* with Husserl. Together with Reinach came his friend, Theodor Conrad, who in 1907 founded the Göttingen Philosophical Society. A group photograph of the society in 1912, a year before Stein arrived in Göttingen, shows among others Reinach, who had remained in Göttingen as *Privatdozent*, Johannes, later Jean Hering from Alsace, Hans Lipps, a student of medicine as well as of philosophy, Conrad, Scheler, who was visiting from Munich, Alexander Koyré from Paris, and Hedwig Martius who was very soon to marry Conrad. It was a circle that continually added and lost members. Dietrich von Hildebrand had already left for Munich, Koyré returned to Paris, and Hering went back to Strassburg to study for his examinations, while Elizabeth Heymann, who had studied with Simmel in Berlin, and Fritz Kaufmann from Marburg added to their numbers. From Lwów came a student of

Twardowski, Roman Ingarden, from Canada Winthrop Pickard Bell. Their meetings were attended not only by philosophers, but also by, for example, Rudolf Clemens, a philologist, Fritz Frankfurter, a mathematician, and the Germanists, Friedrich Neumann and Günther Müller. It was here that Edith Stein immediately found friends as well as fellow students.

There had been and continued to be a wonderful blending of social and intellectual life in those years at Göttingen. A key part in creating it was played by Husserl's remarkable wife, Malvine, née Steinschneider, like Husserl from a Jewish family and like Husserl an undogmatic Protestant Christian. It was Malvine who made Husserl's achievements possible. She had no independent interest in philosophy, but she attended Husserl's lectures and always counted the number of students present. It was she who had designed the house that they lived in, who saw to all the household tasks, who brought up their three children and who created a welcoming and much appreciated ambience for Husserl's assistants and students. Husserl himself was sometimes insensitive and sometimes worse than that, even in his dealings with those whom he liked and valued. Malvine had a sharp and occasionally tactless tongue, but she was also immensely kind, and from the start Edith Stein was to be one of the recipients of her kindness. But this is to look ahead. So I return to Stein's first encounter with Reinach.

It took place in the apartment where Reinach lived with his wife of six months, Anna. Reinach, like Stein, had been brought up in a Jewish family, but one that was at once a good deal more prosperous and more fully integrated into German society than Stein's. His parents seem not to have provided him with a Jewish education and at no time in his adult life did he take the claims of Judaism seriously. At Munich his studies had been in philosophy, psychology and jurisprudence and his doctoral dissertation was on the foundations of criminal law. After pursuing further legal studies at Tübingen—his family had wanted him to become a practicing lawyer—he returned to philosophy, leaving Munich for Göttingen.

His doctoral dissertation had been strongly influenced by his principal teacher at Munich, Theodor Lipps. And his interest in Husserl's work was initially elicited by Husserl's criticism of Lipps. What was it in Lipps's thought that provoked this criticism? Although Lipps occupied a chair in philosophy, psychology was his primary interest and he had founded the Psychological Institute at Munich. His principal aim as a philosopher was to make use of psychology in order to identify and explain the relationship between various aspects of mental life, so as to render intelligible the different types of experience to which he gave the name *'Einfühlung', 'empathy'*. Among the objects of types of empathy are those presentations of colors or sounds onto which we project feelings that are constitutive of our aesthetic responses and those facial movements and gestures of other human beings which we take to be expressive of their inner lives and to which we respond accordingly.

How do we come to experience such objects in these response-eliciting ways? Lipps attempts to answer this question by telling us a psychological story about how attention to what is presented in sense-experience provides thought with objects that we interrogate. When objects are thus put to the question, we may acknowledge that they are what they are by acts of judgment. And just such acts of judgment are presupposed by, even if not wholly constitutive of our empathetic responses. What kind of a story is this and why should anyone want to tell such a story?

Is it a set of factual generalizations about how in fact from sense-experience and thought the empirical conditions for the possibility of *Einfühlung* emerge, generalizations to which there might be counterexamples? Or is it a set of conceptual claims about how such concepts as those of sense-experience, thought, judgment and empathy *must* be understood, if they are to function as they do and to find application as they do? Those, like Lipps, who argued that logic had to be founded on an account of mental activity provided by empirical psychology seem not to have distinguished adequately between these alternative possibilities. And the charge that they had not so distinguished was leveled against Lipps and others by Husserl in his *Logical Investigations*. Husserl himself had been accused of just this confusion by Frege in his 1894 review of Husserl's *The Philosophy of Arithmetic* and, although it is far from clear that Frege's accusation was justified, Husserl thereafter took special pains to distinguish his views from those who were guilty of such confusions, guilty of what he, following Frege, called psychologism.

It is not surprising therefore that at the very beginning of the first volume of the *Logical Investigations*, published in 1900, Husserl set himself in deliberate opposition to psychologism, singling out for criticism Lipps's assertions that logic is a subdiscipline of psychology and that the logician's task is to discover the natural laws of thinking (*Logical Investigations*, tr. J. N. Findlay, New York: Humanity Books, 2000, Vol. I, pp. 91 and 93–94). Husserl later made it clear that it was only Lipps's writings prior to 1902 that he was attacking. "Th. Lipps," he wrote in his foreword to the second edition of the *Investigations* in 1914, "has since 1902 not at all been the man that is here quoted" (p. 47). But some of Lipps's best students naturally enough took note of Husserl's criticisms of their teacher and in the course of so doing discovered in the *Logical Investigations* a work that redefined philosophy for them. Their excitement was very great and a number of them, including Reinach, Conrad, Pfänder and others had formed a group devoted to a close reading of the *Investigations* and to discussion of its implications for their own philosophical work.

It was as a result of these discussions that Reinach had left Munich for Göttingen, where his *Habilitationsschrift* on the theory of judgment had been submitted. Since then, in the years between 1903 and 1913, he had written a short paper on William James and pragmatism, two papers on Kant, one of them a discussion of Kant's misunderstanding of Hume, a long paper on the theory of negative judgment, an article in two parts on the ethical and legal importance of deliberation, and a major work on the a priori foundations of civil law.

His productivity as a scholar was matched by his excellence as a teacher. He was valued by the Göttingen students not only for his teaching, but also for his openness and his kindness, and above all for his ability to mediate between them and Husserl, whom they found unpredictable and at times difficult, even though they greatly admired him. Reinach's class on phenomenology, "Exercises for Advanced Students," was designed to make Husserl's thought accessible to beginning graduate students and generally succeeded in doing so. Indeed Husserl had said of him that he had been among the first who could understand, creatively and perfectly, the distinctive meaning of the phenomenological method. At their first meeting Reinach invited Stein to join his class and made sure that she would be introduced to other student members of the Philosophical Society. As it turned out, Stein was unable to take Reinach's class because she had already enrolled in Max Lehmann's history seminar, a seminar that provided her with her first serious study of politics and an encounter with well-developed views that were very different from her own. So it was to be some little time before she encountered Reinach as a philosopher and her immediate introduction to phenomenology as taught at Göttingen was in Husserl's own classes. (When Husserl interviewed her before the beginning of class and learned that she had read the whole of the second volume of the *Logical Investigations,* he smiled and said, "Why, that's a heroic achievement.")

Some of the questions that Reinach had already addressed in his published work would in the future also be addressed by Stein, although generally in somewhat different contexts. But it will become clear that Stein would have been very unlikely to have made the philosophical progress that she did, if Reinach had not first opened up certain areas of phenomendogical enquiry and in so doing made it clear, as Husserl himself rarely made it clear, what it would be like to learn from Husserl so as to be able to move beyond him. The Husserl from whom Reinach and Stein had both initially learned was of course the Husserl of the *Logical Investigations.* Yet Husserl himself had by now moved beyond the *Investigations.* The Husserl of 1913 was no longer the Husserl of 1900–1901. So for both Reinach and Stein, although in very different ways, the question would arise of whether and to what extent in learning from the *Logical Investigations* they were continuing to move in the same direction as Husserl himself had moved. But to understand how this question became inescapable it is necessary first to understand what it was that the *Logical Investigations* said to those philosophical generations who were so excited by their first reading of it.

3

Logical Investigations:
A New Starting-Point in Philosophy

The two volumes of *Logical Investigations* were published in 1900 and in 1901. The first volume consisted of the "Prolegomena to Pure Logic" and these were largely devoted to refuting the errors of others. Since opposition to the views criticized by Husserl was widely shared among, for example, Neo-Kantians, the response to the first volume was generally favorable. But when, with the second volume, Husserl presented phenomenological views that were distinctively his own, the response was quite otherwise. From the dominant Neo-Kantian standpoint, for reasons that will become clear, Husserl's project seemed deeply incoherent. Yet, especially among younger philosophers to whom Neo-Kantian enquiries had increasingly come to seem barren, Husserl was taken to have opened up a new and unusually illuminating view of what it was possible for philosophy to achieve.

Contemporary readers of the second volume of *Logical Investigations* may well find it difficult to understand their enthusiasm. Husserl's prose style is, even by the standards of philosophical prose, unexciting, and his inveterately theoretical turn of mind often makes it difficult for his readers to recognize what kind of theory it is that he is presenting. For phenomenological theory is the theory of a set of practices and those who have not themselves been initiated into and become skilled in those practices are likely to find it difficult to understand what it is that makes the theory compelling.

In January 1914, Reinach was to deliver a lecture at Marburg that would become famous in the history of the phenomenological movement. The audience could be expected, given the type of Neo-Kantianism that prevailed among the Marburg philosophers, to be notably unsympathetic. And so Reinach was careful to take as little as possible for granted. "To talk about phenomenology," he said, "is the most idle thing in the world, so long as that

19

is lacking which alone can give talk concrete fullness and intuitiveness, namely, the phenomenological *way of seeing* and the phenomenological *attitude*" ("Concerning Phenomenology," tr. D. Willard, *The Personalist*, vol. L, no. 2, Spring 1960, p. 194). What is the phenomenological way of seeing? Reinach compared it to the way of seeing of someone who had learned to see, *really* to see colors. "We start in the world as practically active beings. We see it, and yet we do not see it; we see it more or less exactly, and what we see of it is, in general, determined by our needs and purposes. We all know how laborious a task it is to learn to really see; what work is required, for example, to really see the colors which all along fall in our visual field and are swept over by our glance" (p. 195).

It is worth spelling out this point a little further than Reinach does. Van Gogh once told his brother that he had become able to distinguish nineteen distinct shades of white in the paintings of Franz Hals. Such an ability requires sustained and focused attention on each particular color in each painting. It requires the development and exercise of capacities to recognize minute sameness and difference in color, to exclude from one's attention, while focusing on color, other features of those paintings, such as light, shadow and form, and to notice the same colors in other perceptual contexts outside painting. Learning to see in this way is hard work and not everyone is capable of it. But learning to attend to the character of our own mental acts, such acts as those of perception, memory, imagination and judgment, requires just as much discipline and just as much work.

Consider the range of questions which phenomenologists aspire to answer by focusing their attention on their own mental acts. In doing so they aspire to exclude any feature of those acts that is peculiarly theirs. So that the focus of the phenomenologist's attention is on *the* mental act, not on my mental act. And phenomenological enquiry is therefore a cooperative activity. Insofar as I succeeded in focusing on *the* mental act, my reports will be confirmable by others engaged in attending to the same phenomena, and, insofar as I have failed, my reports will be disconfirmed. What then are the questions asked by phenomenologists? They include questions about how the objects of perception, memory and imagination are each to be characterized, if our description is to be adequate to what is presented in experience. They include questions about what kind of act an act of perception—or of memory or of imagination—must be, if its objects are what they are. They include questions about what it is to think about an object, since two individuals may be thinking about one and the same object, the city of Vienna, yet one of them does so by having in mind the words 'the city of Vienna', while the other does so by having in mind an image of the city as seen from some vantage point. And so they also force upon us questions about the nature of sameness and difference.

Suppose that the object of my perceptual attention is a red house. What properties must the object of my perception possess for it to be *a house?* I imagine this and then that change in what I perceive and, as I do so, I become aware that some changes would make what I perceive *not a house*, but others would make it only a different house. So what is presented as an object of perception is not only *this* house as it is in its concrete detail, viewed by *this* perceiver from *this* particular point of view, but this house as exemplifying what it is to be *a house*. The object of perception is not only this particular, but also the properties that it is necessary for this particular to possess, if it is to be a house, is to belong to the species house. So it is too with the house as a *red* house, when the perceiver focuses on the color, perceiving not only "this aspect of red in the house, but Red as such" (*Logical Investigations*, Investigation II, ch. 1, §1, p. 340). Essences are given to us in perception in and along with the particulars that we see, hear and touch. And these are not the only complexities to which Husserl invites us to attend.

When I perceive this house from this particular point of view, I perceive it as perceivable from a number of points of view and by other possible perceivers. It is presented to me as something that is more and other than an object of my here and now perceptions. It is indeed as just such an object that I here and now see, hear or touch it, but nonetheless I cannot but see it as having an identity and a continuity of its own, as existing independently of my perceptions of it. And, when I pass from perception to memory, or from either to thought, the same is true. The reference of my judgments, whether I am thinking about the red house from which I have just turned away or the city of Vienna which I have never visited, is to objects that I cannot but treat as having a continuing existence apart from and independently of my thoughts, memories or perceptions.

As it is with particulars, so it is correspondingly with essences. What it is for something to be a tree or a house, to be red or to be octagonal, does not depend on how I think about it. The objects that present themselves to us present themselves as the same as or as different from other objects. And one key respect in which two objects may be the same or different is in respect not just of incidental detail, but of essential properties. This house is colored one particular shade of red, that house a somewhat different shade, but both satisfy the conditions for *being a house* and *being red*.

Someone may at this point object by pointing out the undeniable truth that what the words 'red', 'house' and 'tree' mean and the range of objects to which they are applied is a matter of the rules governing the use of such expressions in each particular language. So it may seem that what it is to be red or a house or a tree is linguistically determined. To this it must be said that what is named 'red' or 'house' or 'tree' in English or German or Swahili certainly depends on the rules governing speech in those languages. But what

Husserl was interested in determining was what it was that was presented to us as in need of naming and how it comes about that we are aware of and think about those objects to which we refer by using such words as 'red', 'house', and 'tree'.

Husserl's aim then was to enable us to identify what is prelinguistic in our experience, a project that could not be carried through without an enquiry into the relationship between our uses of language, our acts of perception and memory and the objects of those acts. So in the First Investigation Husserl initiated just such an enquiry. And for this enquiry too it is important that the objects to which we are able to refer, whether the particulars of which we are aware through perception or memory, or the essences exemplified in those particulars, are what they are as independently of our speaking about them as they are of our perceiving them or of our thinking about them.

It was the importance of this aspect of Husserl's phenomenological practice and theory that perhaps most impressed early readers of *Logical Investigations,* who took from it a phrase which epitomized that in Husserl's project with which they identified: "To the things themselves!" In adopting this as their slogan, Reinach and his friends hoped to convey not only what they were *for,* but also what they were *against,* not only their sense of the possibilities opened up by Husserl's program, but also their rejection of alternative ways of doing philosophy as condemned to sterility. The most important of these rejections was that of Neo-Kantianism. Ever since Kuno Fischer and Eduard Zeller had revived the historical and scholarly study of Kant in the late 1850s and the early 1860s, Kantianism had secured the allegiance of the most gifted German philosophers and from the 1870s onwards it had dominated academic philosophy. It became the case that for anyone embarking upon a career in academic philosophy in the major German universities an inescapable first step was: coming to terms with Kant. Kant's texts had to be assimilated and interpreted and Kant's problematic made one's own.

Yet very soon the result of this Neo-Kantian consensus was the generation of increasing disagreement, both about how Kant's texts were to be interpreted and about which elements in Kant's philosophy were to be endorsed and developed and which were to be radically revised or rejected. And these disagreements had proved—at least so far—not to be resolvable within the Kantian framework. From any external vantage point it seemed more and more difficult to identify wholeheartedly or at all with Neo-Kantianism, since it appeared that Kant's philosophy systematically generates problems which it lacks the resources to solve. But what alternative was there?

Husserl had one great advantage over his Neo-Kantian contemporaries. He was from the beginning an academic outsider, someone who had made his own way in the philosophical world, a mathematician by training, who came to philosophy late. His philosophical studies had been not in Heidelberg or Marburg, but in Vienna with Franz Brentano. Husserl had originally been a mathematician, although already with philosophical interests, fostered by his friend, Thomas Masaryk. But after his military service he became Brentano's student from 1884–1886 and became engrossed by Brentano's project, elaborated ten years earlier in his *Psychologie vom empirischen Standpunkte*, of founding a new science of the mind. Mental acts are, in Brentano's view, distinguished from other types of acts by what he called their intentionality. To say that an act is intentional is to say that it is directed towards an object. It is a thought or perception *of* something, a judgment *about* something, a desire *for* something.

"Every mental phenomenon," Brentano wrote, "is characterized by what the Scholastics of the Middle Ages called the intentional (or mental) inexistence of an object, and what we might call, though not wholly unambiguously, reference to a content, direction towards an object (which is not to be understood here as meaning a thing), or immanent objectivity. In presentation (*Vorstellung*) something is presented, in judgment something is affirmed or denied, in love loved, in hate hated, in desire desired and so on" (*Psychology from an Empirical Standpoint*, tr. A. C. Rancurello, D. B. Terrell and L. L. McAlister, London: Routledge, 1995, p. 88). The reference to the Scholastics is not unimportant. Brentano's training as a Catholic priest—he had renounced his priesthood in 1873—had provided him with a scholarly knowledge of the medieval Aristotelians that was rare among German and even Austrian philosophers. And he had studied in Berlin with the greatest of Aristotelian scholars of the nineteenth century, Adolf Trendelenburg. So that his philosophical perspective, his ways of formulating and resolving problems, and his philosophical idiom were very different from those of most of his German contemporaries. And this perspective and idiom he had transmitted to Husserl.

Husserl was also influenced by another student of Brentano, Casimir Twardowski, who in 1894 developed and reformulated some of Brentano's theses in his *Habilitationsschrift*, entitled *On the Doctrine of the Content and Object of Presentations*. Twardowski—who from his chair at Lwów, which he held from 1895 until 1930, became the founder of modern Polish philosophy—began from distinctions that Brentano himself had made. Every mental act is an act of presentation and has an intentional object, and the object is not to be identified with the presentation. The act presents the object as, for example, an act of seeing presents some visual object, an act of hearing some sound. The act is directed towards the object and the object is internal to the act. Brentano uses the expression 'intends' as equivalent to 'is directed towards' and he speaks of the intentional inexistence of the object in characterizing the intentional object as internal to the act. But at once a question arises, a question in answering which interpreters of Brentano have disagreed.

Are we to suppose that Brentano meant that when I think about Vienna the object of my thought is not Vienna, but my thought about Vienna? This supposition clearly imputes an absurdity to Brentano. Yet if the object of my thought is internal to that thought, how can my thought have as its object Vienna? The difficulty is aggravated when we consider that I can think not only about Vienna, but also about Cloudcuckooland, perhaps having the thought 'I would rather live in Cloudcuckooland than in Vienna'. That Cloudcuckooland does not exist does not in the least hinder me from thinking about it. So it may seem to be equally irrelevant to my thinking about Vienna whether Vienna exists or not. But in that case Vienna as the object of my thought will be one thing, the city on the Danube quite another.

These considerations make it clear that here we confront both a problem about how to understand Brentano and a philosophical problem that would have required attention, even if Brentano had never written about it. But in order to consider this problem more adequately, we need to avail ourselves of some distinctions that were introduced by Twardowski. In Twardowski's view it is crucial to distinguish the object of an idea or mental act (*Vorstellung*) from the content that exists in, that is to be found in, that mental act, whereby we are able to refer to the object. We think about realities that are thought-independent, the objects of our thoughts, and we do so by means of signs or images that are mental contents. The content of a thought is what can be studied by introspecting. In a notable simile Twardowski asks us to compare "the idea as an act with the act of painting, the content with the picture, and the object with the subject, a landscape, for instance, depicted on the canvas" (*Zur Lehre vom Inhalt und Gegenstand der Vorstellungen*, Wien: Hölder, 1894, p. 17). Twardowski advances four types of reason for drawing these distinctions, all of which throw further light on them.

The first is that it enables us to understand what gives our thought the content that it has, what makes it a thought of, say, a golden mountain, without supposing that we are thereby committed to belief in the existence or nonexistence of the object of our thought. The content exists wholly within our thought, but the question of whether the object exists or not is not a question about what is in our thought. Among the objects of our thought are not only objects that happen to exist, such as the sun and Vienna, and objects that happen not to exist, such as unicorns and Cloudcuckooland, but objects that could not exist, because they have incompatible properties, such as square circles. Were we not to distinguish content and object, we would be compelled to ascribe incompatible properties to the content of our thought and would therefore have to conclude that the content did not exist. But clearly the content does exist and it therefore cannot have the incompatible properties.

Twardowski's second line of argument is that, while the content of a thought is always and necessarily in the mind, having only properties that are mental, the object of a thought may have physical properties, whether real or imagined physical properties. A gold mountain is made of gold. No thought is made of gold. As with the first line of argument, content and object are distinguished by their very different properties.

The third line of reasoning moves in another direction. The content refers us to the object and one and the same object can be referred to in very different ways. That is, the content can function as a sign in very different ways. My thought of Vienna may have the content of an image of the city's skyline or may consist of the words 'the capital of Austria' or of some other identifying phrase. My thought of Cloudcuckooland may have the content of the words 'the imaginary land in Aristophanes' *Birds*' or just of the word 'Cloudcuckooland'.

Fourthly, I may through a single mental content intend a multiplicity of objects, as when I use the expression 'birds' to refer to all birds that ever were, are, or will be, and I may by some concrete mental content, whether an image or a phrase, refer to some abstract object, as when the content of my thought is the expression 'the triangle', intending the properties of any triangle whatsoever.

These four theses are important in two ways. They enable us to avoid a dangerous confusion and they pose a crucial question. The confusion to be avoided is of course that which assimilates the objects of mental acts to their content. But why is this confusion dangerous? It is so because, by making the objects of mental acts no more than parts or aspects of the content, it reduces them to features of the mental life of the particular individuals whose mental acts they are. It confuses the question 'What are the characteristics of the object of this thought?' with the question 'What characteristics does the thinking of this individual possess?' and in so doing it reduces enquiry into the character of mental acts to a study of the episodes and states of affairs that occur in the mental lives of individual thinkers. And this would make of Brentano's 'descriptive psychology' no more than an empirical study of the contents of particular minds on particular occasions. It is the very same mistake that Frege and Husserl had named 'psychologism'.

About any particular mental act we need to ask at least three distinct questions. The first is: What type of mental act is it? And the answer will be of the form: 'An act of judgment' or 'An act of memory' or 'An act of will' or 'An act of perception' or suchlike. In saying of what type a particular mental act is we will also have said what type of object it has. Indeed, as Aristotle remarked (*De Anima* II, 4, 415a16–22), acts are defined with reference to the type of object which they have. Note that in answering this first question, no reference to content will have been made. And this is also true of the answer to a second question: What is the object of this particular mental act? Here we are indeed speaking of what some particular individual has in mind, but not at all of what has to be going on in her or his mind for this to be the case.

Two individuals may indeed have one and the same object in mind, while what goes on in the mind of one of them is significantly different from what goes on in the mind of the other. Whether in particular instances this is or is not so is a matter for empirical study by psychologists. But their findings will not assist us in identifying the objects of thought or of perception or of desire. To say that two individuals may have the same object in mind is to recognize that we have criteria of identity for the objects of mental acts, and this whether or not the object exists in the physical world. So you and I, for example, may entertain as possibly true the same impossibility, that, say, the number of real numbers is finite (neither of us had come across Cantor's proof to the contrary), or judge to be true the same contingently false belief, that, say, somewhere there is a city made entirely of gold (as some of the conquistadores did). Such objects as the number of real numbers or the gold city exist only as objects of thought, but what is true or false of them is so independently of what any particular thinker judges concerning them. And they share this independence with physical objects. But physical objects are of course independent of mind in another additional way.

For my thought to be a thought of the number of real numbers, its object must satisfy the appropriate criteria. And so too, for my thought to be a thought of Vienna its object must satisfy the appropriate criteria, but in this latter case whether the object of my thought does so or not depends on whether it is or is not identical with a physical object, or rather an aggregate of physical objects, those that comprise the city of Vienna. When I think of Vienna, if it is indeed Vienna that I am thinking of, the object of my thought is not in my or any mind, but on the Danube. And I think truly and accurately about Vienna only insofar as the judgments that I make in my mind are identical with judgments that are true of that city on the Danube.

We may at this point be tempted to suppose that there are two kinds of intentional objects, those that in some sense or other exist in the mind and those that exist outside the mind, on the one hand, the number of real numbers or the gold city, on the other Vienna or cockroaches. But what this way of speaking fatally obscures is that in both types of cases the mind in making this or that the object of its mental acts directs itself to something other than itself. The objects of mental acts are not any of them 'in' any mind. They are realities external to any particular mind with which any mind may engage. They are that by engaging with which the mind has matter for thought, indeed that by engaging with which the mind is able to operate as a mind. It is true that some objects of mind are concrete and physical, while others are abstract. And here there is indeed a problem, a problem about the relationship of the abstract as object of thought to the concrete as object of thought. To this question we shall need to return, but for the moment I put it aside, noting that it is things themselves, whether abstract or concrete, that provide the mind with its objects. The powers of mind are in themselves potentialities, actualized only by being provided with objects.

What is distinctive about this view of the mind and its powers is that on it the mind and its activities are radically incomplete until the mind encounters mind-independent objects. It is of the essence of mind to be open to encounters with what is other than itself and it is constituted as mind only in and through such encounters. This is a very different conception of mind from the Cartesian conception. A third question that needs to be asked about particular mental acts is this: What is it about the content of *this* act that enables it to be the means, the medium, whereby the object of the act is represented as what it is? I noted earlier that I may think of Vienna by using the name 'Vienna', or by using some definite description, such as, 'the capital of Austria', or by entertaining some image of the city. And two individuals, both thinking of Vienna, may employ quite different means to do so. But, in order for anyone's thought to be a thought of Vienna, there must be some relationship between the content of their mental act and its object. The content may of course vary indefinitely. Having been a spy, whose coded messages referred to Vienna by the expression '33', I may, unlike anyone else, continue to think of Vienna by using that expression. And this example should make it clear that it is not what the content of the act of thought is, but how that content is employed intentionally by the particular thinker whose act it is that determines the relationship between content and object.

This then was Husserl's philosophical inheritance from Brentano and Twardowski. But in the use that he made of this inheritance in developing the method and doctrines of the *Logical Investigations*, Husserl exhibited striking originality. And the outcome was a set of positions to which the German philosophical establishment was at first deeply inhospitable, perhaps unsurprisingly, given the break with the past that Husserl represented. The contention that philosophy needs a new starting-point is not uncommon in the history of philosophy and philosophers who advance it always presuppose and generally supply some account of how their predecessors have been misled. In this respect Husserl was no different and the account that he supplied was an account of the genesis of Neo-Kantianism, an account that required a creative reinterpretation of some key episodes in the history of modern philosophy. In the Neo-Kantian view, indeed in Kant's own view, it had been Hume who, by his account of the nature and deliverances of sense-experience, had confronted Kant with the central problem to which Kant's epistemology purported to offer a definitive solution. But it was one of Husserl's central claims that Hume had failed to attend adequately to the deliverances of sense-experience and so had misconstrued the objects of perception, and that consequently Kant's response to Hume rested on a mistake. Therefore, to understand why Husserl's new starting-point for philosophy involved a rejection of the Kantian and Neo-Kantian standpoints it is necessary first to consider the difference between Kant's evaluation of Hume's account of perception and Husserl's evaluation of that account. And to do so we need to chronicle, even if briefly and skeletally, some episodes in the history of modern philosophy, episodes which, although they may seem to take us away from the story of Edith Stein's development, played an essential part in setting the philosophical scene in which she did her work.

4

The Background History:
From Hume to the Neo-Kantians

At the heart of Hume's account of perception is a contrast between the view of the objects of perception taken by plain nonphilosophical or prephilosophical persons and that which is or should be taken by philosophers. Plain persons suppose that their sense impressions, or at least some of them, are of objects that exist independently of those impressions. But philosophers must, so Hume asserts, deny this. "Accordingly we find that all the conclusions which the vulgar form on this head, are directly contrary to those, which are confirmed by philosophy. For philosophy informs us, that every thing, which appears to the mind, is nothing but a perception, and is interrupted, and dependent on the mind; whereas the vulgar confound perceptions and objects and attribute a distinct continu'd existence to the very things they feel or see" (*A Treatise of Human Nature* I, iv, 2, p. 193 in L. A. Selby-Bigge's edition, Oxford: Clarendon Press, 1888). How does Hume arrive at this position? He begins in the opening sentences of the *Treatise* by laying it down that all the perceptions of the mind are either impressions—a class that includes "all our sensations, passions and emotions, as they make their first appearance in the soul"—or ideas. Both impressions and ideas may be simple or complex and complex impressions or ideas are simply complexes of simples. All simple ideas originate from simple impressions and nothing is presented to us in our sense-experience that is not resolvable into some simple impression or set of simple impressions. There is thus no way to compare our impressions with something else. And the notion of comparing my impressions with objects, in order to ask whether my impressions of how objects are corresponds with how in fact objects are, makes no sense within Hume's scheme of thought about sense-experience.

Consider the type of case which the vulgar would describe by saying that some object came into view, passed out of view, and then reappeared. On Hume's account there can be nothing but a sequence of sense-impressions and the opinion of the vulgar which ascribes to the object a continuing and distinct existence, through the stages in which it at first appears, then disappears from view and then reappears, is groundless. For its only ground could be supplied by the senses and "the opinion of a continu'd and of a distinct existence never arises for the senses" (I, iv, 2, p. 192). Nor can it be the work of reason: "our reason neither does, nor is it possible it ever should, upon any supposition, give us an assurance of the continu'd and distinct existence of body" (p. 193). So where does that opinion of the vulgar arise? Hume's answer is: from the imagination.

What is presented to us in sense-experience is one thing, what we imagine to be thus presented is another. We should note at this point that the human imagination is, in the view that Hume takes of it, remarkably uniform in its operations. The beliefs that result from the operations are beliefs on which there is general agreement. And Hume provides an account of how perception, memory, and imagination cooperate to produce belief in "the fiction of a continu'd existence" (p. 209). But the work of imagination extends a good deal further. Our beliefs about causes and effects are derived from our experiences of constant conjunction, from our observations that some type of item in our experience invariably precedes an item of some other type and that items of the latter type are invariably preceded by items of the former type. But the reasoning that we employ in making inferences from the observed facts of constant conjunction to, for example, predictions about what sequences will occur on future occasions arrive at conclusions that go beyond and so cannot be justified by appeal to our past experiences of constant conjunction. Here too imagination has an important part in Hume's account of how we all come to make and to rely upon such inferences, in spite of the fact that they are unjustified.

The details of Hume's psychological account, which have often been criticized, are in the context of my present argument unimportant. What Hume provided and defended was a distinction between what is presented by sense-experience in the form of simple and complex impressions and what is projected onto that experience by the imagination. And what is projected includes not only a conception of the continuing and independent existence of bodies and whatever it is in our conception of and inferences from causal relations that extends beyond an experience of constant conjunction, but also our conception of our own identity as persons.

Some philosophers, Hume says, suppose that they have the idea of a continuing self, a self of whom we are immediately conscious, so that we are certain "both of its perfect identity and simplicity" (I, iv, 6, p. 251). But, Hume asks, "from what impression could this idea be deriv'd?" He answers, "It must be some one impression that gives rise to every real idea. But self or person is not any one impression, but that to which our several impressions and ideas are suppos'd to have a reference" (p. 251). And once again imagination is called upon to supply what is not given in and by perception. "The mind is a kind of theatre, where several perceptions successively make their appearance; pass, re-pass, glide away, and mingle in an infinite variety of postures and situations. There is properly no *simplicity* in it at one time, nor identity in different; whatever natural propension we may have to imagine that simplicity and identity" (p. 253). Imagination leads us into philosophical error, so that while the self is nothing but "a succession of parts, connected together by resemblance, contiguity, or causation" (p. 255), we take it to be more than this.

We are so constituted, that is to say, that we project onto the world conceptions of the identity and continuity of bodies and conceptions of causality such that we impute to the connections between causes and their effects a necessity which they do not in fact possess. Yet, if this is so, we can have no genuine knowledge of necessary and universal laws governing the movement of bodies. Newton's *Principia* becomes in large part a work of the imagination. So a problem was set, the problem of how to combine, if possible, Hume's account of the nature and deliverances of sense-experience with a recognition of the truth of Newton's statement of the laws of nature as laws that hold necessarily of all bodies and all movement. For those laws specify not just what is, but what must be the case, not just what happens to hold true of those physical events that have been or will be observed, but what necessarily holds true of any physical event whatsoever. And their statement presupposes that both the bodies of which they speak and the observers of those bodies possess an identity and a continuity that is no work of the imagination. This is of course the problem that Kant made his own, accepting from Hume his characterization of the deliverances of sense, but providing an account of the mind's contribution to the constitution of our experience which does not make that contribution one of fictions and illusions.

On Kant's account what we apprehend in experience is a world of bodies interacting with each other in space and time, exhibiting those regularities upon which ordinary observers rely and which Newtonian science explains. What makes such experience possible is the joint contribution of two elements. "Without sensibility no object would be given to us, without understanding no object would be thought. Thoughts without content are empty, intuitions [*Anschauungen*, immediate experiences] without concepts are blind" (*Critique of Pure Reason*, tr. N. Kemp Smith, A 51/B 75). Things appear to us as ordered, but just as Hume thought, the order is not itself presented in the appearances. "Thus the order and regularity in the appearances, which we entitle *nature*, we ourselves introduce" (A 125).

The appearances, the phenomena, are the appearances of things, of realities external to our experience, but we know those things only as they appear to us, but not as they are in themselves, as phenomena, but not as noumena. "What the things-in-themselves may be I do not know, nor do I need to know, since a thing can never come before me except in appearance" (A 277/B 333). Kant agrees with Hume that the limits of human experience set the limits of human knowledge. But, unlike Hume, Kant holds that our knowledge of nature permits us to make sound inferences not to what is unobservable, but to what is unobserved, and to draw conclusions about what must be and not only about what is. How is this possible?

The question itself is Kantian. Kant has no doubt that we possess knowledge of the mathematical and scientific truths which hold of all possible experience. The philosopher's task is to identify and explain the conditions that make such knowledge possible. This task is to be carried through by transcendental arguments, arguments which are to demonstrate that such and such must be the case, if so and so is to be possible. And one aim of the arguments of Kant's first *Critique* is to show that, if our knowledge of mathematics and physics is to be possible, then we must have a grasp of synthetic a priori truths, that is of truths that are known independently of and prior to experience, but which are not merely analytic, truths in which the predicate is not already contained within the subject. 'Every event occurs at some particular time' is analytic; 'every event has a cause' is synthetic and since, if it is true, it holds of every possible event, observed or unobserved, its truth could only be known a priori.

Since in knowing a synthetic a priori truth I know that it holds of all possible experience, I know, for example, that "All alterations take place in conformity with the law of the connection of cause and effect" (B 232) and that every new experience will provide further confirmation of this truth. "The proposition that everything which happens has its cause . . . has the peculiar character that it makes possible the very experience which is its own ground of proof, and that in this experience it must always itself be presupposed" (A 737/B 765). We cannot make sound causal inferences as to what is the case beyond the realm of phenomena. The limits of possible experience are the limits of application for synthetic a priori concepts and truths. So we cannot infer from how things appear to what must have caused them to appear as they do. We can have no inferential knowledge of things in themselves or of a cosmic order beyond appearances. We cannot infer soundly to the existence of God.

We do indeed know of things outside the self, if by this we mean what Kant calls *"empirically external* objects," *"things which are to be found in space"* (A 373). But we have knowledge of nothing that is not somehow presented in appearance to the mind. To speak of 'the mind' or rather of 'the understanding' in this way is not to speak of an empirically discoverable self.

"This 'I' is, however, as little an intuition as it is a concept of any object: it is the mere form of consciousness" (A 382). What the 'I' senses and apprehends as ordered experience of nature is only made possible, because another a priori concept has application. "We are conscious a priori of the complete identity of the self in respect of all representations which can ever belong to our knowledge, as being a necessary condition of the possibilities of all representations. For in me they can represent something only in so far as they belong with all others to one consciousness . . ." (A 116). Leibniz had used the term 'apperception' to name the mind's consciousness of itself. Kant distinguishes what is merely empirical awareness by a mind of itself from that transcendental unity of apperception which is the mind's grasp of all its experiences, outer and inner, as belonging to the unified and synthesized experience of a single mind.

We may note in passing the contrast between Kant's view and the view that Husserl had taken in the *Logical Investigations*. For Husserl, as I noted earlier, the mind is radically incomplete until it encounters mind-independent objects and it is in and through its encounter with those objects that mind is constituted as mind. For Kant it is the mind that imposes form and order on objects. They must conform to its requirements in both their presentation and their representation and not vice versa. Objects of perception are indeed mind-independent, but only as things-in-themselves. And as it is with those objects, so it is too with the self.

Insofar as we are aware of ourselves empirically, what we are aware of belongs to the realm of phenomena. But on Kant's account it does seem that we are aware of our noumenal selves as moral agents. As perceivers and observers we apprehend phenomena as universally law-governed, just because the mind imposes the form of law upon what is presented in experience. As moral agents, we prescribe to ourselves actions that conform to universal law, to that moral law to which reason requires a self-imposed obedience. In our obedience to the categorical imperatives of that law our wills are freed from determination by the laws that govern the phenomenal realm, a realm that includes our empirically known inclinations. So reason instructs us that we belong to two worlds, that of law-governed nature and that of the autonomous law-prescribing rational will and its duties.

So very brief and skeletal an account does not of course begin to do justice to the detail and complexity of Kant's positions. But it may serve to identify those areas of Kant's thought in which central problems were to arise for his Neo-Kantian heirs. Neo-Kantianism had been generated in the 1850s and 1860s by a growing shared conviction that Kant's immediate heirs had been conclusively shown to be unsuccessful in their various attempts to think their way through him and beyond him. This negative verdict was not always just. Fries, for example, was for the most part dismissed without having been read. But Fichte, Hegel and Schelling had provided matter for systematic debate,

debate which had put their criticisms of Kant in question in fundamental ways. So that by the 1850s there was widespread agreement that their attempts to displace Kant had failed. It is therefore unsurprising that a sequel to a new set of scholarly studies of Kant, studies that had clarified what was at stake in the differences between Kant and his successors, was a large and enthusiastic response to the slogan: 'Back to Kant!' Yet the Neo-Kantians were of course returning to Kant in an intellectual context very different from that of Kant's own age. Hegel had taught them to think historically, even although they rejected Hegel's version of history. And their attempts to restate Kant's positions in contempory terms immediately encountered problems and reflection upon those problems multiplied disagreements. So the protagonists of Neo-Kantian positions characteristically found themselves involved in debate both with Kant's critics and with others who also defended Kant, but who interpreted him in rival ways and offered alternative solutions to the problems posed from within the Kantian renewal. A number of problem areas were of particular significance.

A first concerned the relationship between what is presented in sense-experience and the concepts and categories through which the mind approaches that experience as structured and ordered. Kant plainly distinguishes between these, between what is given and what is imposed upon what is given. Yet he equally plainly asserts that we never encounter the former apart from the latter. And it is a short step from agreement with Kant on this latter thesis to concluding that the notion of unstructured, unordered experience, of a presentation that is not already conceptually informed, is a myth, the myth that later on in quite another philosophical context Sellars was to christen "the myth of the given." Nothing, said Hermann Cohen, is given. Everything is the work of thought and the history of human experience is a history of thought and of the objects of experience that are internal to thought.

Yet this reformulation of Kant itself presents problems of at least two kinds. First, it is in Kant's own view sense-experience that gives empirical content to our judgments and we can contrast a judgment with such content with one that is contentless. But how can we do this, if we cannot identify what is given in experience as distinct from that which imposes structure and order on it? Secondly, it appears that such identification must be possible, if we are to be able to speak of one and the same set of presentations in experience as structured and ordered in two or more different and incompatible ways. And it seems that we must be able to do this, if we are to take account of developments in the history of physics, developments which constituted a second problematic area for Neo-Kantians.

According to Kant, our synthetic a priori knowledge includes something very close to knowledge of the necessity of Newton's laws of motion—in a somewhat revised version. The forms of Newtonian science are the forms through which the mind constitutes and apprehends nature. But in fact Newton's mechanics turned out to be false, displaced in one area by relativistic mechanics, in another by quantum mechanics. And the same perceptions and observations that had been accorded one kind of significance within the Newtonian scheme were now to be accorded quite another in the physics of Einstein or of the quantum theorists. These historical developments were to confront later Neo-Kantians with a dilemma. On the one hand each major physical theory seems to bring to the data of sense-experience an a priori theoretical scheme within which and by means of which the data are interpreted. But the rejection of Newtonian physics at the very end of the nineteenth century was sufficient to show that what the Newtonian scheme had provided may have been, indeed was a priori, but was not *knowledge*. So there arose a second set of problems about the nature and status of the scientific a priori. They included problems posed by developments in mathematics as well as in physics, especially by the discovery of non-Euclidean geometries and by number theory. What was needed and what Ernst Cassirer was to attempt to supply later was a new account of concept formation in mathematics and the sciences, one that aspired to identify general principles that necessarily govern the construction of any mathematical or physical theory for which the status of objective knowledge can be claimed.

Yet to move in this direction may make it difficult to resist claims that mathematical and scientific theories are in their different ways no more than formal constructions, constructions that can then find application to experience, applications that are justified pragmatically by the manipulative and predictive successes in which they result. So a key problem for the Neo-Kantians was to preserve an account of the synthetic a priori and of its indispensable role in the constitution of knowledge that was both recognizably Kantian and compatible with ongoing changes in physics and mathematics, compatible too with the successive transformations of logic by Frege, by Russell and Whitehead and above all by the intuitionists. With logic the Neo-Kantians had perhaps an easier, if still not an easy task. For the logicians themselves were concerned to identify those characteristics that any logic whatsoever must possess, those theses that constitute logic's minimal commitments. And what Neo-Kantians, such as Cassirer, had to show was that, in moving beyond the logic that Kant himself had employed, the logicians had done nothing to preclude a Kantian account of those minimal commitments. Yet this too required resistance to rival claims, to those of Russell's logicism and later to positions on logic taken by the positivists.

It was not just that Neo-Kantianism had generated problems in these two areas—that of the relationship of concepts and categories to sense-experience and that of the nature of a priori knowledge—but that different Neo-Kantians had responded to them very differently, thus putting Neo-Kantians at odds with each other, as well as with their external critics. And this was also true of

other problem areas. At the very beginning of the Neo-Kantian revival Liebmann had argued for the elimination of the thing-in-itself from the Kantian
scheme of thought. Since the limits of our sense-experience set limits to our
knowledge and the thing-in-itself lies beyond those limits, the thing-in-itself
must, it seems, be unknowable, and we have no reason to ascribe existence to
it. Liebmann took it that Kant's use of this notion had made him unnecessarily
vulnerable to criticisms that could easily be avoided by eliminating it. Riehl by
contrast argued that the thing-in-itself is that of which we have knowledge
through the mediation of sense-experience and that without that notion we
can make no sense of the mind's relationship to the objects that it encounters.
For Cohen the concept of the thing-in-itself was neither the redundant notion
that Liebmann took it to be nor that of an object of knowledge, as Riehl understood it, but rather a *Grenzbegriff,* the concept of an ideal limit to our investigations into how things are.

A similar range of disagreements arose over how to understand the Kantian doctrine of the knowing self in its relationship to empirical discoveries
about the self and about cognition. Natorp made of the Kantian concept of
the pure ego the same kind of *Grenzbegriff* that Cohen had made of the
thing-in-itself. But there were those Neo-Kantians who attempted to show
that the a priori elements in our knowledge are the outcome of physiologi-
cal and/or psychological structures of human perception and cognition that
can be identified and studied empirically. Among these was Edith Stein's first
teacher at Breslau, Richard Hönigswald, who took the self to be able to recognize itself as existing in and as part of that world which it apprehends in
conformity with the a priori structures of the understanding.

One source of this range of disagreements in particular areas of philosophical enquiry was the difference in the projects undertaken and the goals
set by Neo-Kantians in different universities. For some, as with Cohen at Marburg, a primary task was to sustain Kant's enterprise as a philosophy of natural science, while at the same time upholding Kant's ethics. Riehl at Berlin
was similarly preoccupied with issues in the philosophy of science, but in a
way that put him seriously at variance with Cohen. Windelband and later
Rickert at Heidelberg attempted to expand the Kantian scheme, so as to find
a place within it for the historical and cultural sciences, while at Göttingen
Leonard Nelson, taking up a view of Kant that he had arrived at through his
reading of Fries, attempted to provide Kant's scheme of thought with a new
starting-point in introspection, a type of introspection that makes us aware
of the undeniable character of the principles governing experience, principles that can only be adequately expressed as synthetic a priori truths. And
Nelson took it that this understanding of Kant's thought rendered it less vulnerable to hostile external criticisms than did the versions of Kant defended
by his Neo-Kantian rivals.

So in the early years of the twentieth century, Neo-Kantianism dominated the philosophy departments of large numbers of German universities, but what was taken to be of permanent value in Kant's thought as contrasted with what was taken to be problematic or simply in error varied a great deal from university to university. And which view of Kant any particular younger philosopher took seemed more and more to depend upon where he had studied and with whom. A number of Neo-Kantian dynasties had begun to develop. Moreover, there appeared to be no way in which either the interpretative disagreements or the substantive philosophical disagreements that divided the Neo-Kantians could be resolved. Yet generally for those educated within the Neo-Kantian framework and ethos, this was not of itself troubling, not something that threatened either their cultural or their philosophical allegiance to Kant. It was generally only to those educated outside that framework and ethos that the fractures and fissions within Neo-Kantianism suggested the need for a radical break. And it was indeed only when genuine alternatives had been provided that Neo-Kantianism became open to questioning at a fundamental level. One of those alternatives was the Neopositivism that Mach's followers in Vienna defended. Another was Husserl's phenomenology. Both of these were in key part responses to a rereading of Hume and both took Kant's responses to Hume to be misguided, although in very different ways. In the eyes of the Neopositivists, Kant had moved too far away from Hume. From Husserl's perspective, it was the extent of Kant's agreement with Hume that needed to be questioned.

5

Logical Investigations: What Do We Learn from Experience?

What do I hear when I hear a song? The answer, Husserl once said, is that I hear the song, not the notes. I may of course, by focusing on particular phrases or individual notes, hear *them* rather than the melody of which they are parts. But what is presented to me in experience is the whole, a whole composed of parts, and not just a series of auditory sense-impressions. Hume, in Husserl's view, makes two closely related mistakes. He supposes that what is presented in experience is no more than a series of atomic sensory units. And he fails to discriminate the object presented in perception from the perceptual content of the act of perception. So, in Hume's view, neither the unity of the object—a song, a house, a cabbage, a landscape— nor the kind of object that it is are given in perceptual experience. All that is presented are a set of sensory particulars: colored extended patches, shapes, sounds, smells, tactile sensations, everything that for Hume falls under the heading 'impression'.

How then do impressions thus understood stand to ideas? As we have seen, Hume's problem is that while, on the one hand, in his view ideas can derive only from impressions, ideas nonetheless do have contents that could not be derived from impressions, if impressions are understood as Hume understood them. An idea of a cabbage is not an idea of *this* cabbage, yet to perceive some particular cabbage is always and necessarily to perceive both *this* cabbage and *a* cabbage. What it is and that it is are characteristically and generally given in one and the same act of perception, something that Hume cannot acknowledge.

Hume's nominalism thus entangled him in insoluble problems. If impressions are indeed what he says they are, and nothing is in an idea that was not first in the corresponding impression, then it is difficult to understand in what relationship the idea of a home or the idea of a cabbage can stand to the impressions of this or that house or cabbage. Hume tries to elucidate this relationship by telling us a story about abstraction and resemblance, but Husserl argues compellingly that no such story will provide what is needed. Yet Hume's difficulties are wholly of his own making. It is because he begins from an impoverished view of what is presented in experience that he has no credible way of relating the particular and the universal. And this is not the only problem so generated for Hume.

Because he restricts the domain of experience to sensory particulars, he cannot allow that bodies as such present themselves to us in experience, bodies that are wholes with structures and constituent parts, continuous, but changing through time, as both cabbages and houses are, bodies that present themselves as law-governed in respect of change, movement and their relations to other bodies. Acknowledging that all of us commonly take what is presented to us in experience to be more and other than his account of impressions and ideas can accommodate, Hume argues that we do so by imaginatively projecting that more and other onto our experience. And what Hume credits to the projective imagination Kant ascribes to the structure of the perceiving and judging mind, to concepts grounded a priori in the understanding. For Husserl it is what Hume and Kant share that has to be put in question and part of what he aspires to show is that in invoking in the one case the imagination, in the other the a priori structures of the mind, each offers a solution to a nonexistent problem. How does Husserl go about showing this?

In the *Logical Investigations*, Husserl paid most attention to Hume in the fifth chapter of the Second Investigation, which is an extended critique of Hume's theory of abstraction. But his quarrels with Kant and the Neo-Kantians are also quarrels with Hume. For it is Husserl's central claim that the invariant, universal and necessary features of the objects and states of affairs that we apprehend in experience, the features that Kant had ascribed to the a priori structures of the mind, are themselves realities as independent of our minds as are the objects whose features they are. The a priori is not mind-dependent. And this puts Husserl as squarely at odds with Hume as he was with Kant.

Why do I emphasize this? It was certainly not what Husserl himself or most contemporary readers of the *Investigations*—with the interesting exception of Reinach—would have fastened on. But it had and continues to have a peculiar importance for English-speaking readers. For their philosophical tradition is one in which for the vast majority the notion of an appeal to experience as foundational for our judgments and beliefs have been equated with the key doctrines of British empiricism and no empiricist has been more philosophically influential than Hume. So that, when in his review in *Mind* in 1929 of Heidegger's *Sein und Zeit* Gilbert Ryle set out to explain phenomenology to the British philosophical public, he introduced Brentano and

Husserl by making a comparison with Hume. And, had Ryle given his allegiance to phenomenology instead of to language analysis, British philosophy in the 1930s and 1940s might have been enlivened by debates between phenomenologists and empiricists that would have both paralleled and illuminated the earlier German debates between phenomenologists and Neo-Kantians.

The first volume of the *Investigations*, published in 1900, consists, as I remarked earlier, entirely of prolegomena to the study of what Husserl now called 'pure logic'. And, as I also remarked, it was generally well received by those Neo-Kantians who took notice of it, partly because Husserl was understood to refute what he now took to be his own earlier psychologistic errors and the Neo-Kantians too were hostile to psychologism. So they at first took Husserl's positions to be closer to their own than was in fact the case. Moreover some of Husserl's idiom was Kantian or Neo-Kantian. He distinguished ideal laws from merely empirical generalizations, he emphasized what he too called the a priori element in knowledge, and he wrote of how he felt, in respect of his view of the laws of logic "close to Kant's doctrine" (*Logical Investigations*, tr. J. N. Findlay, London: Routledge and Kegan Paul, 1970, *Prolegomena*, §58, p. 215; Findlay's translation is of the text of Husserl's 1921 revised edition of the *Investigations*, and not of the original 1900–1901 edition, but nothing is affected by this in the quotations that I have used). It is understandable that Natorp's comments were favorable, although he might perhaps have noted that in the same paragraph Husserl speaks of "Kant's confusing, mythic concepts of understanding and reason." But, when in a second volume in 1901 the *Investigations* themselves were published, the Neo-Kantians were both puzzled and affronted.

Husserl takes as his aim, just as the Neo-Kantians do, an identification of the conditions of the possibility of experiences of various kinds, and again, just as the Neo-Kantians do, he attempts to distinguish what is invariant and necessary from what is not. But his method is to investigate the invariant and the necessary as presented in experience by means of the discipline of phenomenological attention and inspection, and by reflection upon what that attention and inspection discloses. And for the Neo-Kantians any such project must have seemed crudely incoherent, an attempt to discover in experience what is prior to experience, to investigate the a priori by investigating the a posteriori.

Husserl first set himself to discover how we are able to employ language that affords expression to ideal meanings and to ideal laws, notably to the ideal concepts and normative laws of logic, and in so doing to refer to what is independent of our mental acts, to what is true or false independently of any mind judging it to be so, and to do so through and in virtue of the structure of our mental acts. The intentional structure of our particular mental acts is such that we can distinguish between their matter, that which provides them with content, and their quality, that which makes of each act an act of judgment or of perception or of memory or of imagination or of desire or of. . . . For Husserl there is an indefinite variety of types of mental acts and we investigate what makes each distinctive by higher-order attention to first-order intentional acts. That is, we make first-order intentional acts, or rather aspects of them, the objects of second or higher-order acts. A first-order act is an act of perception or judgment or. . . . Second-order acts supply answers to such questions as 'What is an act of perception?' 'What type of object does it have?' 'What is the object of this particular act?' and so on.

Consider some particular act of perception in which I see something colored. About this act I may ask: 'What is perceived in perceiving the color of this particular?' By doing so I move from considering the object of perception as a whole to considering one of its properties or perhaps a property of one of its parts. What I see is red, but in seeing red I see this particular shade or hue of red, and in seeing it as this red I cannot but also see it as an instance of redness. In so doing I grasp that what is presented to me is both particular and universal or rather a particular exemplifying something universal. I also grasp the truth of certain universal and necessary propositions, such as 'If anything is red, it is some particular shade of red' and 'If anything is red, it is colored'. And in further reflecting upon what it is I have understood in understanding these propositions, I also understand that I have grasped certain logical truths about the entailment relationship of those propositions, about the inferences that we may or must make. (Husserl himself more than once used the example of seeing something red to make some of the points that I have tried to make here, but the spelling out of this example is my own.)

In the *Investigations* as published, Husserl does not begin by considering acts of perception. But in the First Investigation he already presupposes what he had to say about perception in the Sixth and the prudent reader will sometimes be wise to consult the Sixth Investigation in order to understand the First. What Husserl begins from is the thought that it is by and in language that we give expression to what we perceive, judge and the like and enquires how our utterances can embody 'meaning-intention' (*Logical Investigations* I, p. 281). When someone uses some particular linguistic expression, we have to distinguish between what the use of the expression, as Husserl puts it, intimates and what the expression itself means.

> To understand an intimation . . . consists simply in the fact that the hearer *intuitively* takes the speaker to be a person who is expressing this or that, or as we certainly can say, perceives him as such. When I listen to someone, I perceive him as a speaker, I hear him recounting, demonstrating, doubting, wishing etc. . . . Common sense credits us with percepts even of other people's inner experiences; we 'see' their anger, their pain etc. Such talk is quite correct, as long as, e.g., we allow outward bodily things likewise to count as perceived, and as long

as, in general, the notion of perception is not restricted to the adequate, the strictly intuitive percept. If the essential mark of perception lies in the intuitive persuasion that a thing or event is itself before us for our grasping . . . then the receipt of such an intimation is the mere perceiving of it. . . . The hearer perceives the speaker as manifesting certain inner experiences, and to that extent he also perceives these experiences themselves; he does not, however, himself experience them. (*Logical Investigations* I, §7, tr. J. N. Findlay, Amherst, NY: Humanity Books, 2000, vol. I, pp. 277–78)

I have quoted this passage from Husserl at some length, not only because it enables us to understand what Husserl means when he says that the use of a linguistic expression in an utterance "intimates" the mental act of the utterer, but also because it is a passage to which we will have to return in considering Edith Stein's relationship to Husserl. But for the moment what is important to stress is the difference between what, on Husserl's account in the *Investigations,* the other intimates by her or his use of an expression and what the expression itself means.

Where Husserl speaks of linguistic expressions, he seems to mean whole indicative sentences. And when he speaks of the objects that may be referred to in such sentences, he includes under the term 'object' properties, events and states of affairs. About the meaning and reference of expressions, thus understood, Husserl makes two points. The first is, "Each expression not merely says something, but says it *of* something: it not only has a meaning, but refers to certain *objects*" (I, 12, p. 278). Meaning is one thing, the object referred to quite another, but there is no meaning without reference. The second is, "To use an expression significantly and to refer expressively to an object (to form a presentation of it) are one and the same. It makes no difference whether the object exists or is fictitious or even impossible" (I, §15, p. 293). That is, to refer to an object by an expression is to have that object in mind. So I do not fail to refer when the object that I have in mind does not exist.

This differentiates Husserl's account sharply from Frege's, since for Frege, if an expression is used of what does not exist, it fails to refer. And this is not the only disagreement between Husserl and Frege on issues of meaning or sense and reference. But far more important than their disagreements on particular issues was the difference in the directions taken by their enquiries and the consequent divide between those whose investigations were Fregean in spirit and those who followed Husserl. Frege's antipsychologism led him to give an account of logic and of certain aspects of language, which is intended to be independent of any account of the minds of those who argue and conform to or violate the laws of logic, who assert and who refer. Hence the common charge of 'Platonism' brought against Frege. (We need always to remember that 'Platonism' thus used is a curse word and has little to do with Plato.)

Husserl, equally anxious to avoid the errors of psychologism, nonetheless insisted that an adequate understanding of logic and language requires a phenomenological account of the human being who is at once perceiver, thinker—and as such subject to the laws of logic—and language-user. What the phenomenologist provides is fourfold: not only, as we have already seen, an account of those various types of mental acts in which someone perceives, judges, imagines, wishes and the like, and of the types of object of those acts, so that we are able to understand the various different ways in which language can give expression to thought, but also descriptions, if necessary minute descriptions, of those particulars which are the objects of particular mental acts and identifications of those universals which are presented in and with particulars, universals which in their relationship to other universals and to particulars, so it will turn out, can only be grasped through the modal concepts of necessity and possibility.

What is and has remained distinctive in the phenomenological standpoint is its insistence on the givenness of the objects of mental acts. And the importance of this insistence can be brought out by considering what is involved in its denial, a denial that has characterized one strand of analytic philosophy. Consider the objects of acts of perception. For some analytic philosophers—from Sellars to McDowell and Brandom—perceptual experience is relevant to judgments of perception only because it is already conceptually informed. There is no way to go beyond or behind what is conceptually informed to the preconceptual or the prelinguistic. And it follows that nonlanguage-using and nonconcept-deploying animals are understood by such philosophers as no doubt responding differently to different sense experiences, but not as enjoying an awareness that has any further significance.

What is thereby omitted is twofold: on the one hand the richness of what is given in experiences of, say, color or sound, the range of preconceptual and prelinguistic discriminations of, among other types of object, colors and sounds, and the abilities to recognize and to reidentify particular instances of these as being the same or different, and on the other the role that looking and seeing, listening and hearing—and other perceptual activities—play both semantically and epistemologically in founding those concepts which are put to work in our judgments. To grasp what is meant by 'red', to have the concept and the word, certainly involves more than looking and seeing, but without looking and seeing there is nothing to give that concept or judgments employing that concept application. In conceptualizing red we go beyond what is immediately given, extending our applications of the concept indefinitely, so that we can come to speak of someone being red with anger or of their bank account being 'in the red', but we never leave behind those founding applications on which our concept use and judgment continue to depend. Without them there would be nothing to go beyond, nothing to extend. There is no adequate response to a wide range of questions of the form 'What do you mean?' and 'How do you know?' that does not include references to looking and seeing, to listening and hearing, and the like. Before we can cite what we see or hear as a reason for some judgment, we must see what we see or hear what we hear and this is no platitude.

So, it makes sense to ask, as it cannot from the rival analytic standpoint, whether our concepts are adequate to the objects in the world presented to us in sense experience. And it is only when they are so adequate that our judgments can re-present what is thus presented. Lacking such presentation 'red' could not have the sense and reference that it has. And this truth holds of objects other than those of acts of perception.

If by careful and disciplined reflection on the objects of such acts I have understood the relationship of 'red' to particular presentations of red and of 'green' to particular presentations of green, I will also have understood that *necessarily* any surface that is red is not green and vice versa. The necessity presents itself in and through the presentation of the particulars as something that holds independently of my judgments concerning that necessity. So phenomenology enables us to grasp the essential properties of the objects presented in experience.

The attitudes of phenomenologists to their experiences are therefore, as Reinach emphasized in his lecture at Marburg, very different from those of plain nonphilosophical persons. And a precondition for achieving the phenomenological standpoint is a putting on one side, a temporary discarding of the attitudes characteristic of everyday life. Husserl was to speak of a suspension of such attitudes and beliefs as a precondition for achieving both adequate attention to the objects of experience and adequate reflection on what is involved in such attention. Only by such attention and reflection can we distinguish adequately the objects of mental acts from the contents of those acts, the objects which are the focus of our attention from their backgrounds, the differences between what is central and what is peripheral in sense experience, and the like.

The standpoint of the phenomenologist is also very different from that of the empirical psychologist. Phenomenology does not provide those kinds of empirical generalization that are the findings of experimental and observational psychology. And psychology takes it for granted that we know what an act of perception is and how it is to be distinguished from acts of memory or of imagination. It is precisely what empirical psychology, that is, the psychology of almost all academic psychology departments, takes for granted that phenomenology puts in question.

The second of the *Investigations* therefore begins with a discussion of the relationship between particular and universal as discerned in particular acts of perception. The example that Husserl uses is one that I made use of earlier:

that of someone who, seeing a red house, has as the object of his apprehension not this red house, not "this aspect of red in the house, but Red as such"
(II, §1, vol. I, p. 340). And this apprehension of red as such is an apprehension
of an object and of an object that anyone who perceives, and attends to her or
his perception, cannot but be aware of. This awareness is not a result of abstraction, certainly not of abstraction as understood by the British empiricists.
Husserl is particularly careful at this point to distinguish his views from those
of Berkeley and Hume. What abstraction—if by abstraction we mean a focus
upon one attribute of an experienced object to the neglect of all other
aspects—could yield at most would be still particular: red-as-instantiated-in
this-object, *this* red, not red as such, the universal. But in my taking what I am
presented with as not just *this* red, but as exemplifying what it is to be red, my
intentional act has an object that is not a particular.

In grasping universals, in grasping, that is, what it is for anything whatsoever to be red or green or, more generally, colored, or what it is for anything
to be a number, or what it is for anything to be a physical body, we grasp
what is essentially the case with all color or number or body. And the task of
phenomenology is by focused attention to discriminate for each class of objects presented to consciousness in intentional acts the essential from the accidental, and so to arrive at an intuition of essences. We perceive particulars
as having properties that can only be identified and understood, when we
have intuited the relevant essences.

Intentional objects are not only of various kinds, but they present themselves in various ways. The objects of acts of perception are present as bodily presences. The objects of acts of memory are as fully present, but not as
bodily presences, and so it is too with imaginary objects of acts of imagination. (Not all objects of imagining are imaginary.) And in speech-acts we can
refer intentionally to objects without any presentation at all. It would be a mistake to think that, in characterizing the objects of intentional acts in this way
by reference to their mode of presentation, we are committed to holding that
the objects of intentional acts are *only* intentional objects. This is of course
true of, for example, imaginary objects. But in the Fifth Investigation Husserl
took pains to insist that the identity of a presentation is not the same as the
identity of an object: "The presentation I have of Greenland's wastes certainly
differs from the presentation Nansen has of it, yet the object is the same"
(V, §21, p. 590). And the object as presented always may be and often is an
object quite apart from its being presented to some consciousness:

> It is a serious error to draw a real (*reell*) distinction between 'merely immanent'
> or 'intentional' objects, on the one hand, and 'transcendent', 'actual' objects on
> the other. . . . It needs only be said to be acknowledged *that the intentional ob-*
> *ject of a presentation is the same as its actual object, and on occasion as its ex-*
> *ternal object, and that it is absurd to distinguish between them.* (V, Appendix
> to §11 and §20, p. 595)

We are then to understand phenomenology as enabling us, by identifying accurately and by understanding what is presented to consciousness, both in the perception of individuals and in the intuition of universals, to encounter and to recognize a world of particulars and universals that exist independently of and external to consciousness. And this is one of the issues on which Neo-Kantianism is most decisively repudiated in the *Logical Investigations*. Perception yields not just knowledge of how sensible particulars appear to us, but of how they are. For what is presented, what appears, in genuine perception is the thing as it is, albeit presented to a particular perceiver from a particular point of view. No place is left for the Kantian distinction between the-thing-in-itself and phenomena. And so one source of Neo-Kantian disagreements also disappears. Moreover what Kant had taken to be the mind's contribution to experience, those a priori universal structures, that, in Kant's view, impose their ordering on experience, are, in Husserl's rival view, constituted by the necessary relationships between those universals that are also objects of experience. The world that we encounter in experience is a world structured in such a way that it is apt for representation by and through conceptual schemes that we elaborate on the basis of our experience.

The particular sciences, whether physical, biological, or human, presuppose what phenomenology discovers: the concepts constitutive of those necessary and unqualifiedly invariant relationships governing all discourse which constitute the laws of logic, the concepts constitutive of necessary and invariant relationships within a particular domain, such as those of number or of body, and the concepts constitutive of those invariant, but contingent relationships that are identified as laws of nature. For each of these sets a grasp of essential properties is required, a grasp expressed in those linguistic formulations that depend for the evidentness and the exactness of what they say upon the given, upon what is presented to consciousness either as individual or as essence. And this presupposition by the particular sciences of what can only be disclosed by phenomenological attention and enquiry holds of their contingent generalizations (although not of the empirical content of those generalizations) as well as of their necessary truths.

Nature discloses itself to us as a whole, the interrelationship of whose parts is apprehended through grasping the relevant essences, and our knowledge of these is characterized by Husserl as what is a priori in our knowledge of nature. But this is not the Kantian a priori, not only because, as I have already emphasized, it is itself an object of experience, but also because the line between what can be known only by empirical enquiry and what is given to phenomenological enquiry is very different from any of Kant's distinctions: "natural laws . . . do not belong to this *a priori* . . . they have the character not of truths of essence, but of truths of fact. . . . Nature with all its physical laws is a fact that could well have been otherwise" (III, §23, p. 486).

It is then a contingent fact that such and such a set of laws hold. Laws themselves are indeed formulated by scientists not as empirical generalizations, but as holding necessarily. But, as such, they have a provisional character: "All laws of fact in the exact sciences are accordingly genuine laws, but, epistemologically considered, no more than idealizing fictions with a *fundamentum in re*" (*Prolegomena*, §23, p. 106). Further enquiry may always result in their revision or replacement. And Husserl's understanding of laws therefore leaves open such possibilities as the replacement of Newtonian mechanics by quantum mechanics, a kind of possibility that was not allowed for in Kant's scheme of thought and that therefore provided a set of difficulties for the Neo-Kantians. Husserl is thus at one level, that at which experience provides our most fundamental concepts, a thorough-going realist. But in the philosophy of science, at least in the *Logical Investigations*, his realism is qualified.

When I sketched the history of Neo-Kantianism, I identified some central problems that the Neo-Kantians had encountered. What I hope has now become clear is that from the standpoint of the *Logical Investigations*, two of these need not arise. They present difficulties generated only within and by a Kantian scheme of thought. One is the problem of what to make of the concept of the thing-in-itself, the other that of how to reconcile the Kantian understanding of laws of nature with the replacement of Newtonian mechanics by quantum and relativistic mechanics. Here Kant had perhaps provided the resources for a solution, since he was concerned to identify what necessarily holds of *any* space-time experience and could have accommodated an alternative account of the nature of the laws of mechanics within this framework. Nonetheless, freeing up Kant from his Newtonian commitments requires considerable work. There was however another problem central to the Neo-Kantian debates that is of a very different order. How is the knowing self, as understood by Kant, to be related to what is empirically discoverable about the self and about cognition?

This is a problem that arises as sharply for Husserl as it does for Kant or for the Neo-Kantians. For it is not just Kant's particular understanding of the knowing subject that poses the problem. It is an empirical fact that I engage in numerous distinct acts of perception of judgment, of doubt, of desire and the like. What is it then that makes each of them mine? To what does the 'I' of the 'I think that . . .' that is presupposed by all my mental acts refer? How is the identity of the 'I' constituted? Husserl raised some of these questions in the first chapter of the Fifth Investigation, rejecting Natorp's Kantian account of the 'pure ego'. But he did not pursue them at any length and, when he later returned to them, the line of thought that he then pursued was to lead him back towards the Kantian account. For the earlier readers of the *Logical Investigations*, this later development would have seemed unimaginable. What had inspired them was the extent of Husserl's success in providing a new and fruitful way of opening up philosophical enquiry that was a radical alternative to Kant. And, when Edith Stein and her contemporaries began to contribute to the philosophical enterprise, they had before them the instructive example not only of Husserl himself, but also of those of his students who had learned from his investigations how to pursue their own. Foremost among these was Reinach.

6

Reinach's Philosophical Work

Reinach's first substantial contribution to philosophical enquiry was his *Habilitationsschrift* on some of the concepts central to civil law. He then proceeded to pursue lines of thought in the philosophy of logic and epistemology that Husserl had opened up in the *Logical Investigations*, finally returning to issues in the philosophy of law. So I begin this account of his development with considering his more general philosophical commitments, before turning to his seminal work on legal and normative concepts.

In a paper published in 1911, Reinach accused Kant of having failed to grasp adequately a distinction between two kinds of necessity, modal necessity and material necessity, and in consequence of having misunderstood Hume. Modal necessity concerns what Hume called "relations of ideas" and is exemplified in arithmetical and geometrical propositions. Material necessity is what is ascribed in judgments about causal relations, when we assert not only a relation of temporal sequence between one event and another, but also one of necessary connection, not only, that is, that event a occurs after event b, but that, given that event b has occurred, necessarily event a occurred. Hume's account of sense experience did of course exclude the possibility of our encountering examples of material necessity in our experience and so he had concluded that it was a fiction. But Kant had failed to recognize even the possibility.

"According to Kant, Hume saw only two possibilities: either the *foundation* of the causal judgment in pure reason, or the *explanation* of it from experience, i.e., from the mechanism of association and the 'subjective necessity arising from it,' which is falsely taken to be objective. That for Hume there is a third possibility—the immediate grounding of necessity through experience—is overlooked by Kant and, from Kant's standpoint must be overlooked" ("Kants Auffassung des Humeschen Problems," *Zeitschrift für Philosophie und philosophische Kritik* 141, 1911, tr. J. N. Mohanty in *Southwestern Journal of Philosophy* 7, 1976, p. 186). Yet for Reinach it was just this possibility that Husserl's phenomenology had opened up. For he took it that Husserl had provided the means for showing that we not only apprehend essential properties of the objects that are presented in perception, but also those of changes in those objects that occur to them and the necessary relationships that may hold between such changes.

We apprehend, that is, not only this bat and that ball, but also that this bat is striking that ball, and that necessarily, whenever a bat strikes a ball, the ball changes direction. The material necessity is at once a matter of a relationship between ideas and of a relationship between things. And our ascriptions of material necessity are grounded in our experience of what is essential and invariant in the attributes and relationships of moving bodies. Such complex objects of intentional acts—for example, that the bat is striking the ball—Husserl spoke of as categorial objects and in the *Investigations* he says a good deal about such objects and the intentionalities whose objects they are.

Notice that what a phenomenological report supplies is an account fuller than, but not inconsistent with the elliptical reports of ordinary prephilosophical perceivers. 'What did you see?' 'The bat deflecting the ball, so that it can no longer reach the wicket'. What is given in perception, on both the plain person's and the phenomenologist's account, is a single phenomenon, perceivable by any well-placed perceiver, that of the bat striking the ball, so that the ball is deflected away from the wicket. All this occurs independently of its being perceived by any particular perceiver or indeed by any perceiver at all. And the necessity that attaches to the deflection of the ball, given that it was struck thus by the bat, is as much a property of what is given in experience as is the shape of the ball or the movement of the bat. What is not given is a set of Humean impressions, let alone a set of Humean impressions ordered by the structures of the mind, as understood by Kant. And we could only suppose otherwise by failing to attend systematically and minutely to what it is that is perceived and to what it is that is invariant in the given of perceptual experience. The onus here is on the Humean or the Kantian to show otherwise and to discharge that onus they would have to argue us out of a conviction that is at once native to plain persons and as well-grounded as any such conviction can be by the reports of disciplined phenomenological attention.

Of course plain prephilosophical persons do not speak in the idiom of Husserl. They do not use terms such as 'intentional object' or 'material necessity'. But the terms that they do use are consistent with Reinach's Husserlian claims. This is then one area in which the judgments of plain prephilosophical persons are vindicated by phenomenology. Nonetheless, the difference between their reports and those of the phenomenologist must not be underestimated. Reinach was not able to say what he had to say without making a set of logical, ontological, and epistemological commitments, each of which needs philosophical clarification and justification. Let me consider briefly just two of those commitments.

Reinach drew an important distinction between two senses in which we may ascribe to someone a judgment that a is P. We may speak of such a judgment as expressed by some act of affirmation or assertion that a is P and we may also speak of such a judgment as a conviction that a is P. Assertions are events. They occur at particular points in time. Convictions are states that endure through periods of time. Assertions are all or nothing. Either I assert that a is P or I do not. Convictions by contrast admit of degrees. One can be more or less convinced that a is P (see "On the Theory of Negative Judgment" in *Parts and Moments: Studies in Logic and Formal Ontology*, ed. B. Smith, München, Wien: Philosophia Verlag, 1982, p. 319, tr. from *Zur Theorie des negativen Urteils* in A. Reinach, *Gesammelte Schriften*, Halle: Niemeyer, 1921; this paper was first published in 1911 in a *Festschrift* for Theodor Lipps). Acts of assertion have as their counterpart acts of questioning ('Is a P?') and acts of wishing ('If only a were P!'). States of conviction have as their counterpart states of conjecture and doubt. A conviction may or may not issue in an assertion, but an assertion, so Reinach asserted is always "accompanied by an underlying conviction" (op. cit., p. 320). To this it might be objected that it is possible to make an assertion, without any underlying conviction, as when one lies. But in Reinach's view the utterance of a lie is not a genuine act of affirmation—it has the appearance, but not the reality of an assertion.

Having distinguished these two senses of 'judgment' or perhaps these two kinds of judgment, Reinach follows Brentano and Husserl in treating the intentionality of each kind of judgment as its primary characteristic, asking in each case what the judgment is *about* and how it is related to that which it is about. His answer is that in both cases what the judgment is about is the same, but that the relationship of the judgment to what it is about differs. This latter point I put on one side. What judgments are about are states of affairs (*Sachverhalte*). So when someone judges that some particular rose is red, and it is in fact red, it is the state of affairs constituted by that rose's being red about which they judge, and it is that same state of affairs that renders their judgment true.

About the nature and status of states of affairs there has been continuing philosophical disagreement. There are at the one extreme those who hold that states of affairs are no more than shadows cast by true sentences, individuated only as the subject-matter of those sentences. And at the other extreme are those who assert that states of affairs are independent of our linguistic practices and that for every possible judgment there is a corresponding

state of affairs. Reinach defended one version of the latter view and thus committed himself to a variety of highly debatable positions. But I want to attend
only to one aspect of those commitments.

Reinach held that, just as there are both positive and negative judgments,
so too there are both positive and negative states of affairs: "Negative states
of affairs subsist precisely as do positive states, quite independently of
whether or not they are presented to anything or come to be apprehended,
believed, meant, or asserted. *That 2 x 2 is not equal to 5*, this state of affairs,
subsists wholly independently of any conscious subject which may grasp it,
just as much as does the positive *being identical of 2 x 2 and 4*" (op. cit., p.
361). In those acts of meaning in which we make negative states of affairs the
subject-matter of our assertions we are able to present those negative states
of affairs only by negating some positive assertion whose subject-matter is
the corresponding positive state of affairs. Since in this way we apprehend
negative states of affairs *via* positive states of affairs, the latter are linguistically and epistemologically prior to the former. But the ontological status of
negative states of affairs is the same as that of positive states of affairs. Why
should this have mattered to Reinach?

It is in part because of his view that one state of affairs can stand to another in the relationship of ground to consequent. "Everything which we encounter, either in science or in everyday life, as a connectedness of ground
and consequent, is a relation between states of affairs" (op. cit., p. 339). This
relationship is informed by the material necessity about which Reinach
spoke in his article on Hume and Kant. And just as, in order to identify the
logical relationships that hold between propositions, we need to recognize
negative propositions, for corresponding reasons we need to recognize negative states of affairs.

States of affairs can not only be positive or negative, they also vary in
modality. It can be the case that a is P, but it can also be the case that a is possibly P or that a is probably P. And once again the analogy with propositions
holds. But it is important not to confuse propositions and states of affairs.
Every act of assertion is an act of meaning and what is meant by the judgment that I assert about some state of affairs is a proposition. What is presented to me in experience is something with both contingent and necessary
properties and in becoming aware of particulars I become aware of the states
of affairs of which they are constituents and so can assert a judgment whose
meaning is a proposition. Propositions can stand to each other only in logical relationships, objects only in contingent causal relationships, while states
of affairs can stand to each other in relationships of material necessity.

What I have presented so far is a very bare sketch of some of Reinach's
central positions, so bare that each of them invites obvious objections. And
here I am going to do nothing to meet those objections. Every one of
Reinach's lines of thought was, as he well understood, an elucidation and an

extension of Husserl's enquiries in the *Logical Investigations*. But they also bear the stamp of Reinach's originality and, when it came to issues in the philosophy of law, Reinach broke new ground in even more striking ways. Consider first his treatment of acts of promising, a type of act essential to the making of contracts and so one an understanding of which is presupposed by every system of civil law. Four features of promising are salient in Reinach's account in "Die apriorischen Grundlagen des bürgerlichen Rechts," published by Husserl in the first volume of the *Jahrbuch für Philosophie und phänomenologische Forschung* in 1913.

First an act of promising is an act which brings into being both an obligation and a claim. If A promises B that A will do such and such, then A has an obligation to do such and such and B has a claim upon A that terminates only when A does in fact do such and such. The connection between the state of affairs that is A's having at some earlier time promised to do such and such and not yet kept that promise and the states of affairs that are A's now having an obligation to do such and such and B's now having a claim against A is one of material necessity, one of ground to consequent. The necessity is not a matter of the relationship of propositions, although the truth that 'Necessarily, if A promised B to do such and such, and if A has not yet kept that promise, A has an obligation to do such and such, and B has a claim against A' does exhibit a corresponding necessary relationship between propositions. But no proposition can necessarily generate an obligation or a claim and the state of affairs that is A's having made a promise does just that.

A second salient characteristic of acts of promising is that they cannot be reduced to or wholly explained in terms of psychological states of the agent who promises. It is now a philosophical commonplace, although it was not so in Reinach's time, that, although someone who promises to do such and such expresses an intention to do such and such, the expression of an intention to do such and such is not by itself the making of a promise. And what is true of intending is also true of wishing, desiring, hoping and other such psychological acts and states. A third salient characteristic of promising brings out a further crucial difference between these acts or states and promising.

Someone can intend, wish, desire or hope without giving any perceptible expression to their intending, wishing, desiring or hoping. These can be entirely inward acts or states. But an act of promising, while it will always have an inward aspect, that is, the agent's awareness of what she or he is intending and doing in promising, must also receive outward expression, or else it will not be a promise. Moreover it is not that there are two distinct and separable parts to promising, an inward and an outward. These two aspects of the act of promising are integrated into a single unified act that is at once internal and external, bodily and mental. This unity of mental act and physical expression is not unique to promising. A whole range of inner acts and states characteristically receive physical expression, but with some types of act or state it is possible to inhibit the outward expression, so that the feeling or attitude remains within the inner life of the individual. So it can be with shame, regret, anger and the whole range of the emotions. Wittgenstein was later to raise crucial questions about how in such cases inner act or state and outward modes of expression are related. Reinach passes by those questions, moving on to note a fourth distinctive characteristic of promising.

Acts of promising by contrast are members of the class of what Reinach called 'social acts', acts one of whose essential properties is that they are directed towards another self. Other types of social act are: informing, requesting, commanding and questioning. Social acts are, in Reinach's view, members of a larger class, that of what Reinach called 'spontaneous acts'. To say of an act that it is spontaneous is to say that it brings something about. It is not merely a receptive experience of something undergone, as feeling a pain is. Turning one's attention to something is a spontaneous act; being involuntarily made aware of something is not. But only some spontaneous acts are essentially intended to bring something about in someone else, and so a social act is defined as "an action of the subject to which are essential not only its spontaneity and its intentionality, but also its being directed towards alien subjects and its needing to be understood by those subjects" (*Sämtliche Werke*, p. 160).

Just as it would be a mistake to think of an act of promising as essentially an inner mental act which merely happens to receive outward expression in an utterance, so it would also and equally be a mistake to suppose that an act of promising is nothing more than the outward expression, the utterance. Every social act is the expression of an underlying conviction of the subject and a difference in conviction entails a difference in the nature of the social act. "Imparting information presupposes a conviction as to what is imparted. It is of the essence of asking a question that it excludes such a conviction, requiring uncertainty about what is asked" (p. 162). But what then, if I ask a question, when I am not really in doubt? And what, if I tell someone that such and such is the case, but am convinced that things are otherwise?

In the first case, I will be pretending to uncertainty or ignorance and so not genuinely posing a question. In the second case, I will be lying and so not making a genuine affirmation, but only acting the part of one who affirms, as—my example, not Reinach's—an actor on the stage may play such a part. In both cases the social act is other than it is taken to be. What kind of social act I am performing in any given instance is therefore a matter both of outward expression and inner conviction and of these two integrated into a single act. Moreover this unity of inner conviction and outward expression is something that has to be understood by those others to whom social acts are addressed. They have to understand what is said to them as expressive of acts of promising, imparting information, commanding, making a request, questioning and the like. In so doing they not merely hear and understand the spoken words of the utterance, but hear and understand them as expressions of the conviction of the utterer. They may of course be deceived, as when someone is not genuinely questioning, but play acting the part of a questioner, or pretending to impart information, while in fact deliberately misleading. But these cases of error are secondary to and intelligible only in terms of the primary and standard examples of those types of speech act which the play actor or the liar mimics. And in the standard cases, that is in the vast majority of cases, we understand each other very well as makers of promises, askers of questions, and the like.

Reinach made this account of what speech acts are and how they are to be classified the starting-point for a systematic philosophy of law, in which he deals with what it is for one person to represent another, with the nature and origin of legal rights, claims and obligations, with ownership and contract, and with what it is to enact a law. These were of course areas that were remote from Husserl's interests and Reinach's independence of mind, so long as it was exhibited only or primarily in these areas, did not represent any kind of challenge to Husserl. Indeed, as we have already seen, Reinach presented himself to the students at Göttingen above all as an interpreter of Husserl and one whose insightfulness Husserl himself had acknowledged. Yet in three ways at least Reinach's philosophical and pedagogic stances posed questions about his and their relationship to Husserl.

Husserl's achievement was so extraordinary that he does not need to be forgiven for treating his students' projects as parts or aspects of a phenomenological enterprise that was primarily his. He was enormously generous to his students and they varied in their responses to this aspect of his character. But for a few it made their relationship to Husserl a difficult one. So later on, one of the best and certainly the most independent of his students, Hans Lipps, was to suffer from Husserl's philosophical intolerance. By contrast, Reinach in his relationship to his and Husserl's students was not only a generous and agreeable person, but in his attitudes to philosophy someone for whom all that mattered was what was said, and not at all who had said it or who disagreed with it.

At the conclusion of the lecture on phenomenology that he was to give at Marburg in 1914 Reinach first stressed "the peculiar and immense effort required, if we are 'to break with theories and constructions,' so as to return to 'the facts themselves,' to pure, unobscured intuition of essences" (p. 220). But he then goes on to say that, when we undertake this labor "*there* philosophical work is taken out of the hands of individuals. . . . To future generations it will be just as unintelligible that an individual should project a philosophy as today it is that an individual should project natural science" (p. 221). Philosophy, as understood from a phenomenological standpoint, is to become a cooperative project, just as physics or astronomy is, rather than an

arena of conflicting standpoints, each identified with some great philosophical name.

So Husserl's students were summoned by Reinach to find a role for themselves within the phenomenological enterprise, just as he had done. But, if
they were to extend further the lines of thought that Reinach himself had developed, they might well in time find themselves at odds with Husserl's own
understanding of the directions in which that enterprise now had to be
taken. It is true that many of Reinach's key ideas extend further remarks that
Husserl had made in the *Logical Investigations*. The seeds of his conception
of natural necessity are to be found in Husserl's discussion of causal laws in
the second chapter of the Third Investigation. And the seeds of his conception of states of affairs and their relationship to judgments and propositions
are to be found in the third and fourth chapters of the Fifth Investigation. But
the use that Reinach made of these concepts in his analysis of promising and
more generally in his account of social acts gave phenomology a dimension
that had been absent from Husserl's writings.

For Husserl phenomenological enquiry is always from some first-person
perspective. It is *I* who perceive, remember, imagine, judge and what is presented to consciousness in such acts provides the objects of *my* intentionally
directed attention. It is I, the same I, who as phenomenologist attends to such
acts and objects. It is of course true that in attending to such objects I have to
exclude everything that is peculiarly and contingently mine. What is presented to me in an act of perception or memory or imagination or judgment
or in second-order reflection on these acts is what would be presented to any
phenomenologically attentive subject. The 'I' of Husserl's phenomenology is
an impersonal 'I'. And in the decade after the *Logical Investigations*, Husserl
developed more than one account of how detachment from those
prephenomenological beliefs and attitudes of mine that can infect and distort
my awareness of what is presented to consciousness is to be achieved.

Moreover, Husserl from the outset had understood the cooperative nature
of the enquiries on which he was engaged, acknowledging his own debts to
Brentano and Twardowski and expecting his students to carry his work further. And he was to recognize that in identifying something as an object I
identify it as a possible or actual object of minds other than my own. When
he came to write about the history of science late in his life, he understood
very well that the objectivity of science is inseparable from its public and social character. So that in a variety of contexts he found the existence of a plu-
rality of minds unproblematic. Yet the thought seems to have remained alien
to him that some types of mental act—and *therefore* their objects—might require for their being as they are, a multiplicity of consciousnesses, a society
of minds. For Husserl other minds, other human beings, are among the objects of my mental acts. I quoted earlier from the seventh section of the First
Investigation where Husserl allows that we may truly be said to perceive

"other people's inner experiences," their anger or their pain. But that there are such other minds seems to have no bearing on the constitution of the objects of my consciousness, of what is presented to it.

Indeed it was in the next section of the First Investigation that Husserl took a crucial step in excluding any such possibility from consideration. In the seventh section, Husserl considers how expressions, meaningful signs, function in communication and in the eighth how they function "in solitary life," "in uncommunicated, interior mental life." "This change in function," he then says, "plainly has nothing to do with whatever makes an expression an expression. Expressions continue to have meanings as they had before . . ." (p. 278). By contrast, Reinach in his account of social acts, and more especially of promising, had identified a set of cases where this is not so, where it is of the essence of what is said that it is addressed to another person. In promising, for example, the expression 'I promise' has the meaning and force that it has only because it generates an obligation to and a legitimate claim on the part of the person to whom it is addressed. Moreover 'I promise' has the meaning and force that it has only because of a shared understanding of what is involved in promising in general and in making this particular promise. I can understand myself as having made a promise only if certain others also understand me to have made it. Promising is possible only in a particular kind of social setting.

This of course by itself need not suggest that Husserl was mistaken, either in his account of the meaning of expressions in general or in his first-person perspective. Husserl had after all recognized that the use of expressions in acts of communication has to make reference to those others with whom the subject communicates and Reinach's account of social acts can perhaps be understood as developing out of that brief discussion of acts of communication. Moreover Reinach is careful to contrast social acts with those acts in which there need be no reference to anyone other than the subject. So that it may seem that so far Reinach merely extends and does not break with Husserl's thought. But he does raise three questions to which Husserl had provided no answers, questions that Husserl's conception of the phenomenological standpoint seems to preclude him from asking, let alone answering: What are they?

On Reinach's account of social acts there are mental acts in which my understanding of what I am doing includes an understanding that someone else understands my act precisely as I understand it. When, as phenomenologist, I so understand myself as a maker of promises, I am aware of my act as the other is aware of it and of me as agent. Now it is necessary for the truth of these claims that all these uses of 'I', 'me' and 'my' should have the same reference. The 'I' who understands my utterance as having the relevant meaning has to be the same as the 'me' who is understood by others as understanding my own act and the same as the 'I' who is aware of myself in a single act as both understanding and understood. Yet it is difficult, on any account consonant with Husserl's characterization of the phenomenological standpoint, to see how this could be so.

Husserl contrasts sharply what he called "the psychological point of view" with the phenomenological standpoint. From the psychological standpoint, we may treat "an experience of joy, for instance, as an *inner state* of feeling of a man or an animal," as someone's, that is, but from the phenomenological standpoint what is given is "the apprehension of an absolute experience in its intimate subjective flow," as anyone's, that is, so that in "the effective experience of joy as an absolute phenomenological datum" what is manifested is "the state of consciousness of a human ego-subject linked to the appearance we call a body" (*Ideen I*, §53, translated as *Ideas* by W. R. Boyce Gibson, New York: Macmillan, 1931). Notice the disappearance of all personal pronouns in Hussel's characterization of the phenomenological standpoint, as though it were inessential to joy that it is always mine or yours or hers and as though it were inessential to the phenomenologist that the joy on whose experience he reports is his own and that the reference of that 'he' and that 'his' has to be the same. The 'I' of the phenomenological standpoint is always and necessarily subject and not object.

How can this 'I' have the same reference as the 'I' and the 'me' of individuals who are always both subjects and objects? It is of course true that the end purpose of the phenomenologist is to give an impersonal account of the nature of the experience of joy as such, of what it is for anyone to be joyful. But a condition of the phenomenologist's report being true is that what *he* has inspected is *his* joy, for otherwise it would not be "subjective" in the required sense. Yet Husserl's account of the radical difference between the phenomenologist's standpoint and that of any individual who is in fact joyful makes it unclear how this condition could be satisfied, how the 'I' who reports as a phenomenologist could be the same as the 'I' whose mental act is the object of the phenomenologist's attention. Or rather, insofar as they are the same, and clearly they must be, it is unclear how the degree and kind of phenomenological detachment from everything that is peculiar to me as experiencing subject is to be achieved. This is not anything like an insuperable objection to Husserl's thesis. It is just that more needs to be said.

A closely related question, one also suggested by the passage from *Ideen* from which I quoted, concerns the mind-body relationship. In the very next section of *Ideen*, Husserl entertains the possibility of "the whole of nature" being "annulled," so that "there would then be no more bodies" (§54). Yet "my consciousness . . . would remain an absolute stream of experience with its own distinctive essence" and Husserl concludes that even without "the empirical intentional unities," including that of the body, states of consciousness would remain what they are in their givenness. That is, for Husserl there is no essential relationship between my having or being a body and my being the subject of conscious experiences. Yet on Reinach's account of social acts, a condition of the possibility of such acts is that inner mental awareness and outward bodily expression are parts of a single unified act. Subtract what is bodily and what we would be left with is not with a purely mental act, but no act at all. So there must, at least for some types of act, be an essential relationship of inner consciousness and the body in and through which that consciousness is directed.

To these two problems—that of the identity of reference of the relevant personal pronouns and that of the mind-body relationship—add a third that is closely related. When I perceive some physical object, a ball, say, being deflected by a bat, I perceive it as perceivable by others who occupy different physical standpoints. And I perceive it as moving relative to the position of my body, occupying a space partially defined by the position of my body, a space that changes its boundaries as my body moves. How I perceive the movement of that ball as perceived by others is a matter of how I perceive their bodies relative to it and relative to my body. That is, how the physical objects of my acts of perception appear to me cannot be characterized without implicit reference to my body. Subtract this reference and what remains is no longer the object of an act of perception, no longer an object that is at once external to my body and independent of my acts of perception. So even in the most elementary of mental acts the intentionality is that of an embodied consciousness, something that Husserl's account of acts of perception *seems* to find no place for.

I say only "seems," because Husserl himself was to assert this very thesis in his 1913–1914 lectures on "Nature and Spirit," arguing that experience of the world as objective is possible only if individuals, who each experience the world from their own subjective point of view, are able to understand their own point of view as only one among many and are able to learn from others what it is to experience the world from the point of view of these others. The problem for Husserl is this. It appears that from my subjective standpoint other human beings and physical objects can be no more than objects of my experience. Yet it also appears that my experiences of objects can only be what they are, if others too are subjects against whose experiences I must match my own, if I am to have a true view of things. How can both of these be true? That they are true Husserl certainly allows, but he provided no answer to this question, understandably, since to do so he would have to put in question his account of the 'I'. When very much later Alfred Schutz asked him why he had never published the second volume of *Ideen*, Husserl replied "that at that time he had not found a solution to the problem of intersubjectivity. He believed he had done so in the Fifth *Cartesian Meditation*" (Alfred Schutz, *Collected Papers*, Vol. I, p. 140).

Reinach's account of social acts suggests that it is the latter of these two theses that we should accept. But Reinach did not himself pursue these questions.

It was only later that they were to be opened up again in different ways by Lipps, Ingarden and Stein. Hans Lipps, who was a physician as well as a philosopher, insisted from the outset on the bodily dimensions of our experience and on consciousness as constituted through interactions with things, so that the relationship of body to mind and of body to body is of central importance. Roman Ingarden, both in his later work on ontology—in which he was to quarrel with some of Reinach's conclusions—and in his writings on aesthetics, took it to be of some importance to phenomenology that the mind directs itself to and is receptive to physical objects that are what they are independently of our perception and judgment. And Edith Stein in her dissertation developed lines of enquiry that are responsive to these same questions. All of them, Lipps, Ingarden and Stein, took themselves to be faithful to the modes of phenomenological enquiry exemplified by both Husserl and Reinach. But all of them were at some time to clash with Husserl and in their work which led to this clash owed a great deal to Reinach.

7

1913–1915: Stein's Education

The majority of Husserl's students had come to Göttingen only in order to study with Husserl. And the rift between Husserl and his philosophical colleagues made it as easy for them to be as dismissive of those colleagues as many of those colleagues were of Husserl. But in this the students were mistaken, most notably about Leonard Nelson, himself treated as something of an outsider by most of the Philosophy Faculty. He had been appointed *Privatdozent* as long ago as 1909, yet he was not to achieve the rank of *Extraordinarius* until 1919.

Nelson was an unusually effective teacher, a Neo-Kantian, but very much his own man. His philosophical hero was Jakob Friedrich Fries and it was Kant as understood by Fries whom Nelson expounded in both his classes and his writings. For Fries, what the *Critique of Pure Reason* provided was an identification of the limits of human cognition. Those who had developed its thesis in either a transcendental or a psychologistic direction had betrayed their Kantian inheritance. What was needed as a sequel to the *Critique of Pure Reason* was a better account of what is involved in what Fries had called "faith in reason." A central thesis affirmed by Nelson is that no justification for our fundamental claims to knowledge is either possible or needed, since any such justification would involve an appeal to something beyond reason, an incoherent notion. The project of a theory of knowledge, as customarily understood, is therefore always based upon some philosophical mistake and Nelson's lectures were designed to demonstrate the contradictions of which the protagonists of each particular theory of knowledge were guilty. But these negative attitudes to epistemology were not carried over to ethics, where Nelson developed his own version of Kant's categorical imperative and was famous among his students for the extent to which his own life was informed by the precepts that he defended theoretically. (After the First World War he was to become an active participant in the labor movement, founding a school for young people designed to enable them to act constructively and with integrity in that movement.)

Husserl's students did not generally attend Nelson's classes, but Edith Stein was an exception. She was also an exception in the extent to which she undertook studies outside philosophy. And these were to have their effect later in her life. While still in Breslau, Stein had read Max Lehmann's life of that great Prussian hero, the Baron vom und zum Stein. Now she was able to attend Lehmann's seminar on German constitutional history and, in order to do so, had to miss Reinach's introductory lectures. Lehmann had himself been a student of Ranke and had learned from Ranke to present German history in a European context. Moreover Lehmann himself was, as a liberal, suspicious of Bismarck's policies and as a Hannoverian, highly critical of Prussia. Stein herself had remained to this point not only a patriotic German, but also a warm admirer of Prussian character and achievement and it was Lehmann who introduced her to very different attitudes towards German constitutional history and to a view of it whose standards were drawn from English liberalism rather than from any German source.

The paper that she presented to Lehmann's seminar so impressed him that he told her that he would be prepared to submit it in a rewritten version as the thesis required for the examinations prescribed by the state board. Stein was led by this to consider taking those examinations earlier than she had planned. Students were required to take examinations in three disciplines, in Stein's case in philosophy, in history, for which a student had to show a command of Greek, and in German philology. The benefits of this breadth of preparation were not only to the student, but also to the university. It enabled the practitioners of each particular academic discipline to understand and take an interest in the enquiries of their colleagues in other disciplines to a degree that has been rare elsewhere.

Stein's cousin, Richard Courant, for example, had taken his examinations in physics and philosophy as well as in mathematics. He had attended Husserl's lectures and Husserl had been one of his examiners, arriving forty minutes late for the examination, much to the exasperation of David Hilbert, Courant's examiner in mathematics, and then taking up all of the remaining time not by questioning Courant, but by answering a question about phenomenology posed to him by Courant. Needless to say, Courant passed as easily in philosophy as he had brilliantly in mathematics (*Courant* by Constance Reid, New York: Springer-Verlag, 1996, pp. 33–34). But this true tale should not mislead us into underestimating the value of this examination system. Courant is a good example. He not only knew a good deal of philosophy and was able to make informed judgments about appointments in philosophy, but the temper of his mind, as exhibited in his mathematical work, owed something to philosophy, so that Kurt Friedrichs, Courant's assistant at Göttingen and later his colleague in New York, when defending Courant's reluctance to accept what he took to be oversimplified in a piece of mathematical work, said of him that "He is inhibited out of a philosophical insight, so to say" (*Courant*, p. 122).

It was this general academic culture of Göttingen that enabled Husserl to flourish, even with the disapproval of his senior philosophical colleagues. And it was this same culture, with its openness to a range of different academic enterprises and attitudes that encouraged in the students an independence of spirit that protected them from being too daunted by Husserl's single-minded pursuit of his own philosophical projects. There was in any case at the time that Stein arrived in Göttingen a new complexity in the attitudes of some of his students to Husserl.

Those students whose excitement on reading the *Logical Investigations* had brought them to Göttingen had been impressed in part by what they took to be Husserl's commitment to some form of realism and his denial of Kantian or any other form of idealism. They may perhaps also have understood that Husserl's commitment to the mind-independent existence of physical objects and of human beings had coexisted with an anti-Platonism in mathematics and an openness to a range of possibilities in the philosophy of science. But they had not been prepared for and were puzzled by some of the central assertions of the first volume of *Ideas*, when it appeared in 1913. Consider just one short passage.

"Reality, that of the thing taken singly as also that of the whole world, essentially lacks independence. . . . Reality is not in itself something absolute, binding itself to another only in a secondary way, it is, absolutely speaking, nothing at all, it has no 'absolute essence' whatsoever, it has the essentiality of something which in principle is *only* intentional, *only* known, consciously presented as an appearance" (*Ideas*, tr. W. R. Boyce Gibson, New York: Collier Books, 1962, §50, pp. 139–40). On a plain reading this seems to mark an abandonment of any version of realism. And commentators have ever since discussed passages such as this in the course of debating whether or not Husserl radically changed his views during the period in which he was formulating the positions that he took in *Ideas*. (For the strongest case that Husserl remained a realist, see both Karl Ameriks, "Husserl's Realism," *Philosophical Review* LXXXVI, 4, October 1977, and Robert Sokolowski, *The Formation of Husserl's Concept of Constitution*, The Hague: Nijhoff, 1970, p. 159. For the strongest case against this view, see Roman Ingarden, *On the Motives Which Led Husserl to Transcendental Idealism*, The Hague: Nijhoff, 1975, and his "The Letter to Husserl about the sixth *Investigation* and 'Idealism,'" Analecta Husserliana IV, ed. A.-T. Tymienecka, Dordrecht: D. Reidel, 1976, pp. 419–38.) But to some of Husserl's students at least, it seemed clear that a new direction had been taken.

Husserl was "at home" to his students one afternoon a week and at these gatherings anyone could ask him any philosophical question. About the first of these "at homes" that she attended, Edith Stein wrote: "All of us had the same question on our minds. The *Logical Investigations* had caused a sensation primarily because it appeared to be a radical departure from critical idealism which had a Kantian and Neo-Kantian stamp. It was considered 'a new scholasticism.' . . . Knowledge again appeared as reception, deriving its laws from objects not, as criticism has it, from determination which imposes its laws on the objects. All the young phenomenologists were confirmed realists. However the *Ideas* included some expressions which sounded as though their Master wished to return to idealism" (*Life in a Jewish Family, 1891–1916*, p. 250; I have altered Sister Josephine Koeppel's translation of '*Erkenntnis*' as 'perception' to 'knowledge').

The questions that the students raised with Husserl received answers that by and large failed to satisfy them. And this was the beginning of a disagreement between Husserl and some of his best students, who took themselves to have remained more faithful to Husserl's original intentions than Husserl himself. For Edith Stein this issue was to become one of first importance. But for the moment it was only one out of a set of topics that engaged her. Husserl's lecture course, entitled "Nature and Spirit," was on the foundations of the natural and the human sciences, matters that were to receive attention in the second volume of *Ideas*, and at the same time he was engaged in revising the *Logical Investigations*, which had been out of print for a number of years, with a view to publishing a new edition. So that the question of how far *Ideas* was no more than an extension and development of the standpoint of the *Investigations* rather than the expression of a radically new point of view was raised for his students in a number of different philosophical contexts.

At the same time, Stein had perhaps become more aware than previously of political alternatives. Her Prussian conservatism was initially strengthened by her encounter with Lehmann's liberalism, but she was now a good deal better informed about the choice between these rival political perspectives. And she also, for the first time since her early adolescence, began to take seriously the possibility of a belief in God. Here the example of Max Scheler played a part. Ever since she had abandoned her family's Judaism, Stein had taken it for granted that belief in God was a possibility only for those not yet sufficiently educated and enlightened. But now she was confronted by philosophers whose acknowledgment of God suggested otherwise. And among these Scheler was perhaps the most forthright and sophisticated in speaking about religion.

The quiet Protestant piety of the Husserls had in this period no discernible effect on Husserl's philosophy. By contrast Scheler concerned himself philosophically with questions about God. He was not yet a Catholic, but already in 1913–1914 he was impressed by the Catholic conception of the universe and made Stein's mind aware of possibilities that she had not so far entertained. But she was repelled by Scheler himself. Scheler, while teaching at Munich between 1907 and 1910, had elaborated his own version of phenomenology and claimed sincerely and passionately that, insofar as his positions coincided with those of Husserl, they had been arrived at independently. Yet in fact Scheler had almost certainly become acquainted with Husserl's basic positions in conversations that had taken place much earlier, while Husserl was still at Jena. Stein said of Scheler that everyone who knew him knew too "how apt he was to pick up suggestions from others. Ideas slipped into his mind and grew there while he himself was totally unaware of his having been influenced" (p. 259). Stein may well have exaggerated Scheler's lack of self-knowledge, but the equally tiresome vanity that was its counterpart led Scheler during his visits to Göttingen to adopt towards Husserl an attitude almost of condescension. Yet, although in fact deeply indebted to Husserl, he was also capable of brilliant and original insights and his books on *Ressentiment*, on sympathy, and on formalism in ethics, laid the foundations for a phenomenological ethics and greatly influenced Stein's own subsequent work, in spite of her dislike for their author.

What Stein had most urgently to answer at this point was that inescapable question for all students required to write a thesis—the state boards required theses as part of the examinations—what was to be its topic? She had been attending Husserl's lectures on "Nature and Spirit" in which, as I noticed earlier, he had argued that experience of the external world as objective was possible only if individuals were able to learn from others what it was to experience that world from their point of view. But this at once raised the question of what access each of us has to the experience of others. How do I know what someone else is perceiving, judging, feeling, remembering? Though what intentionality can I become aware of the intentional acts of others? Husserl had taken over from Theodor Lipps, who had been Reinach's teacher at Munich, the expression '*Einfühlung*', 'empathy', to name the experience through which we are so aware, although his uses of that word did not always coincide with Lipps's usage. And in the first volume of *Ideas* Husserl had mentioned empathy several times, contrasting what is given to us in empathy with our perception of the outward bodily behavior of others (§1), remarking that the possibility that those other consciousnesses that are posited in our empathetic experiences do not in fact exist (§46), and promising to deal more fully with empathy and with the kind of evidentness that it has in his second volume (§140). But he nowhere says what empathy is. And when Stein proposed this question as a dissertation topic, he was happy for her to fill this lacuna in his thought.

What he first required of her was that she make a study of Theodor Lipps's work, so that her dissertation might have the form of an analytical dialogue with Lipps, something that she agreed to only reluctantly. But Husserl insisted. So Stein began to make a detailed study of Theodor Lipps, becoming gradually dismayed, partly by the variegated uses to which he put his concept of empathy and partly by the discovery that whatever Lipps meant by *'Einfühlung'*, it was something very different from what Husserl had meant by his use of that word (p. 277).

She was occasionally able to discuss her project with Hans Lipps, the fellow student whom she most admired, but Lipps was not always forthcoming and besides he was preparing to join Hering in Strassburg. Reinach however was always available and helpful and, when Stein finally despaired of achieving clarity, it was to Reinach that she went. His evaluation of what she had done so far turned out to be encouragingly and to Stein surprisingly different from her own. We should perhaps be less surprised than she was, when we remember how in his account of social acts Reinach had paid particular attention to the outward expression of inner states and to the ways in which one and the same inner act can be expressed in very different ways. But just these were inescapable topics for Stein in her treatment of *Einfühlung*. So that Stein, although she seems not to have realized this at the time, was carrying further an investigation initiated by Reinach, who sent her away to spend three weeks writing a first draft of what she had done so far, approved it, and then sent her away once more to add to it. What she then showed him was, he said, more than adequate by the standards of the examinations for the state boards. "After these two visits with Reinach I was like one reborn. . . . I felt as though I had been rescued from distress by a good angel" (p. 284). And Stein was then able to resume her other studies for her examinations.

When she went back to Breslau for a short visit with her family before returning to Göttingen for the summer of 1914, her sister, Erna, was in the middle of the onerous state boards examinations in clinical medicine, and everyone at home was trying to be as supportive as possible. At the same time, the marriage of her eldest sister Else had entered a period of crisis and Else's husband, Max Gordon, had demanded that Else should return to her mother and receive medical and psychiatric treatment, if the marriage was to be saved. (She did and it was.) It was Edith who volunteered to go to Hamburg in order to bring her sister back to Breslau and she remained at home during the difficult period that followed. It was a time that tested the close bonds between the sisters, a time during which they were sustained by their shared closeness to their mother.

When she returned to Göttingen, it was to a life of developing friendships with several other women: with Toni Meyer from Breslau who had at the age of thirty-six come to Göttingen to attend Husserl's and Reinach's lectures; with Käthe Scharf, a teacher who was studying with Stein for the history examinations; with Lotte Winkler, her fellow student for the history of philosophy and for Germanic philology; and with Reinach's sister, Pauline, who was just beginning her university studies. And she enjoyed too the friendship of Husserl's other students. Hering had returned to take his examinations, while Bell, the Canadian, was working on his thesis, and there were also a number of newcomers ranging from a retired general to a visiting Russian professor. It was a time both of friendship and of intellectual excitement and it was brought to a dramatic end by the assassination of an Austrian archduke at Sarajevo.

An anxious July followed. On July 30 Stein was due to attend Reinach's lecture at five in the afternoon and an hour earlier she was at her desk reading Schopenhauer's *The World as Will and Idea*, when Käthe Scharf arrived with a friend to tell her that war had been declared and that all lectures had been cancelled. Shortly after this Nelli Courant came to tell her that Richard had been called to his regiment and that she had decided to return to Breslau. Would Edith Stein go with her? Within three hours Stein had been to the bank, paid a bill, made her farewells to Reinach, arranged for Toni Meyer to travel with them, packed, and walked to the Courants, where together they took a car to the railway station and departed for Breslau. Stein never returned to the reading of Schopenhauer.

There was no doubt in Stein's mind or in Courant's or in Husserl's or indeed in that of any of the professoriate or students at Göttingen, with the one possible exception of Max Lehmann, that Germany had engaged in a war that was at once just and unavoidable. Like so many others, they believed that the values at stake in the conflict were those of *Kultur*, values threatened by French cynicism, British commercial self-seeking and Russian barbarism. Almost the entire student body at Göttingen enlisted, among them Hans Lipps and Fritz Kaufmann, both of them good friends of Edith Stein, and so did many of the younger teachers, including Reinach, who was sent to Mainz for artillery training and then stationed near Verdun. Those professorial families who had sons of military age saw it as their children's patriotic duty to offer themselves for military service. Husserl's two sons both volunteered, the younger one, Wolfgang, while still only seventeen years old. Stein herself at home in Breslau was trained as a nurse by the Red Cross, so that she would be available for service in a military hospital. But in that early period in 1914 there was as yet no need for additional nurses.

Stein therefore returned to Göttingen, where classes had resumed, to complete her preparations for her examinations, which she passed "with Highest Honors" early in 1915. The only remaining task before she could begin work on her doctoral examination was that of passing an examination in Greek, for which she began to prepare, while at the same time enquiring of the Red Cross in Breslau whether it might now be possible for her to enter the nursing service. But she received no reply until after she had returned from Göttingen at the end of the semester, when she was asked whether she would be willing to nurse at a Red Cross hospital in Austria. So in April 1915, Stein reported for duty at Mährisch-Weisskirchen in Moravia, where a military academy had been turned into a *Seuchenlazarett*, an isolation hospital with four thousand beds for soldiers with contagious diseases, especially cholera, typhoid and dysentery. And there were many patients who had been wounded on the Carpathian front, where, later in the war, Wittgenstein was to serve.

Edith Stein's mother was at first bitterly opposed to her going to Mährisch-Weisskirchen and her decision to go was the first ever in which she defied her mother, who them relented sufficiently to provide her with her nurse's outfit. It was not only her mother who tried to dissuade her. Geheimrat Thalheim, a Breslau dignitary, when he learned why she was postponing her Greek examination, urged her to follow her mother's advice. Nursing exposed young women not only to disease, but also to moral danger. Stein's response was twofold: that, given these dangers, it was all the more necessary that women with a serious commitment should volunteer and that she had no better right to exempt herself from suffering than had the soldiers at the front. When she arrived at Mährisch-Weisskirchen, she was assigned as a nurse's aide to the typhoid ward.

8

1915–1916: From Nursing to a Doctorate

Edith Stein's time as a nurse was important to her in a variety of ways. She encountered a far wider range of types of human beings, drawn from different social classes, than she had met before, either in the circle of her family's acquaintances, or at school in Breslau, or while a student at Göttingen. Soon after she arrived at the hospital, she, who never touched alcohol, was shocked to find herself the only person sober at a party apart from the host, a Polish aristocrat who was also a physician. Gradually she became less naïve.

Among the patients there were speakers of all the languages of the Austro-Hungarian empire: not only German and Hungarian, but also Czech, Slovak, Slovenian, Ruthenian, Polish, Russian and Italian. The nurses could consult phrase-books for all these languages, but language was not the only barrier to communication, since the variety of languages was matched by the variety of ethnic cultural habits and customs. So there were recurrently problems both about how to communicate to the patients what the physicians or the nurses needed to tell them and also about how to interpret what the patients were trying to communicate or, on occasion, to conceal.

Moreover, cooperation between physicians and nurses and between wards was not always easy. So it was important to present oneself to colleagues as trustworthy and reliable, something that was also important in winning the confidence of suspicious or frightened patients. When Stein had chosen empathy as the subject for her dissertation, it had been because Husserl had so far not given an account of it, and because a good account of it was necessary, if some of his central claims were to be sustained. But now at Mährisch-Weisskirchen, the questions of how to be aware of the feelings and judgments of others and of what it was in one's own speech and bearing to which those others were responding in acting as they did had become questions of daily practical import. And this was not the only area in which Stein's experience as a nurse was relevant to her later philosophical enquiries.

Socrates in the *Phaedo* is represented by Plato as saying that "all who engage in philosophy in the right way practice nothing other than dying and being dead" (64A). And in the subsequent history of philosophy, this Socratic assertion has been transformed into a set of questions about the way in which we should view our own deaths and the deaths of others. To some of these questions, Heidegger was, more than ten years after Stein had served as a nurse, to give an answer and Stein was to be provoked into commentary on that answer. Her commentary appeals to a particular understanding of what it is to be with and to be there for others, when they are confronting the possibility of imminent death. Just such a relationship to others became part of Stein's everyday life during her nursing service, especially when she moved from the typhoid ward to the operating room and to the duties of postoperative care.

Stein went on leave early in September 1915, expecting to be recalled at any moment. While at home she therefore sat for and passed the examination required for auxiliary nursing, an examination that could only be taken after six months hospital experience. She also resumed her studies for her examination in Greek—the only books that she had taken with her to Mährisch-Weisskirchen were *Ideas* and Homer. But while she was still at home reading Homer and Plato, the Austrian victory over the Russians in Galicia ended the need for a hospital at Mährisch-Weisskirchen. And, although Stein remained available for recall by the Red Cross, she never was recalled.

So she was able to engage in extended work on her doctoral thesis and, when she returned to Göttingen for a visit at Christmas 1915, she presented Husserl with a manuscript on which a great deal of progress had been made. The occasion for the visit was Reinach's first leave, which happily coincided with his birthday on December 23. It was for Stein an important visit in at least three ways. Husserl's response to her manuscript was uncharacteristically encouraging and constructive. For the first time she got to know Anna Reinach well, a friendship that was to deepen and was to play a remarkable part in her life. And she was able to come to terms with Richard Courant's divorce. Nelli Courant in her account to Edith Stein of how her marriage had broken down had suggested to her that Richard Courant took a negative view of his cousin. But talk with Richard himself restored their relationship, which from then on was always warm and trusting. Very much later in life Courant would refer to her jokingly—long before her canonization—as "my cousin, the saint."

After this visit Stein returned to Breslau to complete her dissertation. But soon after she returned, she was asked by the principal of her old school, the *Viktoriaschule*, to teach Latin to the senior classes. The younger teachers had gone to the war and their replacement had developed tuberculosis. Because there was no one else available, and because of her love for and gratitude to the school, Stein agreed. There commenced one of the most physically taxing periods of her life. She would teach all day: Latin for the three upper grades and also some German, history and geography. Then, after joining her family for the evening meal, she would work on her thesis until at 10 p.m. she would begin her preparation for the next day's classes. The pressure on her gradually because more intense and during the summer she lost her appetite and twenty pounds in weight. By this time the thesis had been completed. During the Easter vacation she dictated it to two cousins, who had volunteered their services as typists (could there be better evidence of the strength of family ties?) and it was then mailed to Husserl.

Husserl was now at Freiburg-im-Breisgau. The death of Windelband had left the chair at Heidelberg open and Rickert, Riehl's successor at Freiburg, had been appointed to that chair. So Husserl succeeded Rickert. It had been a very difficult time for him. His younger son had been killed at the front and in the families with which the Husserls were most friendly such losses were becoming more and more frequent. But Husserl's response to crises which deeply engaged his emotions was always to immerse himself in work. And so at Freiburg his first semester was one of busy absorption in his new duties. When he received Stein's thesis, he wrote to her at once, expressing his pleasure, but warning her that it might be some time before he was able to read it. And when Stein traveled to Freiburg, in order to take her oral examinations, Husserl told her that he was so busy with his new course that she would have to postpone her examinations until some subsequent visit. At this Frau Husserl expressed great indignation on Stein's behalf and Stein decided to stay in Freiburg and let her efforts take their course.

It was a time for renewing friendships. Stein had traveled from Breslau to Freiburg by way of Dresden, Leipzig and Heidelberg. In Dresden she had met Hans Lipps at the railway station and travelled with him as far as Leipzig, discovering during the journey to her surprise that each thought the other greatly superior as a philosopher. Lipps was, after Roman Ingarden (about whom I have not yet spoken), the most impressive of Husserl's students. He was at that time twenty-seven years old, two years older than Stein. He had qualified as a physician, while also studying philosophy, and he had practiced medicine in Göttingen. He understood his own thought as developing out of Husserl's, but the temper of his mind was very different and relationships between them were not always easy. While Husserl was apt to move at the earliest possible stage of his enquiries to the abstract and the universal, Lipps always insisted on considering the abstract and the universal in terms of their particular and concrete embodiments. He was not an easy conversationalist, given to silences and to short staccato utterances. But at this period Stein valued both his judgments and his friendships more perhaps than those of anyone else.

On her visit to Heidelberg she had been accompanied by Pauline Reinach. In Freiburg her old friend, Erika Gothe, came to be with her during her preparations for her examinations. She also deepened her friendship with Roman Ingarden, whom she had first met in Göttingen. Ingarden was two years younger than Stein. A native of Kraków, he had been a student of Twardowski at Lwów, before he went to Göttingen to study for his doctorate under Husserl. He had also studied mathematics with Hilbert and psychology with G. E. Müller. The topic for his doctoral thesis was the relation between intellect and intuition in Bergson's philosophy. Like Hans Lipps, he was both conscious of his debt to Husserl and also fiercely independent. It was Ingarden who was to formulate most clearly and to pursue most strenuously the charge that Husserl had in *Ideen* abandoned his earlier realism. In 1914 Ingarden had joined the Polish Legion, but had been discharged because of a heart condition. He had returned to Göttingen and then accompanied Husserl to Freiburg.

Stein's patience with Husserl was not in vain. Malvine Husserl insisted that her husband take the time to read Stein's thesis and a date for the oral examinations was fixed. Husserl was however still disturbed by the lack of progress in his own work. He had been writing for some years on a number of topics that he intended to treat in the second volume of *Ideen*, but the result so far was a large collection of papers covered with the messily written Gabelsberger shorthand that Husserl used to record his thoughts, bundled together in no particular order. Husserl badly needed an assistant who knew his thought well and who could read his handwriting, so that this material could be put into some sort of order. But all the younger men were absent at the war. About this Husserl had complained at length to Stein's friend, Erika Gothe.

When therefore one evening Stein and Erika Gothe met the Husserls by chance and Husserl took the opportunity to tell Stein that he had now read a large part of her thesis and was very impressed by it, she felt able to offer her services as Husserl's assistant. Husserl was delighted and it was arranged that when, after her examinations, Stein returned to Breslau, she would fulfill her immediate obligations as a teacher at the *Viktoriaschule* and then end her career as a *Gymnasium* teacher.

The oral examinations took place on August 3, 1916. Afterwards, the examiners conferred and Stein went to a restaurant with Ingarden and Erika Gothe, since they knew that the Husserls, who had invited them for a post-examination celebration, would offer them only dessert. And so to the Husserls, where Stein learned that she had passed *summa cum laude*, a rare achievement at Freiburg. It was the end of the beginning.

9

Stein on Our Knowledge of Other Minds

Stein's doctoral thesis is a work of some philosophical importance, not so much because of the conclusions that she reaches or the arguments that she advances in support of them—important as some of these are—as because of the questions that she raises. These questions are of two kinds. The first concern method. Stein's starting-points and methods are Husserl's. But her use of those methods reminds us that there are two distinct directions in which Husserl's thought can be developed, one that of a phenomenological realism, the other that of a transcendental idealism. Once we have understood this it is unnecessary to enter into the interpretative controversy over whether Husserl himself, in moving towards transcendental idealism, had or had not abandoned some of his own earlier commitments. What matters is that immanent within Husserl's writings there sometimes seem to be two distinct and incompatible philosophies. And among the questions posed for us by Stein's thesis is that of whether the treatment of *Einfühlung* provides grounds for deciding between these.

A second set of questions posed by the dissertation concern its specific subject matter. When Husserl had agreed to assign the treatment of *Einfühlung* to Stein, he had seen this subject matter as one piece of philosophical business that still needed attention, a set of questions that he himself had not yet dealt with in sufficient detail. Insofar as Husserl had concerned himself with *Einfühlung*, it had been in the course of asking what it is that enables us to recognize the body of another as a living body, a body with its own sensations, and through that recognition as the body of another with whom I can communicate. But he had as yet said little about this and he evidently hoped that Stein would in this area act as his underlaborer. What had plainly not occurred to him was the thought that everything for his system might turn upon the success or failure of a phenomenological treatment of *Ein-fühlung*. Yet just this possibility is suggested by Stein's dissertation. How so?

Stein argues that key aspects of my knowledge of myself, of myself as someone with conscious awareness of a variety of objects and of myself as a body in the world, a body among other bodies, are possible only in and through my knowledge of others as those who know me. Yet if this is so, further questions are provoked. Since, if something is presented to me as an object of perception, it is presented as perceivable by others, and perceivable by them as one and the same object that is presented to me, in a space partially defined by the relationship of my body to theirs and of both to the objects of perception, is it perhaps the case that even my judgments of perception presuppose an awareness of other perceivers, embodied as I am embodied? Is it possible to characterize adequately even such basic intentional acts as those of perception independently of and antecedently to characterizing our awareness of such others?

These are not among the questions that Stein herself poses in her dissertation. Indeed it is clear that in 1916 they lay just, even if only just, beyond the horizon of her enquiries. But they are questions that we, her readers, from our later vantage point may well find ourselves asking and we may also need to remind ourselves of how hard Stein had to struggle to make as much progress as she did. Like almost all dissertations, hers is plainly apprentice work. Some important points are made far too briefly, some of the writing is clumsy, and there are passages where her meaning is far from clear. Stein seems herself to have understood its inadequacies not too long after she had completed it and she welcomed Ingarden's thoroughgoing critique. What then did she succeed in saying?

In the thesis as submitted to the examiners, Stein began with a historical survey of the history of the problems with which the thesis is concerned, but in the published version (*Zum Problem der Einfühlung*, Munich: Gerhard Kaffke Verlag, 1980, originally entitled *Das Einfühlungsproblem in seiner historischen Entwicklung und in phänomenologischer Betrachtung*, Halle, 1917, translated by Waltraut Stein as *On the Problem of Empathy*, Washington, DC: ICS Publications, 1989) she omitted this first chapter—it had been trenchantly criticized by Ingarden—and proceeds immediately to questions of philosophical method. Here, because she speaks very much as Husserl speaks, an incautious reader might suppose that there is a complete identity of views. But this would be a mistake. For what Stein does not say is also important.

Stein initially characterizes her project in terms that would not have surprised any reader of the first volume of *Ideas*. The object of her phenomenological investigation is what is presented in experience. That investigation is prior to any experimental or observational scientific enquiry and therefore cannot draw upon the results of such enquiry. And it involves a suspension of prior everyday belief and an exclusion of all questions about whether what is presented in experience does or does not exist independently of and apart from experience of it. The declared aim of Stein's investigation is to identify the essential characteristics of empathetic awareness, awareness of the thoughts and feelings of others. And this empathetic awareness is of some other individual who "is not given as a physical body, but as a sensitive, living body belonging to an 'I', an 'I' that senses, thinks, feels and wills." The body of this 'I' is not only something that is presented to me, but my body is likewise presented to it as part of its world. "It faces this world and communicates with me" (p. 5).

Even at this early stage, two comments are apposite. The first is that in her selective use of Husserl's formulations, Stein nowhere adopts any that commit her to Husserl's developed conception of the transcendental ego. She presents herself at least by default as an Husserlian realist. Moreover, already in this initial statement the 'I' whose acts of empathetic awareness provide the subject matter for her investigation is characterized both as subject and as object and indeed as a subject who is aware of herself as an object of awareness of other subjects. I shall argue later that this recognition committed Stein to a realism even more uncompromising than that of Husserl's earlier writings.

Stein begins her analysis by identifying what is primordial in the experience of empathy; that is, what belongs to it as immediately given, as contrasted with what is mediated by primordial features of some other experience. Consider the difference between what is given in an act of perception and what is given in an act of memory in which the object of some earlier act of perception is called to mind. What at an earlier stage were primordial characteristics of what was presented in the act of perception are, when it is recalled in memory, no longer primordial. In the act of memory, what was once immediately perceived is no longer immediate, although memory of course has its own primordial characteristics. And so it is too with remembered states of feeling. When I remember my having felt joy on some earlier occasion, I no longer feel that joy, and the primordial characteristics of that feeling of joy as I immediately experienced it are not the same as the primordial characteristics of my present memory of that feeling.

Our relationship to the feelings of others is analogous to our relationship to our own past feelings. I may become aware of what another is feeling by trying to put myself imaginatively in his place, but, even if I succeed in this and so recognize that he is feeling great joy, I do not feel that joy. To be aware of the joy of another is not to feel joy. Yet it is also important that the joy—or grief, or anger—of the other can be an object of my direct awareness. I do not in such cases know of the thoughts and feelings of others by some kind of inference.

John Stuart Mill was the most notable of those who had argued that our knowledge of the inner states of others depends on analogical inference. We are aware, in his view, of our own feelings and thoughts directly and we are also aware that our thoughts and feelings are sometimes expressed in our bodily movements. But in the case of others we experience only those outward bodily movements. So we infer, by analogy with our own case, that they too have inner thoughts and feelings that find expression in their outward bodily movements. I am aware both of my own grief and of the tears that express it. I see your tears and I infer that you are grieving. We have good reasons to reject Mill's account over and above these that Stein cites. Were the situation such as Mill pictured it, all such inferences would be unwarranted. For we would be entitled to make such inferences only if we already knew that others resemble us, both in having an inner life of thoughts and feelings and in expressing it in much the same manner that we do. But this, if our situation in relation to others is indeed as Mill pictures it, is something that we do not and cannot know.

What Stein's account brings out is that we are not in fact presented by others with mere bodily movements. There is not something which is the mere outward expression of grief as contrasted with some unobservable inner reality. The grief is present in its expression and, when someone else expresses their grief, what is presented to me, what I become directly aware of, is the grief of the other. And this awareness, although it differs from perception, also resembles it closely. "Perception has its object before it in embodied givenness; empathy does not. But both have their object itself there and meet it directly where it is anchored in the continuity of being" (p. 19). We are at once reminded of the *Logical Investigations*: "Common sense credits us with perceptions even of other people's inner experiences: we 'see' their anger, their pain etc. Such talk is quite correct" (for this passage in full, see pp. 42–43 of this book). Both Husserl and Stein in speaking thus are anxious to distinguish empathetic awareness from knowledge. We can know that someone else is angry or in pain without any empathetic awareness of how they are, although empathetic awareness is of course a source of such knowledge. And knowledge of what another is thinking or feeling always points back "to some kind of experienced, seen act" (p. 19).

What Stein claims here cannot but remind us of her experiences as a military nurse, a nurse whose awareness of the pain, grief and anger of the wounded had been of crucial importance in the exercise of her nursing skills. She is able to write about empathy as she does in part at least because of her own empathetic awareness and of the discriminations that she had become able to make. Moreover, her nursing experience had taught her how nurses may be deceived by their patients, intentionally or otherwise. And in her dissertation Stein is careful to note that our judgments about what someone else is thinking or feeling may always be in error. We can be better or worse at perceiving and discriminating thoughts and feelings, just as we can be better or worse at perceiving and discriminating physical objects and characteristics. And there are some cases where we learn that this particular individual's otherwise unexpressed anger, say, may be indicated by some particular kind of associated movement. When we have learned that this is so, we may make use of this association to infer from such movements that she is angry. But such inferred knowledge of the thoughts and feelings of others always presupposes some prior knowledge derived from empathetic awareness and so it cannot be adduced in support of J. S. Mill's view.

Stein discusses, although for the most part only to dismiss, a number of rival accounts of empathy: not only those of Theodor Lipps and of Mill, but also theories grounded in psychological accounts of the genesis of empathy. Her most extended critical treatment is devoted to Scheler's views and, although she finds valuable observations in Scheler, concerning, for example, mistaken identifications of our own feelings, she accuses Scheler of failing to distinguish adequately what is immediately given to consciousness from what is apprehended only through reflection. About "what I primordially feel" she says that such "experiences of my own, the pure experiences of the pure 'I', are given to me in reflection" (p. 29).

What did Stein mean by "the pure 'I'"? We can best approach this question by first considering further her view of the nature of acts of empathetic awareness. Stein draws attention to a phenomenon already noted by Theodor Lipps, named by him 'reflexive sympathy', but by Stein 'the reiteration of empathy'. "In fact," she wrote, "all representations can be reiterated. I can remember a memory, expect an expectation, fantasize a fantasy. And so I can also empathize the empathized, i.e., among the acts of another that I comprehend empathetically there can empathetic acts in which the other comprehends another's acts. This 'other' can be a third person or me myself" (p. 18). So it is possible for me to be indignant that you are dismissive of your friend's sympathy for my misfortunes. What examples of reiterated empathy bring out is the way in which a certain conception of the relationships between the thoughts and feelings of different individuals is presupposed by our understanding of acts of empathetic awareness. What conception is this?

It is a conception that requires a view of the 'I' as not only unifying disparate experiences, but disparate experiences that are of different kinds. For I not only experience my thoughts and feelings, judgments and wishes, expectations and disappointments as all of them mine, belonging to one and the same stream of consciousness, but I also experience them as someone who not merely has, but is a body, is a psychological unity. My experience and understanding of myself as a unified consciousness, some of whose experiences disclose my dispositions, is incomplete until I understand my self "as always necessarily a soul in a body" (p. 41). And in understanding myself as embodied soul I have to come to terms with the complexity of my experiences of my body. For it is one more physical body, visible and tangible, but also one to which I stand very differently from my relationship to other

physical bodies. I cannot, by moving around it, view it from different standpoints. There are parts of it that I will never see directly, although I may
touch them. Yet my body is not only given to me as a physical body, but also
as a living body of which I am sensorily aware. The 'I' who recognizes that
the body that I perceive as a physical body and the body that is mine as lived
bodily experience are one and the same body is a "zero point of orientation,"
a nonspatial point "within" the lived body. I pick up a stone so that it is no
longer at a distance for my hand. But what distance is it from "me"? It is neither a very small distance nor no distance at all further from me than my
hand is. Distance from me is not the same as physical distance from my
body.

There is thus a double character to the givenness of the body, yet it is one
and the same body that is presented in these two ways. And the complexity
thus engendered extends to the awareness that we have of our own sensations. Consider what is involved in my touching a hard surface, say a table.
There is first "the sensation of touch," secondly my awareness of the hard-
ness of the table which is the object of my act of tactile perception, and
thirdly my awareness of my fingertip touching the table. But if this is so,
there may seem to be a problem. For one and the same tactile sensation, as
it is presented immediately in consciousness is not, it seems, part of the extended world, and yet, as an event caused by another physical event, namely
my fingertip touching the table, it also seems to be part of the extended
world in which such events occur. As such it has, a spatial location, while the
'I' whose sensation it is is nonspatial. Or so Stein claims. And to some of her
readers this has rendered her account problematic.

Walraut Stein, for example, who was Edith Stein's great niece as well as the
translator of her thesis, argued in her 'Translator's Introduction' to the English version of the thesis, "if it is meaningful to say that the 'I' has sensations,
and if sensations are always localized, then it must be possible to say where
the 'I' is" (p. xx). But this argument rests on a misunderstanding not only of
what Stein wrote about sensations, but also of the larger character of her
phenomenological enterprise. As Husserl had defined it, phenomenology is
an investigation into the nature of intentional acts and their objects from a
first-person point of view. The 'I' whose acts provide the subject matter of
such investigation is indeed an impersonal 'I'. The standpoint of the 'I' can
be occupied by any one. But the questions to which phenomenology affords
answers cannot be answered by observation from some third-person standpoint. I can in this view see someone extending her index finger towards a
tree, on one of whose branches a bird is sitting. But what makes it the case
that she is pointing at the bird and not at the branch or at the tree is an act
not accessible to third-person observation.

Husserl made use of this distinction in defining the respective subject
matters of phenomenology and of the natural sciences. Each has its own do-

main into which the other cannot trespass without confusion. It is true that the sciences presuppose some fundamental concepts and judgments the clarification of which and justification of which are tasks for phenomenology. But the natural sciences, in Husserl's view, know nothing of intentionality and phenomenology cannot speak of those causal relationships which the scientist establishes by observation and experiment. Yet this sharp distinction between what can be known only from a first-person standpoint and what can be known only from a third-person standpoint breaks down as soon as we carry our enquiry into what we know about the thoughts and feelings of others beyond its most elementary stages. And we are presented with just such a breakdown as Edith Stein's enquiry progresses. Why so?

Consider, as an example of a sensation, pain (This is my example, not Stein's). I may feel pain in any part of my body. That it is I who am feeling the pain is true whatever part of the body the pain is in and the meaning of the judgment 'I am in pain' is the same whatever part of the body it is that is afflicted by pain. So the 'I' is not locatable as the pain is locatable. It is not at all the case, as Walraut Stein supposed, that the locatable character of pain requires a similarily locatable 'I'. But this mistake is perhaps grounded in another deeper mistake. Our ability to locate sensations as we do is an ability to locate them both from our own first person standpoint and from the third-person standpoint of an external observer. I am manifestly in pain and a nurse asks, 'Where does it hurt?' I in response tell her or point to the place and she in turn informs the physician by pointing to the same place and saying, 'This is where it hurts'. Sensations, that is to say, lead a double life: They are objects both of first-person awareness and of third-person observation and it is one and the same sensation that is the object of both. Someone may say: the external observer does not observe the pain, but only its symptoms. But this is a much too restricted view of what can be observed, a view whose error is the same as that of those who claim that I cannot observe your grief, but only your tears.

It is not only sensations that have this double aspect. Of all our mental activities, of all our intentionally directed thought and feelings, it is true that they are at once possible objects of first-person awareness and possible objects of third-person observation. But it is not just that they have both sets of characteristics. It is also that in characterizing them from a first-person point of view, whether as the agents whose acts they are or as phenomenologists, we cannot but presuppose the truth of certain third-person judgments made from the standpoint of either the lay or the scientific observer and that in characterizing them from such a third-person standpoint we cannot but presuppose judgments made from a first-person point of view. Consider some different types of example.

When I perceive some object, that object must be a possible object of perception both by me and by others. And indeed others will be able to observe

me directing my attention towards that object, perhaps picking it up, taking
time to inspect it and putting it down again. That is to say, the assertions in
which I report my first-person experience of the object will be true if and
only if some set of third-person assertions about how the same object appears to or would appear to others is true, and some set of third-person assertions about how I as a perceiver appear to others is true.

A second type of example suggests an even closer relationship between
first-person and third-person accounts. Here I lay myself open to what is presented to me in a perceptual experience and report what I see. What I see is
a revolving globe with rapidly changing patterns of color. When I report the
successive colors, someone else observing the same globe says, 'Between
the yellow and the green was a very thin line of purple which you missed.
Look again!' I look again and I see the purple. My first-person report is corrigible in the light of third-person reports.

To this it will be said that, insofar as my first-person reports are true reports
of how things appear to me, they are necessarily incorrigible. First of all things
appeared to me in one way and then they appeared in another. If both reports
of these appearances are genuine phenomenological reports, the second report is not a correction of the first. But to say this would be to be in danger of
severing all connection between the concepts of objects-as-perceived-now-
by-me and that of objects-as-perceived-by-others. Yet it is essential to the concept of an object of perceptual acts, as it has been understood within the phenomenological tradition, that unlike objects of imagination, it is perceivable
by others and by me at different points in time. And if they are so perceivable,
then we can bring the experiences of others to bear on what we took ourselves to have perceived with a view to arriving at a more adequate account
of the object of perception.

What these examples underline is not just that one and the same object
may be characterized from both a first-person and third-person part of view,
so that to my statement 'What was perceived by to me in experience was
such-and-such', it can always be retorted 'No! What was presented to you in
experience also had some characteristics that you failed to notice'. It is also
that my acts of perception, like my acts of imagination and of memory, can
be objects both of my own first-person awareness and of third-person observation. Indeed it is as a third-person observer that I can become aware of
someone else's grief as occasioned by their remembering some past loss or
of someone else's pleasure in seeing a landscape. So that, in giving an account of empathetic acts of awareness of the thoughts and feelings of others,
we are bound to move between first-person and third-person reports and to
recognize how one and the same concept may find application to one and
the same object both from a first-person and from a third-person point of
view. And this is something recognized by Stein and not only in what she
says about sensations.

Of peculiar importance here is Stein's emphasis upon how our understanding of ourselves is open to correction by what we learn about ourselves from others through our empathetic awareness of their view of us. But to understand how she arrived at this insight, we need first to follow the line of thought that she developed about the relationship between my body and those other human bodies that I encounter.

In my empathetic awareness of others I move from taking my own standpoint as *the* "zero point of orientation" to considering it as *a* "spatial point among many. By this means, and only by this means, I learn to see my living body as a physical body like others" (p. 63). Yet my body is given to me as a living body only in my own first-person primordial experience, while what I perceive of that same body with the senses is an incomplete physical body. Yet through reiterated empathy I become aware of myself as others are aware of me and so understand my physical body as one and the same as the living body of my lived experience. And so it is that I am for the first time given to myself as "a psychological individual in the full sense." My awareness of myself as embodied mind, which is itself integral to my being an embodied mind, is constituted through interactions with others, most notably those characterized by reiterated empathy.

So others make an indispensable contribution to the constitution of my self-awareness, but not only of my self-awareness. "Were I imprisoned within the boundaries of my individuality, I could not go beyond 'the world as it appears to me.' At least it would be conceivable that the possibility of its independent existence, that could still be given as a possibility, would always be undemonstrable. But this possibility is demonstrated as soon as I cross these boundaries by the help of empathy and obtain the same world's second and third appearance, which are independent of my perception" (p. 64).

Here Stein is careful to note that she is following the lead of Husserl in *Ideas* (§151) as well as that of Josiah Royce in *Self Consciousness, Social Consciousness and Nature*. But in agreeing with Husserl that "empathy as the basis of intersubjective experience becomes the condition of possible knowledge of the existing outer world" (p. 64), she also prepares to go beyond Husserl. For she now recognizes that the double aspect of our mental lives is of importance in understanding the relationship between intentionality and causality. She begins her account by considering how we distinguish in the body of the other spontaneous and voluntary movement from merely mechanical movement, noting that we make the same distnctions in our own case and also that what from my point of view is experienced as a voluntary act may have effects that are and are perceived as mechanical movements by an observer. And so too in the body of another we may be empathetically aware of felt effects of external movements, as when someone else pushes that other or that other picks up a heavy load (pp. 71–72).

So the world that we become aware of is one of independent agencies interacting causally with one another and what is presented to us in consciousness is always liable to be what it is only because the causal impacts on our bodies have been what they are. Stein thus opens up the question of how the intentionality that informs our understanding of others and the causality that is also at work in our interactions with those others are related. She does so in such a way that from the outset any reductive answer is ruled out. But she has also ruled out by implication any too sharp distinction between a realm of the intentional and a realm of the causal, as though these could be clearly demarcated and quite distinct domains of enquiry. In so doing she had once again begun to move in a different direction from that taken by Husserl.

What follows immediately in her thesis is a more extended account of what makes empathy possible, namely the expressive dimensions of bodily movement and of speech. Stein distinguishes between the speaker-independent meanings of sentences and what may be expressed by the uttered sentences of a particular speaker on a particular occasion. To understand those uttered sentences I must not only know what they mean, but also be able, by empathetically putting myself in the place of the speaker, to identify what it is that is expressed in this particular use of them. And such uses of language are of course only part of what is expressive in a speakers' movements: there are also the accompanying gestures or smiles or blushes. Here it is important that, as Stein had already suggested, what is expressed is not an external sign of some inner thought or feeling. It *is* the inner thought and feeling. So a blush is not an external effect of an inner sense of shame. The blush is not caused by the shame as it might be caused by exertion (p. 83). The shame is present in the blushing. And our recognition that someone is ashamed makes their blushing intelligible. For to find an action intelligible is to experience its parts as parts or aspects of a whole. So blushing is intelligible as a part or aspect of shame, laughter as a part or aspect of happiness. "An action is a unity of intelligibility or of meaning . . ." (p. 86).

It is always possible of course for me to misinterpret what someone else is expressing. And we can learn to correct our misinterpretations and to see through concealment or pretence. In so doing we take account of context, of what may have occasioned the thought or feelings that I am ascribing. Someone realizes that he has just made a stupid remark and I correspondingly recognize the source of his blushing. Or he grows red in the face and I impute anger. But suppose that he has just exerted himself and has no occasion for anger: then I will interpret his growing red in the face quite differently. Context is of course not the only guide to correct empathetic judgment. When we come to know someone well, then on the basis of our empathetic awareness of his particular acts we may ascribe character traits to that individual. And later we may make use of what we understand about his character traits in interpreting his particular acts.

We may still of course be deceived. One not uncommon source of error is to substitute for empathetic awareness of the other an inference to what the other is feeling and thinking guided by an analogy with what we ourselves do or would feel or think. We unjustifiably take the other to be like us. But it is not only about others that we may be in error. We may also be deceived about ourselves, something that Scheler had stressed. And I discover that I may be so deceived and what it is about which I am deceived by learning to view myself as someone else views me, by learning how I appear to someone who is empathetically aware of me. "It is possible for another to judge me more accurately than I judge myself and give me clarity about myself" (p. 89). So, while I take myself to be acting from pure generosity, someone else may notice that what I am really looking for is approval. And I may learn from that other to see myself as I am. "This is how empathy and inner perception work hand in hand to give me myself to myself."

I know myself then in part only as I know and am known by others. Earlier in her thesis Stein had suggested that in memory and fantasy I may see myself as others see me, seeing, as it were, a mirror-image of myself. And she speculated that mirror-images have the significance for us that they do just because of this. But now she is advancing a stronger thesis, one according to which the ability to move from perceiving myself from a first-person point of view to perceiving myself from a third-person point of view and then back again is an essential human characteristic. The human being so constituted inhabits both the order of nature and that of *Geist*, spirit. And the study of human beings as *Geist* takes a different form from that of the natural sciences. (Here Stein follows Dilthey, albeit critically.) This is in part because empathetic awareness is essential to the comprehension of the world of *Geist*. What those engaged in the *Geisteswissenschaften* have or should have as their goal is the writing of a certain kind of history, a history that enables us "to relive the spiritual life of the past." We make the past of our culture intelligible by learning how to put ourselves in the places of those who created the works of culture and we are able to do this only because of what we have in common with them. What we have in common with them is an understanding of human acts as occurring in rule-governed sequences, an understanding that enables us to interpret the actions of others as either conforming to or deviating from canons of intelligibility, canons that Stein calls "rational laws of *Geist*" (p. 97).

To treat someone in the fullest way as a human being, as a person, is to interpret their actions as motivated in such a way that their motivations express their values. Of those motivations in ourselves we are immediately aware, since they take the form of felt emotion directed towards an object. When we perceive an object, characteristically and generally we are aware only of the object and not of the act of perception. To become aware of the act we have to redirect our attention. But in the case of felt emotion no such redirection is necessary. We are characteristically and generally immediately aware both of the emotion and of the object to which it is directed. And characteristically and generally emotions presuppose evaluative judgments. If I grieve a great deal more over the loss of this than I do over the loss of that, I treat this as more valuable than that. And reflection upon my virtues and their objects allows me first to identify and then, if I find it necessary, to revise the evaluative judgments to which my emotions give expression. So, if my emotions are in good order, I will grieve less deeply over the loss of a piece of jewelry for its own sake than I will over the loss of that same piece of jewelry when it is a souvenir of a loved one (p. 101).

This is a point in the thesis at which Stein breaks off her discussion, when a good deal more is still needed. She says, for example, of someone who is excessively disturbed by the loss of his wealth that his feeling is "irrational" (p. 101: this is one passage in which Walraut Stein's translation is misleading). Yet she does not tell us either what the standard of rationality is or how it is applied. So she needs some further account of the distinction between rational and irrational evaluations. But she does not provide it. Instead she moves on to consider in more detail how we become aware of ourselves as beings who express a range of emotions and who will their actions just because they are motivated as they are by those emotions. "Willing," she had said, "is by its essence motivated by some feeling" (p. 97).

Empathetic awareness allows us to understand others in the same way. In so doing we are able to identify their values and their attitudes towards their emotions and their values. And just as in the case of certain others we find ourselves, after we have become aware through iterated empathy of how they view us, compelled to put in question what we had hitherto taken for granted about our own motives, so, by similarly becoming aware of the evaluations of others, including their evaluations of us, we may be compelled to question our own evaluations. Once again Stein's discussion is in important respects incomplete. But, if with hindsight we consider these latter parts of her thesis in the perspective afforded by the work that she undertook subsequently, they can be read as setting an agenda, as advancing no more than preliminary and provisional conclusions, valuable as much for the questions that they provoke as for the answers that they suggest. And although the final sections of the thesis are an incomplete piece of work, they do provide just the kind of account of empathetic awareness that the *Geisteswissenschaften* need. (I have spoken of the human sciences as '*Geisteswissenschaften*' because there is no good translation of this expression in contemporary English. But it is worth noting that the word was first coined in German to translate the English expression 'the moral sciences', as used by J. S. Mill).

There is one more respect in which Stein's thesis needs to be read as pointing towards her future. In my all too brief and selective exposition of her thesis, I have emphasized how her account of empathy enabled her to recognize the double aspect of so many characteristics of human agents. And this recognition does of course generate problems. In the final section of her thesis Stein returns to one of these, that of the relationship of human beings *qua* inhabitants of the realm of *Geist* to their corporeality. On the one hand, the expressions of *Geist* always take corporeal form. "We meet the spirit of the past in various forms, but always bound to a physical body" (p. 117). Yet on the other, there are a variety of claims that spirit can exist apart from body: claims about divine grace or guardian angels or Socrates' statements about his *daimonion* (although Stein warns us against taking what Socrates says too literally). What would it be to take oneself to have awareness of such a spirit? Would this be "genuine experience" or instead the deluded outcome of confusion about our own motives rooted in a lack of self-knowledge? We need, Stein says, further study of the religious consciousness to address such questions. How we should formulate them is not yet clear. It is evident from her closing paragraphs that at this stage, issues of religion remain for Stein impersonal and theoretical. But it is also evident that between 1913 and 1916 she had become genuinely open-minded about religious questions, a state of mind that may be rarer and harder to sustain than we are apt to suppose.

I have emphasized in my account of Stein's thesis aspects of her argument which need further development, in some cases a good deal of further development. The thesis as a whole is incomplete in two other ways. First, it would have been useful for her to have entertained a wider range of objections to her central positions. Responses to objections from different standpoints would have both clarified and strengthened her arguments. Secondly, she does not consider—and indeed within the terms set by her thesis it would not have been possible to consider—the implications of her conclusions for the larger phenomenological enterprise. I have noted points at which a certain independence from Husserl emerges, even although she is always and self-consciously in his debt. But like Reinach three years earlier, she does not as yet face up to the extent to which she has taken a direction very different from that in which Husserl was now moving and opened up questions that could only be answered from a significantly different standpoint.

10

1916–1922: The Complexity of Stein's History

Any biographer of Edith Stein faces a problem about how to narrate the events of her life between 1916, when she successfully defended her dissertation and became Husserl's assistant, and 1922, when she was received into the Catholic church and prepared herself for a life outside universities. It was a period of a remarkable transformation and this not only with respect to religious commitment. And it had as its background the deprivations and sufferings of the last two years of the First World War, the experience of Germany's catastrophic defeat and the end of Imperial Germany, the political struggles to establish the Weimar Republic, and the economic disorders of massive inflation, of working-class hardship and of the impoverishment of large sections of the middle class.

Unsurprisingly then, one dimension in Stein's transformation was political. Her conception of the state and of her own relationship as a citizen to the state was significantly different by 1922 from what it had been in 1916. A second dimension was of course philosophical. The originality that had marked her doctorial dissertation reappeared in her treatment of the philosophy of psychology and of the *Geisteswissenschaften* in the thesis which she prepared for submission as her *Habilitationsschrift*. And it also enabled her to raise questions about some of Husserl's key concepts that Husserl himself had not raised, most notably concerning the concept of constitution. Here Marianne Sawicki's brilliant philosophical detective work, about which I will be writing further in chapter 12, has provided strong grounds for asserting that Stein's interventions played a key part in Husserl's development. She became much more than the scribe and editor that she had been hired to be.

This period of Stein's life was one that ended in academic defeat, in her inability to find a university that would accept her as a candidate for *Habilitation*, although in retrospect it became clear that it was providential good fortune that she had been freed from the limitations of academic life. But at the time it was a matter of disappointed hopes and expectations, followed by an openness to new possibilities as to where she would move and what work she would do.

Her story is then a narrative of political change, of philosophical growth, and of academic frustration. But it is also a narrative of changing friendships and other personal relationships. The steadily increasing number of deaths on the Western Front left Stein, like so many Germans, with a life partially defined by painfully felt absences. For members of Husserl's circle the most notable of these was that caused by the death of Reinach. Then there was Stein's changing relationship with Husserl, in part a matter of Husserl's failure to be open—except very occasionally—to her constructive philosophical suggestions, so that she was reduced to tasks of secretarial drudgery and finally resigned her position. But her attitude to Husserl was also affected by his fallings out with some of her close friends, most notably with Hans Lipps.

Add to these the changes brought about by the everyday arrivals and departures, so characteristic of academic life. Fritz Kaufmann returned to Freiburg from military service in Romania and Russia to resume his studies. Jean Hering was in Freiburg from time to time. Roman Ingarden, on whom Stein had relied heavily for intellectual support—it was he and not Husserl who provided her with a sustained critique of her doctoral dissertation—returned to a newly independent Poland. But the most important of these comings and goings were those of Hans Lipps.

Lipps was not always an easy person. The focused intensity of his conversational manner sometimes alienated listeners and he was frank and unguarded in what he said. He had recurrently irritated Husserl, perhaps in part at an earlier stage because Lipps's reformulations of Husserl's theses sometimes opened up questions that Husserl had taken to be closed. But during the period of Lipps's military service the philosophical differences between Lipps and Husserl became more fundamental. Quite a number of years later Lipps was to tell the Danish philosopher, Knud Eiler Løgstrup, who had become his student in 1931, that during his time in the trenches Lipps had carried a copy of *Ideen* everywhere with him. "But then as a result he arrived at the conclusion that it was no good. Husserl was a master of singular investigations such as those in the *Logische Untersuchungen*, not of a system as in the *Ideen*. Lipps kept to himself, went his own ways, loyal and distant, that was my impression" (from an autobiographical sketch by Løgstrup, quoted in the "Introduction" by Hans Fink and Alasdair MacIntyre to the English translation of Løgstrup's *Den Etiske Fordring, The Ethical Demand*, Notre Dame: University of Notre Dame Press, 1997, p. xvii).

Lipps was not yet at the point of developing his own distinctive mode of phenomenological enquiry. But his negative verdict on *Ideen*, a verdict that perhaps anticipated positions that Stein was to take up later on, would have been sufficient to antagonize Husserl, had he voiced it. Husserl however seems in this period to have become all too ready to take offense and was difficult and unhelpful to a number of those who had learned from and relied on him. Of his relationship to both Lipps and herself, Stein wrote to Kaufmann "that at times it is not easy to maintain the right attitude. . . . But one must keep reminding oneself that he himself suffers most because he has sacrificed his humanity to his science. That is so overpowering and the amount of gratitude that we owe him for it is so incalculable that, in view of that, any kind of personal resentment should not even arise" (Letter no. 32, November 22, 1919, in *Self-Portrait in Letters, 1916–1942*, ed. L. Gelber and R. Leuven, O.C.D., tr. J. Koeppel, O.C.D., Washington, DC: ICS Publications, 1993, p. 32). Lipps had some difficulty in achieving *Habilitation* and received no help from Husserl. The story of how he did succeed and of Stein's part in his success will be told later. Yet Lipps, like Stein, remained deeply grateful to Husserl.

Of the warmth of Stein's feeling for Lipps there can be no doubt. Later she referred to a period in her life in which she had taken herself to be moving towards marriage with someone whom she did not name. This may have been either Ingarden or Lipps (on her relationship to Ingarden, see Hugo Ott, "Edith Stein und Freiburg," *Phänomenologische Forschungen* 26/7, 1993). But in the case of Lipps it proved impossible for her to become as close to him as she had wished. "Will our good Lipps ever find rest?" she wrote to Kaufmann. "One sees so clearly what he lacks and, at the same time, that one does not have the chance to help him. And one is so terribly eager to do so" (Letter no. 31). But Lipps had his own personal difficulties at this time and distanced himself from Stein.

Stein's own changing beliefs were also to draw her apart from rather than closer to Lipps. Her political evolution may have been one element in this, but even more important was her religious conversion. Lipps seems to have had no sympathy for nor any understanding of any type of religious belief. And the view of human nature that he was to develop offers no place at all for distinctively religious possibilities (see, for example, the first part of ch. 22 on *"Die Geistigkeit"* in *Die menschliche Natur, Werke III*, Frankfurt am Main: Vittorio Klostermann, 1971), while Stein's conversion was not only a matter of her theological beliefs and her religious practice, but also of her conception of human nature and of human relationships.

What then is the story to be told about her conversion? In one way there is relatively little to be told, because of how little she herself told us. She underwent an initial conversion to Christianity while staying with Anna Reinach in 1918. And she became convinced that her devotion to Jesus Christ required her to enter the Catholic Church while staying with Theodor and Hedwig

Conrad-Martius late in 1921. To chronicle these two events is in one way no great task. But their significance in Stein's life becomes a good deal clearer if we situate them in the overall narrative of that life from 1916 to 1922.

This suggests that the best way to proceed might be to write a single complex history of Stein's life in those years in which the different strands of development that I have identified would be woven into a single whole. But there are two difficulties in attempting this. First, although different types of change in Stein's life were related in more than one way, there really were distinct and to some degree independent types of change going on. And, secondly, the interest is always in the detail and to move between sufficiently detailed accounts of Stein's political history, of her philosophical progress, and of her religious and personal life is likely to produce a dislocated rather than an integrated narrative.

Therefore I propose to proceed as follows. First I will trace the changes in Stein's politics. Then I will tell the story of her development as a philosopher and suggest a relationship between her philosophical activity and other aspects of her life. And finally I will discuss her conversion to Catholic Christianity, placing it in the context of her personal relationships and drawing upon what has been said about her politics and her philosophy, in order to identify the several dimensions of her transformation. I therefore now turn to her politics.

11

The Political Dimension

Edith Stein had acquired first from her family and then from her school teachers a patriotic devotion to Imperial Germany. She added to that a strong sense of gratitude for the educational opportunities that she had been afforded. Her initial conservatism and regard for traditional Prussian ideals had already by 1914 been put in question, first by her feminism and then by her encounter with the teaching of Max Lehmann at Göttingen, whose liberal constitutionalism made him an advocate for a very different set of attitudes. But Stein had no time to think through the issues raised by Lehmann's teaching before the outbreak of war in 1914 reinforced her patriotic commitments and her conviction that the cause of the *Rechtsstaat* of Imperial Germany demanded an unconditional allegiance.

Early in 1917 she wrote from Freiburg to Ingarden, who was then in Göttingen, that "we can become aware of our relationship with the wholes to which we belong . . . and can voluntarily submit to them. The more lively and powerful such a consciousness becomes in a people, the more it forms itself into a 'state' and this formation is its organization. A state is a people conscious of itself that disciplines its functions" (Letter no. 7, p. 9). And Stein goes on to argue that the self-consciousness of a people is connected with its tendency to develop and that organization is a sign of inner strength, concluding that *Volk* is most perfect "which is most a state. And I believe I can assert objectively that since Sparta and Rome there has never been as strong a consciousness of being a state as there is in Prussia and the new German Reich. That is why I consider it out of the question that we will now be defeated."

Seventeen months later in July 1918 Stein's tone had changed. She wrote to her sister, Erna, that "one has to get accustomed to the idea of possibly not living to see the end of this war. Even then one may not despair. . . . After all,

93

it is quite certain that we are at a turning point in the evolution of the intellectual life of humankind; and one may not complain if the crisis last longer than is acceptable to the individual" (Letter no. 24, p. 27). And she writes of the contemporary social and political conflicts that "Good and evil, knowledge and ignorance, are mixed on *all* sides and each one sees only the positive of his own side and the negative of the others. That holds for peoples as well as for parties . . . life is much too complex for anyone to impose on it even the most clever plan for bettering the world. . . . ."

Significantly, she sends her sister an article by Walter Rathenau, identifying her opinions about the outcome of the war with his. Rathenau was among the most powerful of German Jews, an extraordinary figure who headed one of the two firms that dominated Germany's electrical industry, the AEG (*Allgemeine Elektrizitätsgesellschaft*), while also having great influence in the financial sector. In August 1914 it was he who had first proposed and then implemented a plan to bring all industrial production for the war and all strategic raw materials under central control. And in sustaining Germany's war effort, no one perhaps played a more important part.

Yet Rathenau's patriotism did not prevent him from seeing the flaws in the German Empire with great clarity. A man of broad liberal culture, he had been a contributor to Maximilian Harden's *Die Zukunft*, a review that was, at least in its editorial voice, the most persistent critic of Imperial German pretensions. And, although Rathenau worked strenuously to sustain Germany's war effort, so long as there was any point in doing so, he was among the first to recognize the finality of the collapse of the Imperial regime. Five days after the Armistice in November 1918, a new political party, the German Democratic Party (DDP), emerged, pledged to the creation of a democratic republic and to cooperation with all other parties who were so committed. It was led by intellectuals, including Alfred Weber and the editor of the *Berliner Tageblatt*, Theodor Wolff. And it was here that Walter Rathenau found his new political home.

So also did Edith Stein. Rose Bluhme Guttmann, who had studied with her at Göttingen remembered how she and Stein "worked together for the Democratic Party" (Edith-Stein-Archiv, Karmel Köln, quoted in Waltraud Herbstrith, *Edith Stein: A Biography*, San Francisco: Harper and Row, 1985, p. 13). And when her brother-in-law to be, Hans Biberstein, finally returned from the Front, it was to find that his fiancée, Stein's sister, Erna, was already a member of the Democratic Party, as was his mother. Stein comments, "The elections left him with no alternative but to choose it as well, for, as a Jew, he could expect no sympathy any further to the political right" (*Life in a Jewish Family, 1891–1916*, p. 229), although his own devotion to Imperial Germany had survived both the defeat and the Emperor's abdication. The elections to which Stein refers, those of 1919, were the first in which women had been able to vote.

Erna and Edith Stein did not move to the Left, unlike Stein's cousin, Richard Courant, who was a declared social democrat. In the turbulent period immediately after the war, he had been one of the few officers to be elected to the Soldiers' and Workers' Councils that were set up. And he continued to speak for the Social Democratic Party and to envisage a socialist future for Germany (*Courant*, pp. 71–75). By contrast, the primary concern of the Democratic Party was with the creation of new institutions that would enable all Germans to participate in a common civic and social life, institutions that would make it impossible for this or that section within the nation to be excluded from playing a part. And one threat of exclusion was that aimed at Jews. Unsurprisingly therefore it was in this period of her life that Stein was forced to recognize for the first time that she had a political interest "as a Jew."

Open expressions of anti-Semitism had in the first decade of the twentieth century become a great deal less acceptable among upper class and educated Germans. And the growing tendencies towards assimilation within the Jewish community expressed a recognition of this fact. In 1914 German Jews had been indistinguishable from other Germans in their patriotic willingness to make sacrifices for the Reich. But in 1918 the need for a scapegoat to blame for Germany's defeat allowed the latent anti-Semitism of the Right to become once again manifest, so that anti-Semitism and hostility to the Weimar Republic became closely linked. And among the poisonous effects of this was the assassination of Rathenau, while foreign minister, in 1922.

By that time, Stein had already redefined her political attitudes in the course of writing a long essay on the state—although completed in 1921, it was not to be published until 1925. That essay relies to some degree on concepts and distinctions more fully elaborated in the treatise "On Individual and Community" that was part of her work for her *Habititationsschrift*, but it can be read as a work standing on its own. It is a philosophical work, one not engaging directly with the political issues of the moment. But part of its interest is that it makes it evident how far Stein had moved from the positions that she had taken in 1917 ("Eine Untersuchung über den Staat," *Jahrbuch für Philosophie und phänomenologische Forschung*, Vol. 7, 1925). Three features of her conception of the state are especially notable.

First, whereas in 1917 she had spoken of the state as the form taken by a *Volk*, when it organizes its life, she now in 1921 distinguishes sharply between *Volk* and state. A *Volk* can survive and even flourish without a state. (The example that she gives is that of the Polish people.) And a state may survive and flourish as the state of a number of peoples. Neither ethnic nor cultural homogeneity is needed to sustain the political bonds and the common purposes required for the life of a state.

Secondly, Stein argues that the state cannot be understood either in terms of *Gemeinschaft* or *Gesellschaft*. The purposes served by the state she takes to be neither those of community nor those of associations that serve external and antecedent ends. And the status of a citizen is a distinctive status. What distinguishes the state from other forms of association is sovereignty and for the state to define itself as sovereign, as it must do if it is to act as a state, it must be recognized freely as sovereign by its citizens. But, if it is to be so recognized, it must in turn recognize the freedom of its citizens, that is, its exercise of its sovereignty must be limited. Yet sovereignty is not self-sustaining. What is required to sustain the sovereignty of a state is continuing recognition of that sovereignty by its citizens, a recognition deriving from shared underlying agreements expressed in shared communal goals or in movement towards such goals. There is therefore a relationship between political stability and the values of *Gemeinschaft*, but the type of community required is not that of a single *Volk*. Where there is too little in common between on the one hand the goals pursued and the values upheld by a state and on the other the goals and values that inform the communal lives of its citizens, the state will rest not on agreement, but on the use of coercive force.

Thirdly, in Stein's view, to be sovereign is to have both the authority and the power to make, to interpret, and to enforce laws. The end served by legislation is the common good. We have a conception of law as such and of timeless and unvarying precepts that are the precepts of law as such, holding for all times and all places. But the positive laws enacted and enforced by the state vary from state to state and how far they agree with the timeless precepts of law as such also varies.

It is about the state thus conceived that Stein raises the question of the relationship between the state and ethical norms and values. The state is not an abstract entity. It acts and suffers only as those individual agents through whose actions the functions of the state are discharged act and suffer. And it is their actions that conform to or violate norms and values. So the state is only in a secondary sense a person and an actor and it is so only because and insofar as individual persons who have the authority to do so act in its name. It follows that the state is just or unjust, protective of those whom it ought to protect or failing in its duty towards those whom it ought to protect, and scrupulous or unscrupulous in its dealings with other states, only insofar as the relevant individual persons have these properties. Moral predicates apply to the state only insofar as they apply to the relevant individuals.

These positions put Stein at odds with a variety of positions taken in the history of political theory. She is not a contractarian. She does not hold the kind of liberal position according to which the state should be neutral and impartial between rival conceptions of the moral life. And most importantly she rejects the historical role assigned to the state by Fichte and by Hegel. The state does indeed have a moral history, but it is a history of individuals working through the state so that the freedoms conferred by the state and by the role of law are themselves rooted in the free agency of the individuals who brought them into being and who sustain them. Moreover, growth in freedom is not the only index by which the historical progress of a state is to be judged. It is rather by an openness to a whole range of values that the institutions of the state exhibit the moral chararcter both of the state and of its citizens.

There seems therefore, to be on Stein's account no place for any conception of raison d'état, of there being a justification for actions by agents of the state, acting with its authority, which would be morally unjustified, if performed by individuals without that authority. Moral and ethical norms and values are a seamless web. Indeed the meaning (*Sinn*) of the state just is the realization of values. In asserting this Stein raises a serious question. For it is clear that no state in the modern world—and the subsequent history of the Weimar Republic afforded strong confirmation for this—can secure the rule of law and liberty for its subjects, unless it is prepared to perform types of action which it would be quite wrong for a private citizen to perform for her or his own individual ends. There is therefore at the very least a case to be made for asserting that the morality of the state cannot be either identical with or derived from the morality of individual persons. If this is so, then someone who holds Stein's moral views is bound to have a more ambiguous relationship even to a democratic state than Stein seems to have recognized.

Finally, we should note that the values and norms that, in Stein's view, are to find expression in the life of the state are secular values and norms. The state is one thing, religion another. The state owes to its citizens and to their practice of their religion liberty. The church owes to the state respect for and conformity to its laws, when these are compatible with respect for the law of God, but disobedience, when these violate the law of God. When there are conflicts between religious believers and the state, the state must have a prudent regard for the conscience of its citizens and for its own sovereign authority. Stein had thus broken finally with traditional Prussian attitudes. And the change more generally in her political attitudes between 1917 and 1921 is striking both in its own right and for its apparent independence of her change in religious belief. Yet some of the questions that Stein asked about politics are closely related to questions that she asked about religion.

In both areas questions that she asked suggest an underlying more general question: through what kinds of social relationship are the ends specific to this or that type of experience and activity to be achieved? That is to say, part of her project is both to distinguish and to relate the different ways in which individuals can through their relationships with others participate in a variety of enterprises with each other. This is why in the philosophical work done for the *Habilitationsschrift* she paid such close attention to the notion of *Gemeinschaft*.

Ingarden ascribed Stein's long-term interest in this and related concepts to a psychological trait. "What interested her most was the question of defining the possibility of mutual communication between human beings, in other words, the possibility of establishing community. This was more than a theoretical concern for her; belonging to a community was a personal necessity, something that vitally affected her identity" (*Über die philosophischen Forschungen Edith Steins, Freiburger Zeitschrift für Philosophie und Theologie*, Vol. 26, 1979, p. 472). Ingarden stresses the effect on her of her experience of the close-knit philosophical community at Göttingen and he then says that she also "needed to belong to a natural community" and refers to her wartime patriotism. "During the time she worked as Husserl's graduate assistant, she wrote me letter after letter asking whether she had the right to waste her time on philosophy and other such nonsense when there were people out there dying whom she should be helping." This is misleading in more than one way.

First, Ingarden did not realize how much her political commitments had changed after 1917 and how much less important political ties had become relative to other ties. Moreover, during the time that she was writing to him from Freiburg, she remained liable for recall to service as a nurse at any moment and whether she was to serve or not was not up to her. What Ingarden seems to have interpreted as expressions of guilt, rooted in patriotism, were, I am inclined to think, doubts about the value of philosophy in the perspective afforded by war and by the urgency of its casualties. We should in any case be careful not to ascribe to Stein any longing for closeness and intimacy as such. She was indeed capable of close friendship, but intimacy did not come easily and her conception of community is badly misconstrued if understood primarily as an expression of her own psychological needs.

What then was her conception of community? To understand it, we first need to consider her enquiries into the structures and power of the individual human *psyche*, enquiries that became central to her philosophical projects. And those enquiries can themselves only be understood in the context of her philosophical development from 1916 onwards. I therefore turn to the history of that development.

12

1916–1919: Stein and Husserl

Stein became Husserl's assistant in October 1916. Husserl had been without an assistant for quite some time and drafts of what were to become sections or parts of sections of the second volume of *Ideen* had accumulated, together with revisions of drafts of the as yet unpublished Sixth Investigation. Husserl worked unsystematically and the stacks of handwritten paper seem to have been in no particular order. Moreover, Husserl wrote in Gabelsberger short-hand and the illegibility of his handwriting would have tested anyone's patience. Stein had therefore to undertake three kinds of work on the manuscripts, all of which required familiarity not only with Husserl's vocabulary, idioms and syntax, but also with his philosophical thought.

First there were the secretarial chores of deciphering and transcribing. Then there was the matter of constructing an order within which each of the texts could find its place, so that something like an overview of Husserl's argument began to appear. But these only opened the way to a third set of tasks: those of identifying sentences or paragraphs in need of rewriting for the sake of clarity, gaps and obscurities in the overall argument, passages that were in need of expansion or revision or of additions without which the treatment of this or that topic would be seriously incomplete.

No one could have carried out these last tasks without raising some substantive philosophical questions about what meaning Husserl had intended to convey in this or that passage. But Stein found it very difficult to get Husserl to review her work and to approve or disapprove of what she had done. He much preferred to continue writing, providing even more disorderly material for his assistant to organize into some coherent shape. So in January 1917 Stein wrote to Ingarden, who was in Göttingen, that Husserl "is now busying himself with the constitution of nature (of course without any review of the draft). In the meantime, I have continued working on that draft on my own authority, without running into any opposition about that, and am as far as 'Person.' The natural consequence of this is that we hardly talk together any more. For me this is very painful, for matters are very complicated and the material that I have at hand is altogether incomplete" (Letter no. 5).

I have already noted that the materials upon which Stein worked included revised and again to be revised drafts of the Sixth Investigation and first and second drafts of sections of what was to become *Ideen II*. In the finally published versions of these, her work would receive no acknowledgment and it was therefore natural for scholars to assume that, while Stein may have had an indispensable role in preparing the manuscripts so that these were in a fit state be submitted for publication, the philosophical content of those manuscripts was Husserl's and Husserl's alone. But Marianne Sawicki in an extraordinary piece of scholarly and philosophical detective work has put us all in her debt by showing that Stein's contribution was much more than this and that it was through debate with Stein, while she was his assistant, that some important aspects of Husserl's thought were shaped. (See Marianne Sawicki, "Making up Husserl's Mind about Constitution," presented at the American Philosophical Association Eastern Division Meetings, New York, 1995—I am indebted to Dr. Sawicki for making the text of that paper available to me—and also her *Body, Text, and Science: The Literacy of Investigative Practices and the Phenomenology of Edith Stein*, Dordrecht: Kluwer, 1997.)

In July 1917 in a letter to Ingarden, Stein expressed her frustration at Husserl's delays in getting around to various tasks. She then goes on: "Recently I have been putting more and more bundles in order. I have just come upon the bundle on *Zeitbewusstsein* [time-consciousness]. You know best how important these matters are: for the theory on 'constitution' and for the dispute with Bergson and, it seems to me, with others as well, e.g. with Natorp" (Letter no. 15). It is on just this question of what Husserl had meant and was to mean by 'constitution' that Sawicki identifies Stein's contribution to the development of Husserl's thought. What then had Husserl meant by 'constitution' and why did problems arise?

The history of Husserl's changing conceptions of constitution has been told by Robert Sokolowski in his *The Formation of Husserl's Concept of Constitution* (The Hague: Nijhoff, 1964). Husserl had first introduced the concept of constitution in the *Logical Investigations*—although there he does not always use the word '*Konstitution*'—most importantly in order to characterize the relationship between the sensations that a perceiving subject undergoes and the object that he perceives. The object stands to the sensations as unifying form to disparate matter, a unification that has two aspects: first, at any given moment the form of the perceived object unifies visual, tactile and other sensations, so that we perceive not a string of various and varying sensations (*red* plus *hard* plus *round*), but rather a single hard, round, red object, and, secondly, through successive moments of time successive sensations are unified in a presentation of one and the same enduring object. Hence the relevance of the notion of time-consciousness to that of constitution. So the perceived object may be said, in Husserl's later terminology, to be constituted as the unifying form of the sensations. But Husserl had become dissatisfied with this conception of constitution as early as 1904–1905.

His dissatisfaction was twofold. Later on he would refer to this earliest conception as 'static constitution', because he believed that it did not allow us to recognize how constitutive acts occur over time, so that the constituted object is the outcome of a process of development. He therefore replaced it with a conception of constitution as genesis, one designed also to deal with a second source of dissatisfaction, the impossibility of giving an account in terms of static constitution of how certain objects of inner consciousness are constituted. (Here I am indebted to Sawicki's account, but depart from it at important points; she must not be held responsible for my formulations or inferences.)

In *Ideen I*, Husserl made use of both conceptions in different contexts and it was not until 1929, according to Sokolowski's account, that he finally abandoned the static conception for the genetic. (The first published material in which the genetic conception has fully replaced the static is from 1929. But Professor Sokolowski has referred me to Iso Kern's *Husserl und Kant*, The Hague: Nijhoff, 1964, where Kern shows that it was around 1918 that Husserl began to understand its importance.) Each of these two rival conceptions fosters its own idioms. The genetic conception finds its natural expression in verbs and nouns that enable us to speak of constitution as an activity, as though consciousness brought into existence the intentional objects presented to it (see, for example, what Husserl says in *Ideen*, §55, about how the objective unities of regions and categories are constituted). Yet Husserl also speaks of constitution in idioms that remain closer to the static conception and its realistic presuppositions. Writing to W. E. Hocking in 1903, Husserl had asserted that "The recurring expression that 'objects are constituted in an act' always signifies the property of an act which *makes the object present (vorstellig)*, not 'constitution' in the usual sense!" (quoted in W. Biemel, "The Development of Husserl's Philosophy" in *The Phenomenology of Husserl*, ed. R. O. Elveton, Chicago: University of Chicago Press, 1970, p. 158), so that to say that consciousness constitutes an object is to say no more than that that object is present to consciousness. And these alternative idioms reflect still unresolved tension in Husserl's thought in the period in which Stein was his assistant. He had at this point left open different possible ways of clarifying and systematizing what he meant by 'constitution'.

How this was to be done depended in key part on how the 'I' in and for whose consciousness objects are constituted was to be conceived. In the *Logical Investigations*, that 'I' is the 'I' of anyone whatsoever, an 'I' whose standpoint is the standpoint of anyone who perceives, judges, wills or desires. But the questions of how that 'I' is itself constituted and of how it relates to the 'I' of everyday life and discourse remained in the background. When Husserl finally posed those questions, he moved gradually towards a conception of the 'I' as transcendental ego, self-sufficient and self-constituting, whose relationship to the objects that present themselves to consciousness can be defined without reference to the multiplicity of egos that inhabit the actual world.

Stein in her dissertation however had provided compelling grounds for skepticism about any such conception of the 'I' and this in two respects. Our awareness of ourselves, so she had argued, is constituted in key part in and through our empathetic awareness of others. And our orientation to those others and hence to ourselves depends on the situations of our bodies in relation to the bodies of those others and on our bodily awareness and responsiveness. If Stein is right, no 'I' can have the self-sufficiency and the self-constituting properties that Husserl ascribed to the transcendental ego. Moreover, it had become clear to her that the objects of perception that present themselves to us in consciousness present themselves as objects presented both to ourselves and to actual and possible others; that is, as objects independent of any particular consciousness. And they present themselves as objects in a spatial field defined for us by the location of our bodies and by the spatial and temporal relationship of our body to other bodies, including the bodies of other perceivers. Perceptual objects are constituted, that is to say, against a background awareness of others and perceptual judgments presuppose the existence of other perceivers.

The differences between Stein and the Husserl who had come to understand perception in terms of the self-sufficiency of the transcendental ego are evident. For Husserl there is the 'I' and the set of objects that present themselves to it in consciousness, among them those objects that are the bodies of other perceivers. But what it is for an object of perception to be constituted as such an object can be specified without any reference to other perceivers. Indeed at this stage of the phenomenological enquiry the question of whether there are other perceivers and of how solipsism is to be avoided have not yet arisen. For Stein by contrast empathetic awareness of others and of their acts of perception, memory and imagination is not just one more phenomenon waiting to be studied. It is only through an adequate phenomenological account of empathetic awareness and of the indispensable part that bodies have in such awareness that we can understand how the objects of perception are constituted as objects of consciousness.

Yet it would be a mistake to define the relationship of Stein's views to Husserl's at this stage only in terms of this contrast. For one thing, Stein understood herself as having developed a line of enquiry that was entirely faithful to Husserl's earlier thought. For another, she believed that even the latest developments of that thought needed the insights derived from her own enquiries, if they were to become adequately coherent. She saw herself as someone cooperating with Husserl, not primarily as someone arguing against him. Yet she also recognized the crucial nature of her disagreements.

Matters came to a head during February 1917. Stein was then engaged in dealing with sections of *Ideen II*. Husserl and she discussed the relevant issues during a long walk on the outskirts of Freiburg—Husserl had for several years made it a habit to go on such philosophical walks with colleagues and graduate students—and, so Stein wrote to Ingarden on February 3, "as a consequence I have experienced a breakthrough. Now I imagine I know pretty well what constitution is—but with a break from Idealism. An absolutely existing physical nature on the one hand, a distinctly structured subjectivity on the other, seem to me to be prerequisites before an intuiting nature can constitute itself" (Letter no. 6). And she adds, "I have not yet had the chance to confess my heresy to the Master. . . ." (Stein in this period always refers to Husserl as "the Master," sometimes "the dear Master" without more than an occasional trace of irony.)

What Stein said to Ingarden in this letter has very great interest quite apart from the light that it throws on her relationship to Husserl. For the thought that she expressed is an Aristotelian thought and this in itself is not surprising when we remember Husserl's debt to Brentano and Brentano's to Aristotle. But it is also, although Stein did not as yet realize it, a Thomist thought, one that anticipates theses that she was later to discover in Aquinas's *Quaestiones Disputatae de Veritate* and one that reveals a direction in her own thought of which she was not yet fully aware. But of course her immediate concern was with how Husserl would respond. Ingarden was apprehensive.

On February 20 Stein was able to report to Ingarden the effect of her newly formulated views on Husserl. "Recently I laid before the Master, most solemnly, my reservations against idealism. It was not at all (as you had feared) a 'painful situation.' I was deposited in a corner of the dear old leather sofa, and then for two hours there was a heated debate—naturally without either side persuading the other" (Letter no. 8). Husserl told Stein that he would be quite prepared to change his mind "if one demonstrates to him such a necessity. I have, however, never yet managed to do that." So Husserl had at least become aware that he should once again revisit this issue, although he postponed doing so. Meanwhile, Stein continued to think through her differences with Husserl, writing to Ingarden a month later that "I have begun to examine more closely one of the points in which the Master and I differ (the necessity of a body for empathy)" (March 20, 1917, Letter no. 11).

In the months that followed, Stein edited, revised and, by adding passages, provided continuity to what were to become substantial parts of *Ideen II*.

Sawicki has argued compellingly that Stein was responsible for, among other passages, crucial parts of §18, where in consequence Husserl no longer is a consistent defender of the self-sufficient ego, and of §43–47 in which Husserl now recognizes the part played by empathetic awareness of the bodies of others and of the relationship of those bodies to my own body in constituting my awareness of the natural world and the objects that compose it ("Making up Husserl's Mind about Constitution," Sections 3 and 4, and *Body, Text and Science*, chapter 4, pp. 153–65; see also pp. 73–89). And in a similar fashion Stein produced a revised and coherent draft of Husserl's manuscripts on time-constitution, a draft that Heidegger later published with his own name as editor and no mention of Stein (see Section 5 of *Body, Text and Science*).

The outcome of course was a presentation of Husserl's views that was not wholly consistent. But it is important to emphasize that Stein was not merely inserting her own views into Husserl's manuscripts (and Sawicki nowhere implies that this was the case). It was rather that Stein was developing a line of argument already implicit and very occasionally explicit in Husserl's writing, but one that was at odds with another line of argument that had become increasingly dominant. And I have already suggested that disputes about the interpretation of Husserl may be due to the fact that there are in fact immanent in Husserl's writings two incompatible philosophical standpoints. Stein recognized this more insightfully and sooner than anyone else. For she understood not only the problem of reconciling the realist Husserl with the idealist Husserl and the problem of rendering coherent Husserl's various thoughts on empathetic awareness, but also, what no one else had understood as yet, the relationship between those two problems.

Two questions therefore need to be posed about Stein's own positions. First, was she right in her interpretation of Husserl? Here the last word so far has been said by Sawicki and I refer the reader to her writings. Secondly, and more importantly, was Stein philosophically in the right? The answer to this question I shall postpone, because it needs extended treatment. For the moment I note only its crucial importance. Stein was at the time unable to pursue her own thoughts further, because of the demanding character of the duties that Husserl imposed upon her. Ingarden had sent her an extended constructive criticism of her dissertation, identifying those parts in which her concepts or her arguments were unclear and needed further work. And the first chapter, he suggested, in which Stein had provided a summary treatment of the work of her predecessors on empathy, was wholly inadequate. Stein did not disagree. And she replied to Ingarden that she had seen the dissertation as no more than a beginning in "a plan I would fulfill in the course of a life time." But then she adds "since I have come here, I sometimes have the scary feeling that I no longer have my life as firmly in hand as I used to. For one thing the problems that lie close to my heart are dependent on the conclusion of the *Ideen*. Then, my duties as assistant make such demands on me that it is impossible to think of doing any intensive and undisturbed work on the side."

Yet she feared that without her "the Master simply would not publish anything more" and spoke of how "the Master tires easily and is so slow. . . ." Her conclusion was that she must not resign because "I consider the publication of his work more important than any possible products I might eventually present to the world" (Letter no. 13). But in this generally bleak period she did find one source of philosophical consolation.

It had been Reinach's habit in Göttingen to give a set of introductory classes on phenomenology to those students who had newly arrived to study with Husserl. Husserl now welcomed the suggestion that Stein should offer a similar course in Freiburg. This Stein referred to as her kindergarten. Its initial membership consisted of three women and four men, one of whom was a Protestant pastor and another a Benedictine monk. "Of course," Stein wrote, "no trace of philosophical companionship, rather strictly ABC instruction. But it is fun nevertheless." And, given Stein's gifts as a teacher and, above all, her clarity of mind, it must have been very enjoyable for the students too. What Stein taught in these classes can perhaps be partially reconstructed from the manuscript entitled *Einführung in die Philosophie* (now published as Band XIII of *Edith Steins Werke* with a foreword by Hanna-Barbara Gerl, Freiburg: Herder Verlag, 1991), but the relationship between the manuscript and the lectures given by Stein is not clear. But Stein's work on it at this time does provide evidence that Stein was no longer prepared wholly to sacrifice her own projects in order to please Husserl.

By February 1918, Stein's relationship with Husserl had reached a point of crisis. Husserl now wished to exert a degree of detailed control over her editorial activities which she found intolerable and she explained to him that "I . . . can only continue with this occupation if I do something original on the side. . . . I offered to remain on in Freiburg and to help him with the editing of the *Jahrbuch* and similar things, only not as his assistant in works for which I am unable to find meaning" (Letter no. 19). She had expressed her dissatisfactions to Husserl in writing and feared that Husserl might take offence, indeed that she might, like Hans Theodor Conrad, one of Husserl's earliest students at Göttingen, who now taught at Munich, together with his wife, Hedwig Conrad-Martius, fall into disfavor for some time. If this happened, she planned to return to Göttingen. But she hoped that Frau Husserl might intervene on her behalf. And in fact she succeeded in resigning without any rupture in her relationship with Husserl, something that reflects well on Husserl as well as on Stein.

So she was able to report to Ingarden on February 28, "The Master has graciously accepted my resignation. His letter was most friendly—though not without a somewhat reproachful undertone" (Letter no. 20). And she also sent news of her resignation to Fritz Kaufmann, who was still serving with the army in Romania, telling him that she was now able to resume her own work. "So, as I told you, I am working at present on the analysis of the person" (Letter no. 21). The work to which she refers was in one way a continuation of the project of her dissertation, but it was to break striking new ground. It is likely that at this time she was working both on the manuscript of her *Einführung in die Philosophie*, which was to remain unpublished, and on the material that she intended to submit for her *Habilitationsschrift*. Husserl's true opinion of this latter can best be gauged by the fact that he accepted the completed text for publication in the *Jahrbuch*, the highest honor that he ever accorded his students. It is all the more shameful that, when Stein submitted her application for *Habilitation* at Göttingen, Husserl's letter of recommendation was not in fact a letter of support.

Originally Husserl had told Stein that she was not to submit such an application, although his daughter Elizabeth argued with him about it (Letter no. 8). When she did apply in October 1919, he wrote a letter on her behalf to his former colleagues in which he spoke of her doctoral dissertation as "excellent," praised her teaching and her work as his assistant and declared that "her capacities for independent scientific research and teaching are beyond question." But he concluded by saying that "If the career of university teaching were supposed to be open for ladies, then I would be the very first to recommend her warmly for admission to *Habilitation*."

This letter in effect invited the Göttingen committee to reach a dual verdict: that Stein was intellectually qualified for *Habilitation*, but disqualified because she was a woman. Such a verdict however would not have been possible for a Göttingen committee. For they had before them the example of Emmy Nöther, a brilliant mathematician who had achieved *Habilitation* at Göttingen in the face of prejudice quite as great. The discussion among the mathematics faculty had been fierce and they had been unable to reach agreement until the hitherto silent Hilbert was asked for his opinion and responded that they were the faculty of a distinguished university and not a swimming-pool club. Nöther was at once accepted for *Habilitation* (Heinz Pagels, *Perfect Symmetry,* New York: Simon and Schuster, 1985, p. 189).

The philosophers at Göttingen had no Hilbert among them. And they fumbled badly in refusing to accept Stein for *Habilitation*. First the faculty met, not as the committee that would evaluate Stein's work, but informally in order to decide whether to meet as such a committee. They seemed to have decided against so meeting, principally at least because of what they thought of as the difficulties in accepting a woman. The head of the department then notified her by letter that she had been rejected, just as if the faculty *had* met in committee, but then realized that the department had not followed the prescribed procedures. So he had a conversation with Stein in which he explained that she had been rejected out of kindness at this preliminary stage, so that she would be spared having her *Habilitation* turned down as a result of the negative intellectual attitude of Georg Müller, professor of both philosophy and psychology, who had declared that Stein's work "would throw psychology as it is done here out of the saddle" (Letter no. 31).

It was probably not only Müller who felt that his own views were put disturbingly in question by Stein. She herself ascribed the principal opposition to her to Georg Misch, the Dilthey scholar and disciple. (In her doctoral dissertation, Stein, although acknowledging the importance of Dilthey in opening up certain questions, had spoken of Dilthey's "unclarity" and of his "mistaken expositions.") Misch, so Stein believed, was anxious not to antagonize either Müller or Husserl and had presumably thought that a decision not to proceed to a decision might achieve this.

Stein took this blow remarkably well. "You may tell . . . Husserl . . . that I am not crushed," she wrote from Göttingen to Fritz Kaufmann, who was now in Freiburg. And she proceeded to explore an alternative possibility. She had at some point come to know Heinrich Scholz, perhaps after he took up the chair of systematic theology and philosophy of religion at Breslau in 1917. Scholz had by 1919 become professor of philosophy and head of the department at Kiel. Scholz wrote to Stein that if the three applications for *Habilitation* at Kiel that were then in hand were rejected, he would be happy to have her submit her application there, since he himself preferred her to any of the present applicants. But the possibility that Scholz had envisaged did not arise.

At the time of her rejection by Göttingen, Stein was about to visit her sister Elsa in Hamburg and she told Kaufmann that she intended to ask her former teacher and continuing friend, William Stern, for his advice. What she could not do, she felt, was to ask him about the possibility of submitting an application at Hamburg "since philosophy in Hamburg is already represented by two Jewish professors" (Letter no. 31). Stein's presumption was that this would make a further Jewish presence impossible and that Stern, who had suffered the effects of anti-Semitism earlier in his career, would at once have told her if this was not so. This is a significant moment, the first time that we have evidence of an awareness in Stein that she was liable to unjust discrimination as a Jew as well as as a woman.

There is of course one remaining question about Stein's rejection for *Habilitation*, a question that she herself asked and answered in the same letter to Kaufmann. When friends in Breslau and Göttingen heard about her rejection, they gave her what they took to be "good advice: why don't you go to Freiburg!" What those friends did not realize was that at Freiburg the rejection would be by Husserl himself. It is a mark of Stein's remarkable character that she did not allow this to change her attitude to Husserl. She continued to regard his work with the same admiration and to feel and to express immense gratitude for what she had learned from him. There is no trace of bitterness in her letters, no hint that the work that she had done in order to achieve *Habilitation* had been any the less worthwhile because she had failed to achieve it. The one good thing is to emerge from the history of this unhappy episode is a recognition that it was the philosophical work itself about which Stein cared most of all. And so she continued to do her philosophical work, returning to Breslau and earning her living as a private tutor to undergraduates and graduate students, as much as ever a philosopher, even although without an academic appointment.

13

Stein's Conception of Individual and Community

What then was that philosophical work? In the discussion of Stein's political theory in chapter 11, it became clear that, in order to understand key aspects of her theory, it is necessary first to understand her conception of community. That conception is elaborated in the second part of the book that was the final outcome of Stein's *Habilitation* thesis, *Beiträge zur philosophischen Begründung der Psychologie und der Geisteswissenschaften* (first published in the *Jahrbuch für Philosophie und phänomenologische Forschung*, Vol. 5, Tübingen: Max Niemeyer Verlag, 1922, tr. M. C. Baseheart and M. Sawicki as *Philosophy of Psychology and the Humanities*, Washington, DC: ICS Publications, 2000; my page references are to this translation and my quotations are taken from it). But Stein found it necessary to preface her account of community with an enquiry into the psychology of the individual, enquiry directed by concerns that only become explicit in the second treatise. What are they? Imagine two individuals who encounter the activities of some ongoing community. One of them becomes caught up in its life. She finds herself energized by so doing and makes the purposes of the community her own, finding the reasons advanced for identifying with those purposes good reasons. She shares the community's hopes for its future prosperity and, when the community is apprehensive of or saddened by setbacks, she too is apprehensive or saddened. The other by contrast is unmoved by her contacts with this community. She forms relationships with some individuals who happen to be members of the community, but this fact about them is irrelevant to her interactions with them. In no way does she become part of the community.

Two sets of questions arise. The first concerns what it means to speak of the purposes or hopes or fears or grief of a community. What is the relationship between the purposes, hopes, fears and griefs of individuals which are theirs qua individuals and those which are theirs qua members of a community? A second set of questions concerns the differences between the two imagined individuals. What is it for an individual to be open or not to be open to those experiences that are communal? What is it for an individual to identify or to fail to identify with the purposes of a community? What kind of changes in an individual might membership in a community bring about?

Stein takes it that we will only be able to answer either set of questions, if we begin by identifying the relevant features of individual experience and the relevant powers of individuals. What she therefore provides in the first of two long essays is a catalogue of those features and powers as disclosed to phenomenological awareness, the awareness of an 'I' conscious of and reflecting upon what is presented to it. But a presupposition of Stein's phenomenological reports is that the 'I', the subject, inhabits a natural and social world that impinges upon it in a variety of as yet unspecified ways. At the beginning of the second essay Stein remarks that what had begun in the first essay as an investigation of the individual *psyche,* as though it were a world to itself, had had to take account at an early stage of aspects of that *psyche's* consciousness which can only be understood as the result of external impacts and influences. Any adequate account of the *psyche* would be one that situated it within a network of natural and social objects and occurrences.

Stein's idiosyncratic use of the word *'psyche'* was borrowed from her friend, Hedwig Conrad-Martius. The word 'mind' would not have served her purposes, since she was concerned not only with phenomena that are usually classified as mental, but also with aspects of our bodily existence that are inseparable from them, and with the nature of the relationship between these. And the word 'soul' has too many irrelevant overtones. So she took over the Greek word as less question-begging and the title that she gave to the first treatise was "Psychic Causality."

Much of it is not easy reading. Stein gives the impression in both parts of the book that she is still working out her thought and in some passages that she had only learned what it was that she wanted to say by writing it down. Her intended readers were her then colleagues in the phenomenological movement and the treatises were published in 1922 in volume 5 of the *Jahrbuch für Philosophie und phänomenologische Forschung* to celebrate Husserl's sixtieth birthday. In some of Husserl's subsequent work, the influence of some of Stein's ideas in these treatises is evident, although Husserl never acknowledged their source.

Part of the interest of the book lies in Stein's complex relationships to the views of a number of writers on both the empirical and philosophical psychology, including her former teacher, William Stern. She is well aware that the direction of her thought is very different from theirs, but she is not afraid to take from them what she needs. And in this respect she is again different from Husserl. Nonetheless she understands her work as building on Husserlian foundations and prefaces it with an acknowledgment of how much she has learned from Husserl's unpublished as well as published work.

Stein begins with what seems to be an elementary and relatively uncontroversial account of some constituents of experience, auditory, visual and affective. Experience (*Erlebnis*) flows, as it were, in currents, and "the unity of a current of experiences" is constituted by successive phases of, say, a set of tones or of changing colors, or of both, and perhaps also of my first increasing and then decreasing enjoyment of what I see and hear. The relationship between such phases is not causal. And how we experience what we experience is affected by what Stein calls life feeling (*Lebensgefühl*). "If I feel myself to be weary, then the current of life seems to stagnate. . . . It creeps along sluggishly, and everything that's occurring in the different sensory fields is involved in it. The colors are sort of colorless, the tones are hollow. . . . Every color, every tone, every touch 'hurts'" (p. 14). And here in the effects of weariness or vigor we discover within our given experience causality, analogous to, although not precisely the same as, physical causality.

The academic style of Stein's writing may have the effect of concealing from the reader the interest and the originality of what she is saying. When philosophers write about mental acts and mental states their examples are generally of acts or states in which the mind is lucid, focused and self-aware. Stein by contrast begins from the experience of fatigue (the Cartesian mind never seems to suffer from fatigue). And by beginning here she reminds us of the mind's vulnerability, of how the quality of our perception, our feeling and our thinking depends upon factors external to, but impinging upon consciousness. Every aspect of our experience may vary in intensity. I may experience more or less intense color and my perception of that color can also vary in intensity. I may only mildly enjoy some intense color or I may enjoy it intensely.

Variations in the quality of our experiences is an effect of the ebb and flow of life feeling. And this is not only a matter of degrees of vigor and weariness, but also of such states as those of heighted alertness and irritability. Heightened alertness and feverish activity may accompany the taking on of a dangerous job or some decisive moment in one's life or they may instead be effects of nicotine or caffeine—the translators remind us in a footnote that in her autobiography Stein told us how a nurse she had resorted to strong coffee and cigarettes. And she contrasts such states with those that are expressions of vigor and both with experiences of fatigue and exhaustion.

So "weariness can be present (perhaps betray itself to others through my exterior) without my knowing anything about it myself. . . . Not until a state of total exhaustion sets in . . . do I notice as I'm bringing the state to givenness for myself, that it already existed before now . . ." (p. 21). What is already present to me in consciousness may go unnoticed, if I am excited or absorbed in some activity. And the same object that is present to me in consciousness may be also an object of the perceptions of others. Here Stein first recognizes that what is given in experience sometimes can only be characterized adequately in terms that takes us beyond that experience, in terms that presuppose some external point of view from which what is given in experience has to be understood. And so it is with another aspect of psychic causality.

The changing life-feelings that have effects on how we experience what we experience are to be understood as manifestations of life-power, the power that we draw upon as living beings. Among the effects of variations in life-power is varying receptivity to experience. The powers that I bring to my discriminations of features of my experience are themselves manifestations of another and more fundamental power, that of life itself. And this stands as cause to effects that I encounter in experience.

The vocabulary of 'life-feelings' and 'life-power' Stein took over from Dilthey. In her doctoral dissertation she had discussed Dilthey's view of empathy and noted how close her position was to his. But it is important to recognize how little Stein has committed herself to so far by her use of that vocabulary. She herself raises questions about the nature of the life-power of individuals and replies that these questions cannot be answered within her present framework of enquiry, concerned as she is to characterize only what is given in experience. She envisions the possibility of a type of experience from which causality would be wholly absent, in which there would be only contiguity and succession. But our experience in fact has "that variation of the 'coloring' and intensity of experiencing which we recognized as what was specifically causally determined" (p. 28). 'Life-power' is at this point the name of an otherwise unknown cause, variation which produces variations in its effects. "Whether I'm capable of receiving sensory data, and with what intensity the data impose themselves on me, depends upon the level of my life-power at the moment. But *which* data present themselves, whether sounds or colors, and which colors in particular, that's independent of my life-power" (pp. 32–33).

Life-power is not completely under the subject's control. And so a consideration of life-power raises the question: how far is the life of the *psyche* causally conditioned? Stein entertains the possibility of formulating a set of empirically grounded causal laws analogous to those prescientific physical generalizations on which we rely, so that just as we can infer from the humidity of the air that visibility will be good, we can infer from feelings of fatigue that some mental tasks will be for the moment beyond us. She does not pursue these questions, since all that she wants to establish at this point is that certain features of consciousness which the phenomenologist reports are open to causal explanation. In so doing she rejects at least in part, although without ever alluding to it, Husserl's sharp distinction between the phenomenological standpoint and what he called the psychological standpoint. The observations of empirical psychology now become grist for the phenomenologists' mill.

What Stein has so far been describing are experiences that the 'I' has, whether or not it attends to them. Such experiences belong to the passive side of mental life. But when we deliberately make them objects of our attention, when, the 'I' directs its gaze so that that to which it is directed becomes an object for it, then the intentionality is that of an act, of an apprehension. With such acts the life of *Geist* begins. The types of object to which the mind may thus direct itself are various. But, when we make those acts and their objects the objects of our phenomenological attention, we discover that they present themselves as moments in sequences and that they have to be understood in terms of the part that they play in such sequences. What kinds of sequences are these?

They are not mere temporal successions of states and events and the links between the items that compose them are not a matter of association. Nor are they causal sequences in which the later stands to the earlier as effect to cause. Stein gives the name '*Motivation*' to the relationship between earlier and later, borrowing this use of the German word—it was a word that had been taken over from French fairly recently—from the Munich phenomenologist, Alexander Pfänder. (Later on Husserl was to discuss *Motivation* in the *Cartesian Meditations*.) So she says that the lightning, which I have just perceived, motivates my expectation of thunder. And the joy that I presently feel is motivated by the arrival of a letter that I have been anxiously awaiting. The expressions 'motive' and 'motivation' are of course used very differently in English, so that we have to be careful in translating or expounding Stein not to suggest irrelevant associations. And Stein's examples make it clear that a wide range of attitudes, feelings and acts can be constitutive elements of such sequences. Of any mental act or attitude or state of feeling we can ask: What is its motive? It need not have been the case that prior to this we were aware of whatever it was that provided that act or attitude or state with its motive. Retrospectively we may be able to make the motive explicit, even though we had not previously attended to it. But once we have identified the motive we are able to ask certain types of questions about the relationship of motive to act, attitude or state. "Here you can talk about accuracy and falseness, discernment and obtuseness, in a sense that does not even come up in the sphere of 'actless' consciousness" (p. 46), the sphere of passive experience.

The sequences that Stein calls 'motivations' include, but extend far beyond trains of reasoning. For motivation, as Stein understands it, is, in Marianne Sawicki's words, "the principle of coherence of the world of meaning" (private communication). Certainly when, having previously judged the premises of some deductive argument true, I infer to the truth of its conclusion, this act of judgment has as its motive my previous judgment about the premises and I can evaluate the movement from premises to conclusion by the canons of deductive logic. But in most of the sequences that make up our active and conscious mental life the transition from motive to act or attitude or state is not of this kind. What *is* always the case is twofold.

We can always ask, in some broad sense of 'warrant', whether the motive is sufficient to warrant the act or attitude or state. And sometimes the motive that an agent herself cites may be insufficient, as when a mother, against all the evidence that her child has died in some catastrophe, yet believes and asserts that her child is alive. It is in relation to such cases that Stein distinguishes 'motive' from 'ground'. When I become aware of the inadequacy of what I have taken to be the ground of my act, then I look for some motivating factor over and above the ground. In such cases motive and ground diverge. If I recognize this, but continue nonetheless to treat my act as warranted, I not only act unreasonably, but I have reached the limits of intelligibility. Yet there is a cure for unreasonable and even unintelligible acts and attitudes. That cure is: to provide them with an explanation.

Turn now to attitudes, including among attitudes beliefs. An attitude is something that I find myself to have. I cannot decide to have or not have it. What I can decide is whether or not to allow it to influence my actions. Finding in myself, for example, some prejudice whose warrant is quite insufficient and whose motive I regard with suspicion, I may act so as, in Stein's phrase, to neutralize it (p. 49). Or, if, on the other hand, I find my attitude warranted and my suspicion of it mistaken, I may adopt and endorse it.

Acts in which some attitude is endorsed or rejected are experienced as acts in which the 'I' is the master, determining what is to be. Adoptions and rejections do not happen to the 'I'. They are acts of the 'I', and the 'I' in a full sense, the 'I' of the *Cogito*, as Husserl would have put it, emerges for the first time in such acts. Because they are not determined by antecedent conditions, independent of the 'I''s understanding of ground and/or motive and of its verdict upon these, they are free acts.

Affirmation and denial are free acts. Affirmation presupposes conviction and conviction is inseparable from the acknowledgment that some state of affairs holds. Yet even when I am convinced that and acknowledge that such and such is the case, I am free to take or not to take the further step of affirmation, expressing that affirmation by uttering an assertion. I may of course utter an assertion, even when I lack conviction and do not acknowledge that things are as my assertion represents them to be. This is the case when I lie. A liar presents what is in fact a sham affirmation as though it were a real one. Someone may object by saying: the liar has at least made a real assertion. But for Stein, as earlier for Reinach, the utterance of an assertion is not itself an affirmation. And what the liar presents to me is not just an assertion, but an assertion presented as though it expressed an affirmation, when in fact it does not.

Here it is not just that Stein has arrived at a conclusion that Reinach had already reached in his discussion of social acts, but also that she has taken over much of his vocabulary. When she uses the verb 'to adopt' (*übernehmen*) or the noun 'attitude' (*Stellungnahme)* or the verbs 'to acknowledge' (*anerkennen*) or 'to reject' (*verwerfen*) with respect to a 'state of affairs' (*Sachverhalt*), when she speaks of 'conviction' (*Überzeugung*) or 'affirmation' (*Behauptung*), she is making Reinach's idiom her own. But she is carrying the enquiry significantly further and in a different direction. For where Reinach was concerned with acts that are essentially social, Stein is providing an analysis of free acts as such, one that will enable her later to open up new questions about the relationship of the individual and the social. What matters for Stein at this point is to identify the relationship of free acts of will to inclinations and impulses.

Acts of will are one, but only one type of voluntary act. All voluntary acts are responses to some ground that constitutes the motivation for the act. What makes those responses voluntary is that nothing external to my act determines it. I am offended by someone's wrongful action. I then discover that that agent is deeply remorseful for what he did. I respond by an attitude of forgiveness that I express in an act of forgiveness. The act is determined wholly by my grounds for so acting, grounds that are internal to the structure of my action. So the act is voluntary, issuing from a resolve so to act, yet it does not involve the kind of decisive moment that is an act of will.

Consider two contrasting ways in which I may respond to some inclination. I may on the one hand have a desire and act accordingly and immediately. I do not treat the desire as affording me either a warrant or a motive for so acting and I do not take into account what motivated the desire. Here there is action, but no act of will. Suppose on the other hand that I, as it were, step back from the desire and recognize that I also have motives for acting otherwise than as the desire inclines me. It is then by an act of will that I decide not after all to act on the desire. It is the will which determines which of my two motivations is effective. And this is also so in a third type of case in which a desire is present and, although I have no contrary motives, I do not act on that desire.

Inclinations may be motivated or unmotivated. Unmotivated inclinations Stein calls 'impulses'. To be aware of an impulse is to be aware of oneself as impelled, as energized, as exuberant or restless, but without any direction towards particular goals. How strong or weak it is and in what forms it appears is a matter of causally effective forces—forces that flow from what Stein calls the lifesphere, the forces of life-power—outside our control, indeed outside our immediate experience.

It is insofar as they become grounded or motivated that impulses are transformed into goal-directed inclinations. And, as goals become more precisely specified, they provide a ground or motive for more determinate inclinations. I feel love for someone and want to give evidence of my love. "Then it strikes me that a gift would please him" (p. 63), and so now I want to find an appropriate gift. Or I judge a picture to be beautiful and want to own the picture. So the question arises: whether perhaps motives may supply direction, but cannot by themselves move to action. We may, Stein suggests, have sufficient grounds and motives—these may of course be the same—to warrant our acting and nonetheless not act. What is lacking? A first answer is: the relevant inclination to act. But strength of inclination itself depends on life-power, so that, without the relevant life-power, inclination too will be insufficient. Can what is lacking in inclination be made up by the power of the will? After all the 'I' on occasion has the power to will independently of inclination. But, in Stein's view, this cannot be the answer. For "an act of willing requires a certain amount of life-power in order to take place" (p. 87).

Stein is then committed to the thesis that grounding and motivation, inclination and will are neither separately nor jointly sufficient to generate action without life-power. And similarly intellectual capacity and sensory powers without intellectual life power are insufficient for achieving that receptivity which is required for the life of the mind. Presented with a work of art, a state of feeling, another human being, we may recognize what is presented, but yet not experience its worth or lack of worth and so remain unresponsive to it, unless our intellectual capacities are energized by intellectual life-power (pp. 83–84).

Stein now has two sets of problems and not just one. She has sketched a philosophical psychology whose starting-point, like Husserl's, is the experienced contents and objects of a single consciousness, of an 'I' reflecting upon and reporting what is presented to it. In so doing, unlike Husserl, she has had to recognize causal relationships between changes in that consciousness and agencies in the social and natural world impinging on it. And she has taken account of those relationships in cataloguing the parts that perceptual receptivity, intellectual receptivity, motivation, impulse, inclination and will play in generating thought and action. But, as she herself recognized, what she has provided is as yet no more than a catalogue, a catalogue however that enables her to formulate a set of important question: How is the life of the mind determined? Which aspects of its activities are predictable and which are not? How far and in what ways are we dependent upon the ebb and flow of life-power? How far is our vitality in turn dependent on how we live and act? She does not as yet have answers to these questions, but happily for her immediate project what she needs are the questions, not the answers. From them she is able to move to the further questions that she wishes to raise about the relationship of individual and community.

A second set of issues had also become inescapable. Given that a human being has capacities for sensation, perception, judgment, feeling, desire, resolve and decision, and that these function as they do in part because of the vitality, the life-power of the individual, what is it that enables these capacities to be exercised in a unified and coordinated way in the perceptions, thoughts, judgments, desires and decisions of a unified individual? What unifies? In what does the unity of this or that particular individual consist? These are problems which Stein was only going to address systematically later on. But from now on they are part of her philosophical agenda. For the moment however she was able to put them on one side, turning to questions that were immediately more urgent for her, concerning the relationship of individuals and communities.

About the first essay two things need to be said. One is that as a phenomenological enquiry it breaks new ground. For the 'I' of the enquiry now knows itself not only as known by others, but as the 'I' of a *psyche* that inhabits a natural and social world, an 'I' whose consciousness has features that can be accounted for only by causal relations to forces outside it that partly shape it. But at this point Stein seems to have reached the limits of purely phenomenological enquiry. In order to go further she needs to supplement her phenomenological findings by moving to some philosophical standpoint that would enable her to ask how an embodied consciousness can be understood from a third-person rather than a first-person point of view. Phenomenology is the practice of disciplined self-awareness of embodied human consciousness. But such embodied consciousness can also be viewed from without as the consciousness of a natural and social being interacting with other such beings. To acknowledge this is to acknowledge that phenomenological enquiry is by itself always radically incomplete. And this acknowledgment Stein was not yet ready to make explicit.

The philosophical psychology that she constructed in the first essay is also incomplete in another way. What she provided was a first sketch, one that drew not only on Husserl and Dilthey, but also on Wundt and Bergson, integrating elements from each into a single account. And she contrasts her conclusions with those of some associationist psychologists and with the account of psychology given by Hugo Münsterberg. But, as in her dissertation, she did not consider adequately and most often not at all the key objections that might be advanced against the view that she is taking. So her next philosophical step should perhaps have been to enter into critical dialogue with at least some rival accounts. This she did not do.

Even so she was able to open up seminal questions about community. From the outset she insists that we should not be misled into thinking of communities as though they were literally superindividuals. A community has no consciousness of its own "in any strict sense" (p. 140). To speak of communal consciousness is to speak of one aspect of the consciousness of those individuals who are members of some community and who constitute it by what they share. What then can they share?

The intentionality of the mental acts and states of individuals can be directed towards common objects, objects of shared feeling, objects of common understanding, objects of shared values. So individuals may share grief or joy, may understand some task in which they are engaged with others by exchanging views of that task from different standpoints, may use a common idiom to describe and analyze what they are doing together, and may find it worthwhile for the same reasons. But individuals can share in these ways without constituting a community. What then is specific to communal sharing?

Here Stein acknowledges a debt to the insights of Ferdinand Tönnies's classic work of 1887, *Gemeinschaft und Gesellschaft*, for her understanding of community. (Tönnies, although for most of his academic career he did little teaching, continued to hold the rank of Ordinarius at Kiel until he became *Emeritus* in 1921.) Tönnies had distinguished two ideal types of social formation, community (*Gemeinschaft*) and association (*Gesellschaft*). The social relationships of community are relationships within which I find myself directed towards the end of *Gemeinschaft*, so that I make its ends my own. The social relationships of *Gesellschaft* are relationships into which I enter so that I may further my own individual ends by furthering the ends of the association. The relationships of *Gemeinschaft* are characteristically small scale, local and face to face, and the role-structures of *Gemeinschaft* are generally governed by custom. By contrast the relationship of *Gesellschaft* are characteristically contractual, entered into by individuals who may differ widely in belief, but recognize that they need the cooperation of other individuals to achieve their ends. Such relationships are characteristic of the private and public bureaucratic institutions of modernity and of the market economies which provide those institutions with their social environments. The history of modern social change has been in part a movement from the institutional forms of *Gemeinschaft* to those of *Gesellschaft*, but in every social order, both are to be found.

Stein understands Tönnies's distinction in the following way. In relationships of *Gesellschaft*, each individual treats the other as object, as someone from whom it is important to elicit those responses that will be a means to that individual's ends. In relationships of *Gemeinschaft*, each individual is equally a subject in solidarity with others in a common life, that is, a life whose ends are shared. Stein follows Tönnies in recognizing that many relationships involve elements both of *Gemeinschaft* and of *Gesellschaft* and she illustrates this by contrasting two kinds of politician, the demagogue and the *Volksmann*. The former wants the crowd, the unorganized mass, to direct itself so that it will serve his individual purposes. But, in order to do this successfully, he will have to speak the language of *Gemeinschaft* and to further communal sentiments that can then be channeled in the direction that he desires. By contrast, the *Volksmann* who genuinely wishes to strengthen communal ties may need to construct organizations whose forms are those of *Gesellschaft*, through which the politics of community may be advanced. To be genuinely involved in communal relationships requires of leaders that they subordinate themselves and their ends to the wishes, needs and interests of the *Volk* whom they aspire to serve. To be effectively ambitious for power in a mass society may require one instead to wear the mask of *Gemeinschaft*.

The paragraphs from the introduction to the second essay in which Stein compares the demagogue with the *Volksmann* have been viewed by some readers as a prophetic anticipation of some features of the politics of the Weimar Republic. What Stein had already grasped was the extent to which Germans in their public life had become "a crowd," a mass of individuals waiting for someone to give their political relationships direction and organization. And that someone might have been Walter Rathenau, a true *Volksmann,* or it might turn out to be—as it did—someone as yet a shadow waiting in the wings for his demagogic opportunity.

From now on in the second essay, Stein therefore distinguishes three rather than two forms of social relationship, those of the members of a crowd as well as those of *Gemeinschaft* and *Gesellschaft*, although her focus is always on *Gemeinschaft*. She begins by asking what the components of communal experience are. Although all sense-experience is the sense-experience of individuals, when it becomes an ingredient in observations, the making of which requires "memories, expectations, conjectures, conclusions, and so forth" (p. 148), it contributes to the activity of a community of observers, to projects that are not merely our own; Stein is clearly alluding to the experience of scientific communities. And she goes on to suggest a different type of example: "we all also know a fantasy world that we take to be common property: Sleeping Beauty and Red Riding Hood," like other figures of the German fairy tale, are part of the cultural landscape of the German people (p. 149). Shared projects of observation and storytelling are constitute of communities.

Stein then asks what characteristics acts of thought must have if they are to be communal. Acts of thought are acts in which objects encountered in individual perception are categorized and classified in terms that have a common meaning for any thinking subject. The ways in which different individuals think about this or that object may differ, but the meanings through which they grasp the objects that are part of their shared experience are the common property of individuals. And the experience of any given individual can have the coherence and unity that it has only because of this participation in some particular realm of common meanings.

Of central importance are *Gemütsakte*, affective acts, for it is through these that individuals encounter values. Such acts have two elements. In them we are presented with objects as bearers of value, as goods, and those values elicit from us affective attitudes. Our states of feeling are responses to and presuppose the value of the objects presented to them. Moreover, although the value of such an object is always the value of some state of affairs, the beauty of a landscape, for example, or the badness of someone's bearing a grudge, it is not that we first apprehend the fact and then adopt an affective attitude towards it, although we may be tempted to suppose that this is so, since different individuals may agree on the fact, but disagree in their attitudes towards it. But this would be an interpretative mistake. "Every fully constituted object is simultaneously a value-object" and whether we do or do not see and understand it as such depends on our orientation (p. 160). But different individuals respond to values in different ways or fail to respond at all, perhaps because they are blind to some particular value, perhaps because, although not blind, they find themselves unmoved by it. And Stein remarks upon the relationships of the ego to objects that afford pleasure or pain or give reason for gratitude and trust or anxiety and despair.

For Stein's immediate purpose, what matters is that the same value can elicit responses from others so that it becomes a communal object. My admiration for a work of art is an acknowldgment of my recognition of the claim that this work makes on me. But, insofar as I take myself to be a member of a community devoted to the arts, my admiration may also express a recognition of a claim that this work makes on the attention and regard of the whole community. So the experience of being engrossed by a work of art is potentially a shared, communal experience. By this stage in her argument Stein has offered us a number of examples of types of community: military units, nations and families, as well as scientific and artistic communities. Each of these is a community only insofar as it has a continuing and more or less continuous history. And we should therefore expect Stein to provide some account of the continuities of communal experiences. As she now proceeds to do.

There are, least importantly, continuities constituted by association, by happenstance. But there are also and more importantly those continuities that derive from the fact that "experiences of different individuals mesh with one another" (p. 169) and do so in ways that result in motivational coherence. An individual's thoughts may provide someone else with reasons for further thoughts that then become part of our common thinking, including our scientific thinking. But not all motivational coherence is intellectual. The desires of one member of a community may provide other members of that community with reasons to act, reasons that they would not have, were they not members of the same community. And different individual motives may contribute to the same communal end, so that, as Stein notes, someone whose own natural scientific enquiries are motivated by intellectual curiosity about nature may contribute to a scientific enterprise whose principal motivation is the advancement of technology.

There is yet another level at which individual and community may inter-act: that of life-power. Individuals may be energized by participation in the life of some community and the vitality of a community can be enhanced or diminished by the way in which individual members of the community re-late to it. And the temper of a community may vary with its life-power. Weari-ness, feverish excitement, endurance, and vigor or lack of it can all be ex-hibited by communities as well as by individuals.

When Stein first introduced the concept of life-power into her discussion in the first of the two essays that make up the *Beiträge*, it was in part to iden-tify those aspects of experience which have to be understood in causal terms. So once again, when she discusses the ebb and flow of life-power within communities and between individuals and communities, she once again treats these phenomena as susceptible of causal explanation. And, as she did with individuals, she understands life-power as informing a range of communal acts and experiences, including those forms of cooperation through which communal experience is constituted. Many individuals may by their actions contribute to a common and communal goal. So the mem-bers of a parliamentary party may individually act so as to implement a de-cision by the party and their acts are or contribute to acts of the party.

Is it then the case that the party is responsible for its acts in the same way as individuals are for theirs? Can the party incur collective guilt for its actions? Max Scheler had answered "Yes" to these questions in his *Der Formalismus in der Ethik und die materiale Wertethik* which Husserl had published in the second volume of the *Jahrbuch für Philosophie und phänomenologische Forschung* in 1916. (It also appeared as a book in the same year.) Stein did not agree. "The community as such is no 'free' subject, so neither is it 're-sponsible' in the same sense that individuals are. Individuals bear the ulti-mate responsibility for the community's actions, which they perform in its name" (p. 194). When individuals act for and on behalf of their community in ways in which they would not have acted qua individuals, they are re-sponsible for those actions. Stein suggests that one source of the disagree-ment between her and Scheler is that she is specifically concerned with one particular type of community, that whose members are and remain free sub-jects, while Scheler has quite another conception of the relationship between a community and its members. But she acknowledges this disagreement only to put it on one side.

If the first of her two essays was no more than a prologue to the second, the first part of the second, which concludes with Stein's remarks about Scheler, is no more than a prologue to its second part. Indeed it is only at this point that it begins to become clear why Stein has proceeded as she has done. The theses for which she has argued so far turn out to be theses pre-supposed by the enquiry which she is now ready to undertake. And it is that enquiry which gives point and purpose to the whole.

So far I have followed Stein's order of exposition in pedestrian fashion, even if selectively. And the effect on the reader may well have been: 'To what is all this leading?' It will perhaps clarify matters, if I begin with conclusions that Stein only arrives at later, conclusions that provide her enquiries with their goal. Those conclusions concern the relationship between the character of individuals and the character of the communities to which they belong. Communities derive their character in key part from the individuals who participate in their activities. But those individuals become the kind of individuals that they become in key part because of the communities in whose lives they participate. So that to ask: 'What kind of person should I become?' is always also to ask: 'Of what kinds of community should I be a member?' Types of community that do not enable their members to develop as free subjects will disable those members in their responsiveness to ethical, aesthetic and religious values. Individuals who insist on their self-sufficiency by refusing to recognize their dependence on a range of communities will deprive both themselves and their communities of badly needed resources and become the victims of debilitating and disabling forms of social relationship. Like Tönnies therefore Stein became unusually aware both of the limitations of the individualism characteristic of the social relationships of *Gesellschaft* and of the dangers in the collective mentality of the mass or herd. And, in this too like Tönnies, she as a result had resources for recognizing the potentialities and dangers of National Socialism.

Having suggested that communities are distinct forms of social reality, Stein then returns to her discussion of individuals and their development, but now in the context of community. She reminds us of the place of life-power in the individual *psyche*. Our abilities, our capacities for perception and feeling, our intellectual powers, our power of will, all of these have to be developed through training. Each individual *psyche* has an "original predisposition" (p. 199) from which and in accordance with which the powers of that individual are developed through such training, training that requires both the right kind of energies, of life-power, in the individual and the relevant opportunities in what is offered to individuals in their social and communal environment. Aesthetic powers require one kind of opportunity and stimulus for their development, mathematical powers another. In thus characterizing the *psyche*, Stein distinguishes it not only from body and mind, but also from soul. To have a soul is to have certain kinds of power, just as to have a body and to have a mind is to have certain kinds of power. To be a human *psyche* is to have the possibility of a centered self, a core self out of which the determinate powers develop.

Stein is now able to consider various ways in which individuals, both members of a community and those who are outside a community, may contribute to a community's life-power, both in living out their individual lives and in playing their part in the community and how at the same time they may be energized by the influence of others. As a member of a community I may find myself able to undertake tasks that I would not be able to, were I not strengthened by the energies of communal life (pp. 205–6), which have resulted from the action of other individuals. But it is not only by other members of my community that I or my community may be energized. Confrontation and conflict with outsiders may have similar outcomes. What Stein says here should remind us of Simmel's thesis that the stranger is one who may impact on a group, so that its members partially redefine themselves over against him and in so doing become more aware of what they have in common, but do not share with the stranger, yet also of what they do share with the stranger. So Stein considers how conflict either between one individual and another or between one community and another may result in interaction so that each becomes "open to all the influences that are emanating from the other. Thus they form a unity of life in spite of the chasm that exists between them" (p. 207). A different type of interaction is that in which a nation receives an economic impetus as a result of transactions between some of its individual members and individuals who belong to a more vigorous and advanced economy. Here what changes in a hitherto economically sluggish society is the overall temper of economic life, but the changes are brought about entirely by the actions of individuals who had in mind only their own economic advantage.

Communities may also draw life-power from other sources. By learning about some other community or by engaging in the study of the past history of their own or other communities, individuals can on occasion revitalize aspects of their communal life. How is this so? Stein answers by considering the part played in energizing both individual and communal life by affective attitudes and by the values that are their objects. Values, as we have seen, are in her view objective and on encountering them we respond with emotion, so that we are first aware of valued objects as objects to which our affective attitudes are directed. And value is always something realized or to be realized by some state of affairs. When Stein spoke of values in the first treatise, she had remarked that it is part of the meaning (*Sinn*) of something known as valuable that it presents itself "as something that ought to be" (p. 43), so that, if it is in my power to bring about the realization of some value, the norm dictates that I should act accordingly. Not all values are positive. Some actual and possible states of affairs are bad. And in our affective responses to value we express attitudes that may be positive, negative or indifferent. Positive attitudes include love, trust and gratitude, negative attributes distrust, aversion and hatred. Such attitudes not only provide us with motives, they are effective causal agencies, increasing or depleting the powers of those whose attitudes they are and of those on whom such attitudes impact. It is in these ways that values become a source of changes in life-power both in individuals and in communities in which those individuals participate.

Individuals make of the social wholes of which they are part objects of their attention and regard, objects which thus became a focus for evaluative and practical attitudes. So a nation can become a valued object of love on the part of individual citizens, who then communicate this attitude to fellow citizens, so that they "inspire patriotism in them too and thereby increase their powers and supply those enhanced powers to the community" (p. 215). Very different factors may also influence the life and life-power of a community. The harsh soil of mountainous country requires demanding labor and influences the directions in which life-power is exerted. The visual quality of a mountain landscape impresses itself on the inhabitants. And a range of different types of aesthetic, ethical and religious values, together with personal values inherited from their pasts, not only provide grounds and motives for action, but also enhance or diminish the life of a community, although only if the members of that community are sufficiently receptive. Yet where there is a rich cultural inheritance, where you have "a well formed morality, a well developed law, and a literature as a national common good," these are not accessible only to those who are especially receptive, but the works and deeds which embody them bear "testimony of the susceptibility and the creative power of the people" (p. 220) as a whole.

Stein is now able to present a more general and developed account of the relationship of individual to community. Individual human beings are to be characterized in a number of ways. They are first of all bodies, subject to physical law, but also sentient beings whose senses and sensory states enable them to be receptive and responsive to what is presented to them, and in reflecting on these intelligent beings whose powers of perception and understanding enable them to classify and to investigate what is thus presented. They are moreover beings of impulse and inclination who find themselves with motives and/or grounds for directing themselves to certain ends, beings whose powers of will allow them to act or to refrain from acting as they are motivated to act, beings whose recognition of values elicits affective attitudes issuing in inclinations and in acts of will, and beings the depth of whose 'I' is the soul. How one makes values one's own and how one acts in relation to them, how one is happy and how one grieves and suffers, depend on the state of one's soul.

'Soul' is not used as a theological term. It is what someone is in the depths of her or his being and "those depths do awaken in affective and dispositional life" (p. 227). For it is in the affective and dispositional life that our openness to values and our ability to act on them appears: "we see what the person *is* when we see which world of value she lives in" (p. 227).

The relationship between soul and character is initially presented in terms of a contrast between the soul, on the one hand, and, on the other, that in us which is the source of the development of those dispositional properties which are virtues and vices and which issue in good and bad actions. External circumstances determine whether or not training of the kind required for the development of the virtues is available to this or that individual, but such external circumstances have no effect on the soul. And what anyone can do about the condition of her or his soul is very limited. One can "suppress negatively valued deeds and stirrings of one's soul and fight against the disposition to them, or even prevent them from arising and instead open oneself to positive values. But one can neither instill the qualities of one's soul into oneself nor break oneself of them" (p. 233). Is then change in the soul impossible? If it does occur, it must result from some intervention from without, from some power that is external to all the natural relationships in which the person is caught up.

In what Stein said about the soul she was following, often closely, an article by Hedwig Conrad-Martius, "Gespräch von der Seele," first published in the journal *Summa* in 1917 and then in a later version of her book, *Metaphysische Gespräche* (Halle: Max Niemeyer, 1922). And she began from remarks by Conrad-Martius in describing different relationships in which the soul can stand to the outwardly displayed qualities of the self. Our capacities come to be through interaction with the world around us. The soul's history is not like this. It gradually awakens and imprints its peculiar mark on the developed properties of the *psyche*. Interaction with the world can provide occasions for the awakening of the soul, but, unlike the training of intellectual or aesthetic or physical capacities, there is no way to say in advance what kind of event will produce such an awakening.

When the soul is fully awakened, every aspect of individual personality is changed. Now life flows to the exercise of intellectual and other powers and that exercise is marked by an individuality that is the expression of *this* soul. So on the contrary when the soul, perhaps in emotional distress, withdraws into itself, the behavior of the individual is no longer genuinely marked by individuality, even if some outward signs of it remain. The soul is itself one source of life-power and the power that flows from it strengthens the development of those qualities in each individual which that individual was predisposed to develop. Moreover the depth of our responsiveness to values depends upon qualities of the soul. So how the core predispositions of each individual are transformed into intellectual, moral and physical qualities depends on how the soul acts, both in the inward depths of the personality and in the outward manifestations of its life. Superficiality and depth are characteristics of individuals which exhibit how it is with them and their souls.

Stein is now in a position to pose and answer questions that have been implicit in her enquiry from the outset, questions of two kinds. She has provided the materials for asking in what ways communities and other forms of social relationships are founded upon the characteristics and abilities of individuals. And she is also able to ask what it is in the formation of individuals that is due to their participation in communal and other forms of relationship.

Stein begins from a distinction that she had also drawn earlier between that in our experiences and in the exercise of our capacities which is solely individual and that in the structure of our experiences which we share with others, so that there are experiences in common, some shared by all rational individuals and some shared by those who are directed towards this or that specific good or value. So members of religious, artistic or scientific communities may exemplify types of personality apt for each of these common pursuits and such a "type is one constituent of the individual personality" (p. 240).

The first kind of social grouping that Stein considers is that of the mass, composed of individuals who by a kind of contagion feel and act in concert with others in a way that presupposes failure to exercise either their powers of decision as free individuals or their powers of thought. Yet what are transmitted from one individual to another through such contagion are not only states of impulse and feeling, but also on occasion ideas. The example that Stein gives of what she takes to be the pathogenic transmission of ideas is that of the spread of Bolshevism in the years after 1918. And this example raises a more general question about the transmission of groundless or ill-founded ideas and beliefs.

Stein notes that few of our well-founded ideas and beliefs derive from firsthand experience. We depend on others for much that we believe and we are for the most part justified in so doing. But what about ill-founded beliefs? What makes us credulous? Stein notes that, where we do not have grounds for some particular belief, we may still have motives, but goes on to raise the question of whether there may not be motiveless beliefs. What she is suggesting is that there may be individuals who, while without any particular motive, have a propensity to adopt beliefs in a way that is independent of the content of the beliefs in question. Just as there are cheerful people with "a natural readiness to break out in smiles at the drop of a hat," so there are people with a certain readiness for conviction, people with "a desire to be filled with a conviction" (p. 250), who are, so to speak, belief-prone.

Add to that a readiness to adopt the particular convictions of others around them and we have the phenomenon that Stein called 'contagion'. Contagion by itself is not sufficient to explain how groundless ideas are propagated, for contagion by itself involves no intellectual apprehension, not even a minimal grasp of an idea. Yet, when some idea has been grasped, it may take a firm hold just because of the effects of contagion. Stein quotes Simmel on how in a crowd a number of influences may operate, so that "there develops a great nervous excitement at the expense of clear and consistent intellectual activity" and individuals become capable of acts that they would not be capable of apart from membership in that crowd. No place is left for reflective or critical thought (pp. 252–53). And this is how the relationships of a mass are. But there may be a further complexity in the social relationships involved.

When, as is often the case, ideas are supplied to the mass that come from those who aspire to direct its activities, the relationship of these would-be leaders to their mass following involves a kind of reciprocal understanding very different from the relationships of the mass of individuals to each other. In sharing goals and directions some aspects of the relationship of leaders to lead may take the form of communal rather than mass relationships, so that an external observer could be misled as to what is going on.

More generally Stein insists that no actual social formation is ever an entirely unmixed case of mass or of *Gesellschaft* or of *Gemeinschaft*. And she puts this insight to use in a discussion of *Gesellschaft* which follows. There are at least two ways in which the social relationships characteristic of *Gesellschaft* need to be informed and sustained by relationships characteristic of *Gemeinschaft*. Individuals come together in the forms of association characteristic of *Gesellschaft* for their own purposes, treating other individuals as instruments for the achievement of the purposes of the association. But nonetheless, says Stein, they bring with them to these new relationships habits of living together with others that do not allow them to treat others *only* as such instruments. And in the course of their working together with others further sympathies are engendered that motivate the treatment of those others in ways characteristic of *Gemeinschaft* rather than *Gesellschaft*. No association, no matter how well organized, no matter how faultless a social mechanism, could continue to function, if it were no more than the norms and values of *Gesellschaft* require it to be (p. 254).

So too in relationships of *Gemeinschaft* sustained over time elements of *Gesellschaft* often enter in and indeed one and the same set of people—a class in a school, for example—can be simultaneously an instance of *Gemeinschaft* and an instance of *Gesellschaft*. Yet Stein also emphasizes the extent of the differences between these two kinds of social relationship. She reminds us that communities, like organisms, serve no purpose external to themselves, that they are not brought into being or dissolved by acts of choice, that they develop, each in its own distinctive way. The flourishing of no individual is indispensable to the flourishing of the community to which she or he belongs. And the character of a community is neither the same as nor the sum of the characters of the individuals who compose it. There are indeed character traits typical of this or that community, but even those individuals who exhibit them have something more to their character as well as those traits. And that something more is the distinctiveness of their personality, their individuality. This distinctiveness is one of the sources of communal relationships.

This may seem paradoxical. For we might expect community to be founded on what individuals have in common rather than on what is distinctive about them. But in Stein's view of *Gemeinschaft* as a community of free individuals, it is on what distinctive individuals have in common that community is founded. There is here a reciprocity. Although the character of a community turns out to be dependent on the distinctiveness of its members, it is also true that the individual may be determined in his character by the community, with traits that are intelligible only in the context of communal life (p. 284).

The communal relationships in which we participate affect our development as individuals. Stein had suggested earlier that how our original predispositions develop depends on the opportunities for development that our environment affords. And a communal environment affords opportunities that might not otherwise be available. But there are other ways in which the development of individuals may be affected by communal life, not all of them good. We may, for example, too easily take over the attributes and emotions of others. Contagion can occur in communal as well as in mass relationships. So "I can be infected with anger and disgust, love and hate for my surroundings, and feel them without their originating from my personal ego" (p. 267). But these states of feeling are not genuinely my own. The personal qualities that they foster are artificial and not rooted in the self. In a similar way artificial moral and religious attitudes can be generated. And indeed someone's whole character can thereby come to lack individuality.

Contrast with this what happens when communal relationships enable one person to open up to another, so that qualities hitherto dormant in me are allowed to develop and the individual becomes what she or he always had it in them to be. Yet whether I develop the characteristics of an artificial personality or whether I develop genuine qualities remains in key part up to me. Through acts of will I am free to choose—at least up to a point—what environment to inhabit, which influences to admit and which to reject, which tendencies in myself to foster and which to curb.

A community always has its own aims and objectives. And what distinguishes the members of a community is that they make its aims and objectives their own. In so doing they are apt to develop new and distinctive character traits. But here too things can go well or badly. In an attempt to accommodate oneself to relationships to others in a common life, individuals can thwart deep tendencies in themselves, becoming victims of their own struggle to achieve a measure of inner identification with the community that is not possible for them. And what such struggle achieves is the simulacrum of a common life, not the real thing.

Genuine community can be achieved at a number of levels. So a community devoted to scientific research, for example, is possible without its members being engaged by each other at the core of their being. But there are possible forms of community in which it is the soul of the individuals who participate that is engaged so that, on the one hand, "the one who acts is no longer the discrete [member], but rather the community in him and through him" (p. 272), and, on the other hand, the distinctive character of the community is realized in and through its members. We sometimes speak of the *Geist* of a community and also of its soul. What do we mean by these expressions and how are they related to one another? To speak of the *Geist* of a community is to say more than that it shares a *Geist*-informed life, a culture. It is to ascribe a certain kind of unity to that life. To speak of a communal *Geist* is analogous to ascribing distinctiveness to an individual. "When the center of this unitary fashioning of the individual or the community lies within the individual or community itself, then we ascribe a 'soul' to it" (p. 275). But it is on the souls of the individuals who compose them that communities depend for their centeredness, for their rootedness.

Stein is now able to differentiate her position from Scheler's and she does so by a classification of types of community. The highest form of community is that is which every individual member of the community acts as a free person and as a member of the community, taking responsibility for her or himself and for the community. Such free persons have within themselves just that centeredness and depth that makes them at one with their souls. Next in order is the form of community where only some members are of this kind, determining the mind of the community for its other members, and taking responsibility for themselves and for the community. Then comes that form of community in which some of its members are free persons and it does indeed have a common mind, but its present members have played no part in determining that mind, as when that common mind was formed at some point in the past and has now simply been taken over by the present generation (p. 278). What then of the case where a community contains no free and responsible persons? Can it still be in any sense a community? Stein takes it that both children and certain types of animals are able to participate in communal relationships, sharing in the directedness of a common life, even though we cannot ascribe responsibility to them, and so her answer is "Yes."

Stein believed that Scheler had blurred distinctions on which this classification of types of community depends and in so doing had lost sight of the crucial part played by those individuals who are able to assume responsibility both for themselves and for their community. Every community of the higher kinds is able to carry on its life only through such persons and therefore it is important to identify what it is to be a 'carrier' of one's community. Stein contrasts two extremes. There are individuals who are members of some scientific or artistic community, but who pursue only their own individual goals, isolating themselves, so that their achievements do not contribute to communal life. And there are by contrast individuals who not only wear themselves out for the community, but who experience whatever they encounter as a member of the community and who take that place within the community that will enable them best to serve its purposes. Some forms of communal relationship—Stein cites friendship and marriage—require that anyone who participates in the relationship be a carrier. But for many forms of communal life this is not so. What is necessary is that some individuals should function as carriers and "The more carriers a community has to support it, and the further that their devotion to it extends, the more secure its substance" (p. 281).

Stein at this point returns to Simmel's remarks about mixed modes of social relationship and among these considers one that involves a quite different application for the word '*Gesellschaft*', used as it sometimes is in German, just as 'society' sometimes is in English, to speak of 'polite society'—a felicitous choice of expression by Stein's English translators. In referring to polite society, Stein is speaking of that upper layer of society which has its own customs and standards, membership in which is valued precisely because so many are excluded from it, a caste whose members are able to recognize who belongs to it and who does not. To belong to polite society one must have the social standing that accompanies a high rank in society at large. But it is an assumption of polite society that only those with its attitudes and personality structure will be able to fill the positions that carry high rank.

Polite society has some of the essential characteristics of community. It was not brought into being to achieve certain purposes and its members share certain inner attitudes. Yet its social relationships also resemble those of the mass. Both polite society and mass are class phenomena, in which acceptance by others is a matter of unreasoned conformity in attitude as well as of social rank. To fail to conform is in both cases to be excluded. But that this is so is merely incidental to the life of the mass, whereas for polite society "the shutting out of others is one component in its *inner* feeling of belonging together" (p. 289), so that those who belong feel themselves different from others. We have to remember that all social life is a kind of theatre, an aesthetic spectacle which both conceals and excludes much of life, including much of the life of those who participate in it, so that "under the surface of theatrical and stylized human relationships a maze of primitive and naïve relationships crisscrosses: relationships that would be impossible inside of polite society" (p. 290). To understand this is to understand that polite society is after all an artificial construction and as such its relationships have something in common with those of *Gesellschaft* in its original sense.

One of Stein's major preoccupations throughout the two parts of her book has been to emphasize not only the openness of individuals to social relationships of various kinds but also that aspect of individuals which is other than and cannot be explained by reference to their social relationships. Hence derives her account of the *psyche* in which is rooted the distinctive individuality of each human being, an individuality which may find or fail to find expression in the development of those qualities from which actions issue. Membership in and openness to the values of communities may play a key part in determining success or failure in this respect. But, important as this is, it is also important that individuals are always more than their social relationships.

Anyone who advances such a view may be misunderstood, for it may be thought that they hold that the individual is one thing, her or his social relationships quite another, so that the roles that individuals play in social life are no more than external trappings behind which the true self is concealed. But this is not Stein's view, as she makes clear in an all too brief discussion of social acts, social types and the forms of self-presentation that social life requires of us. By social types she means what others have meant by social roles. When we are cast in the role of friend or of foe, of employer or of laborer, of holder of this or that office in this or that association, certain typical behavior is expected of us and we generally respond to these expectations by acting in the required way. Yet just how we respond, how we play out our assigned roles, will be in part determined by our individuality. One person will play the role in this way, another in that. Although role-playing is not generally the assumption of a mask that conceals the true face of the individual, individuality and the requirements of some particular role can on occasion be at odds, so that the result is an inner conflict. Or conflict can result from an attempt to occupy two roles that are in tension. The resolution of such conflicts depends on the individual. And in the end what forms of social life are generated depends upon individuals. For new social types can unfold only from and through the creativity of distinctive personalities who are not content merely to adapt themselves to roles and types that are already available. "Thus, all social life and all social modes finally refer back to the core of the person, which is beyond the reach of all the influences of reciprocal communication" (p. 294).

I spoke of this as her "last word" and it is indeed the thought that concludes her overall argument. But in saying this, she had, as she well realized, taken up a position in an ongoing dispute about the nature of the social and human sciences. Among the Neo-Kantians, Windelband and his successor at Heidelberg, Rickert, had distinguished those sciences which aspire to discover universal law-like generalizations from those sciences which are concerned with what is irreducibly individual, assigning the natural sciences to the former class, the historical sciences to the latter. Psychology however they classified as a natural science. But in Stein's view the *psyche*, the person and the body all play a part in the development of individuality and what emerges from this development can only be characterized in part by empirical generalizations, and moreover by generalizations which "never can have the character of exact natural laws" (p. 304). Moreover insofar as individual personality comes to expression in the works of human culture, in the realm of *Geist*, it can only be understood by the distinctively human sciences, the

Geisteswissenschaften. "Thus for any fundamental investigation of the human *psyche* psychology and the *Geisteswissenschaften* must work hand in hand" (p. 304).

How psychology therefore should be conceived, what its relationship to the *Geisteswissenschaften* is, and how her views compare with those of Rickert are therefore discussed by Stein in a concluding section entitled "The distinction in principle between the being of *psyche* and that of *Geist*, between psychology and the *Geisteswissenschaften*." But her discussion, although interesting and suggestive, breaks off at the point at which she confronts Rickert's central thesis. She had partially defined her position over against the Baden Neo-Kantians, but her critique of their position had still to be fully spelled out. We should therefore perhaps put on one side what she has to say in these concluding considerations, returning instead to the title of the two treatises, where she had announced her topic as "The philosophical grounding (*Bergründung*) of psychology and the *Geisteswissenschaften*." What is it to supply these disciplines with a philosophical grounding and how far did Stein succeed in supplying one? We can answer that question best by considering how it was that Stein came to ask it and what it was in her intellectual development that had made it an inescapable question for her.

14

What Kind of Story Is the Story So Far?

In her two long essays on individual and community, Stein asks and answers four sets of questions. The first concern what it is in ourselves that we can only understand as the impact upon us of external causal agencies, whether natural or social. A second set concern the nature of those acts that we can only understand as free acts, acts that can be sufficiently or insufficiently grounded, rationally or irrationally motivated. A third set of questions are about what it is to act either in response to or in concert with others and more especially to act in response to or in concert with those others who stand in certain social or communal relationships to oneself. And a fourth set of questions ask both what it is in ourselves that comes to be only in and through our responsive relationships to such others and what it is in ourselves that is prior to and independent of all such relationships.

In each case, Stein is attempting to identify the foundational concepts and judgments to which any substantive answers to those questions must appeal. To speak of a concept or judgment as foundational is to say three things of it: first, that it is indispensable, if we are to give an adequate account of some particular subject matter; secondly, that it is not reducible to some other concept or concepts, judgment or judgments, by which it could be replaced without significant loss; and, thirdly, that we can identify those objects of our mental acts in and through whose presentation we find primary application for those concepts and primary grounds for so judging. It is in this sense that Husserl took phenomenology to provide foundations for the particular sciences. And it is in this sense that Stein attempted, by answering these four sets of questions, to identify what is foundational for psychological and social science.

How far was she successful? Alfred Schutz in his 1959 paper on "Husserl's Importance for the Social Sciences" (reprinted in Vol. I of his *Collected Papers*, The Hague: Martinus Nijhoff, 1967) wrote of Stein's "naïve use of the eidetic method in analyzing the problems of social relations, of community, and of the state" and castigated her "formulation of certain apodictic and purportedly aprioristic statements which have contributed towards discrediting phenomenology among social scientists" (pp. 140–41). What Schutz meant by this criticism can be inferred from his accusation that Stein was among those students of Husserl who "believed that concrete problems of the social sciences could be solved by direct application of the method of eidetic reduction to unclarified notions of common sense thinking or to equally unclarified concepts of the empirical social sciences" (p. 140). It is a twofold accusation: first, that Stein had moved from the experience of particulars to what she took to be the identification of essential properties of the kinds of things exemplified by those particulars illegitimately (this is the alleged "naïve use of the eidetic method"); and, secondly, that she had allowed "unclarified notions," whether drawn from common sense or from the social sciences, to obscure the character of the particulars presented in experience. How far was Schutz in the right?

Stein did indeed sometimes borrow uncritically and as a result rely on notions needing further clarification. Yet she also shows insight in her borrowings. Consider her use of Tönnies and her treatment of the social relationships characteristic of *Gesellschaft* with its recognition that such relationships must always involve some degree of *Gemeinschaft*. Those others who present themselves to me as coworkers in some organization over some extended period of time never present themselves as only coworkers, but always to some degree as individuals with whom I may develop empathetic relationships and who thereby may elicit my sympathies and modes of solidarity of a communal kind. On this what Stein says is certainly too brief, but, if we fill out our account with what she wrote elsewhere, she provides important phenomenological confirmation of Tönnies's insistence that the relationships of *Gesellschaft* are never purely or only those. Here phenomenology usefully complements a very different mode of social enquiry.

A second area relevant to Schutz's criticism is Stein's treatment of the notion of life-power at various points in both treatises. Here again she starts from concepts used by Dilthey and others. But this borrowing has point and purpose. For the notion of life-power—and she develops it with originality— is a surrogate for a certain kind of biological explanation which we do not even now know how to give. Consider the context in which Stein first introduces the notion. It is that in which she makes an important and original phenomenological point, that the quality of our experiences is affected by fatigue and vigor. Distinguishing between what it is to experience an intense red and what it is to experience some red intensely, she reminds us that intensity or the lack of it is already related to and sometimes characterized by our energy or lack of energy. And this is relevant to distinguishing the content of some of our experiences from their objects. But this aspect of the content of our experiences presents itself as in need of causal explanation, as one of the features of consciousness that derives from the causal background to consciousness, and more immediately from the biological background to consciousness.

So here too Stein moves forward from positions taken by others—in this case from Dilthey and Bergson—but in such a way as to open up further enquiry not within phenomenology, but concerning the relationship of what phenomenological observation discloses to what biochemistry can tell us about the causes and the effects of vigor and fatigue, a story that will be in part about adrenalin flow. And in recognizing how phenomenology poses questions to the biological and other human sciences, Stein identifies a sometimes overlooked dimension of phenomenological enquiry.

A third relevant area is that in which Stein discusses the relationship between that in each of us which is constituted, at least in part, through our relationships to others, and that in us which is prior to and independent of such constitution, that which is the source of our individuality, our uniqueness. Here, as in her discussion of fatigue and lack of energy. Stein was breaking new ground. She poses the question: What is it about my courage or cowardice, my generosity or meanness, that makes them peculiarly mine? And she recognized that external circumstances may be such as either to foster or to suppress individuality. In so doing she made it clear that the nature of communal relationships cannot be adequately spelled out unless the individuality of those who enter into them is taken into account and that different types of communal relationship will exemplify different modes of individual expression. Here again much more needs to be said than Stein was able in this period of her life to say, but she had identified issues that are crucial for further enquiry.

We have to conclude then that Schutz's accusatory generalizations about Stein's treatises are greatly exaggerated. Nonetheless he directs our attention to weaknesses in her arguments. And, if we retort, as I have done, that he failed to notice her insights and her strengths, it has to be with this qualification, that what is valuable in her work is too often both insufficiently self-critical and insufficiently developed. Yet we can identify a set of important conclusions at which she had arrived which carry further a line of philosophical enquiry first developed in her dissertation. Consider six theses to the assertion of which by this stage Stein was committed.

First, that the 'I', whether as perceiver or as agent, is partially constituted in and through relationships with others in which each of those others is also recognized as an 'I'. This recognition involves situating myself bodily in relation to others and to those objects which are shared objects of perception by myself and by those others. Consciousness is always understood as embodied consciousness, just because consciousness of self is always consciousness of a self in relationship to others who are embodied consciousnesses.

Secondly, my self-knowledge derives in part from others and from what they know of me from their external standpoints. And the knowledge of myself that I arrive at, whether through disciplined attention to my own mental acts, the knowledge of the 'I' as 'I', or through what I learn about myself from others to whom I am other, the knowledge of the 'I' as 'other', is the knowledge of a self bodily situated within a nexus of social and natural relationships.

By affirming these two theses Stein had separated herself decisively from both the Cartesian and the Kantian traditions. (We should note, as Karl Ameriks has pointed out to me, that Kant himself had insisted that all determinate self-knowledge requires that one gets beyond one's individual self, although not that this involves an awareness of other minds.) And in this of course she was at one with a number of her phenomenological contemporaries. Scheler was to argue that it is only because our experience is that of a 'We' that we are able to have experience of the world. And Heidegger was to argue that there is no possible understanding of human existence except as existence in relation to the world and to others. But Stein, who could in this at least have agreed with both Scheler and Heidegger, had arrived at her formulations of her positions on her own—Husserl was of course to deal with these issues in *Ideen II* and Stein is always indebted to him, even when she is most independent—and in such a way as to be able to move on from them in a very different direction from that taken by Scheler or by Heidegger.

Her direction is signaled by a third and a fourth thesis. The third asserts that what we become, what qualities we come to possess, aesthetically, morally, intellectually, is in key part a matter of our responsiveness to our social and natural environment. Stein is not here making an empirical assertion about causal interactions between individuals and their environments, although what she says presupposes some account of such causal interactions. She is rather speaking of those of our qualities that can only be characterized, whether by us as agents or by external observers, by reference to our relationships to others, such qualities as aversion to . . . , affection for . . . , openness to . . . , appreciation of. . . . Such qualities are elicited by being presented with objects and what types of objects are presented to them depends upon the character of our social and natural environment. It is not of course that in relation to our environments we are purely passive, since among those qualities are some such as openness to . . . and curiosity about . . . that issue in active engagement with our environments.

A fourth thesis is closely related: that the different types of social relationship into which we enter make a significant difference to the kind of human being that we become. But once again individuals are not passive. They affect in various ways the character of some at least of the social relationships into which they enter, sometimes transforming both themselves and the institutions in which they participate. And here a fifth thesis, one of which we have already taken note, is relevant. The character both of our qualities and of our social relationships is necessarily marked to greater or lesser degree by our individuality. And at the same time the ways in which and the extent to which our individuality is expressed in our qualities and social relationships, and, that is to say, also in our actions and choices, depends in part on the kind of relationships into which we have entered.

Sixthly and finally, Stein asserts that our judgments of value and the attitudes and actions which issue from or presuppose those judgments are intelligible only in terms of the account of individuals and their social relationships that she has sketched. Stein is an objectivist about values. It is indeed through our affective responses to objects that we give expression to our judgments of value. But what we are expressing is a response to objects as value-endowed, as goods. We may however on occasion be blind to certain values or, on perceiving them, find ourselves unable to respond to the claims that they make on us. And how far and on what types of occasion this is so depends upon what kind of person we have become and the qualities that we have developed or failed to develop.

About these six theses, developed at varying lengths in Stein's dissertation and in the *Beiträge*, a range of philosophical questions arise. Some of them were later to provide Stein with a new philosophical agenda. But they already define not just a distinctive philosophical standpoint, but one which portrays human life as essentially problematic. And I take it that it was no accident that, during the period in which she was elaborating this standpoint in her philosophical writings, she was also compelled to understand her own condition as problematic in just the way portrayed in her philosophical account. How so?

From the standpoint that Stein had developed each of us has a story to tell about how we have come to have the perspective that we have on the world, on ourselves, on others, and on the social and national landscapes that we inhabit. What Stein had identified in her philosophical writings, and more especially in the six theses that I have abstracted from them, were those characteristics of individuals and of their social relationships without which neither our present perspective nor the past history that has made that perspective what it is can become intelligible. And it is this same set of characteristics that are salient when we recount Stein's history up to this point. Stein had become what she then was through a formation in which four sets of communal relationships had played a notable part. There was first of all her relationship to her family, especially to her mother and to those sisters to whom she was close. There was next her identification with the wider Germany society encountered in the institutional settings of school, of university and of a military hospital. There were thirdly her immediate relationships to many colleagues, patients, and physicians in that hospital. And finally there were her relationships to her philosophical contemporaries and to her and their teachers, first at Göttingen and then at Freiburg. In each of these cases there was a formative period which opened up possibilities of greater self-knowledge for Stein, followed by a period in which she was compelled to move beyond and, to varying extents, to leave behind the relationships that had been so important to her.

Consider first her relations to family members. Her ties with them had not so far been broken and indeed they never would be broken, but they had already been and would be further tested and transformed in unpredicted ways. Two things had tended to separate her from some members of her family and, most painfully, from her mother: her abandonment of belief in God—which she had so far concealed from her mother; when at home she still accompanied her mother to synagogue—and the interests and direction that had resulted from her education. But she had no problem in identifying herself as Jewish and did so, for example, when anti-Semitic remarks were made in her presence (*Life in a Jewish Family, 1891–1916*, p. 343), as sometimes happened in the military hospital. And she remained deeply affectionate towards her mother and several of her sisters. Yet it is clear that her separation from her family was closely bound up with the quiet independence that she had first exhibited in early adolescence. Stein was to an unusual degree someone who was able to feel great affection for someone else and yet refuse to be influenced by them. One example of such a relationship is that with her mother. Another is that with Hans Lipps.

From adolescence onwards she had identified herself both as Jewish and as a German with peculiarly German loyalties. But here too a change took place with her movement from a pride in the values of Prussian conservatism to the democratic commitments at which she arrived in 1918. Those commitments put her at odds with many of her fellow citizens—even with many of them who now professed democratic convictions—and, although until she became a Carmelite she was always to some degree a politically engaged person, she developed a suspicion of and a skepticism about the forms of political solidarity to which so many Germans were attracted. Thus politically, as well as in her family life, her independent judgments separated her to a significant degree from those around her.

At the military hospital, that independence of judgment was from the outset an important characteristic of her relationship to her colleagues, her superiors, and her patients. Her strong patriotic sense of duty made it easy to obey orders. Her genuine and increasingly informed concern for her patients made it easier than it would otherwise have been to perform unpleasant and menial tasks. The difficulties of communicating with many of her patients

made her unusually self-aware as to the part that empathy played in her relationships to them. But she would also have had to become aware of two
distinctions that reappear in her philosophical writings: that between that in
ourselves which we can and should adapt in response to the claims made
upon us by others and that in ourselves which we can but should not so
adapt, and that between that in ourselves which we can so adapt and that
which it is not in our power to change. It is important that practically effective clarity about these distinctions is necessary for right action. If we do not
know how to make and apply the first distinction, we will not know when
and about what to be intransigent. And if we do not know how to make and
apply the second distinction, we will have an unrealistic view of our possibilities for self-transformation. A capacity for certain intransigence and an
unusual realism about herself became permanent marks of Stein's character.

Finally, there is the effect on Stein from her earliest student days of that
web of philosophical and personal relationships spun by the phenomenologists at Göttingen, although growing out of earlier encounters and relationships at both Munich and Göttingen. It was of crucial importance for these
relationships that philosophy was understood by that generation of phenomenologists as a cooperative enterprise in which the whole was greater
than the contributing parts. This was above all Reinach's vision of philosophy, embodied in his practice as well as in his theory. And it was a vision
powerful enough to withstand the tensions and conflicts that from time to
time Husserl's way of dealing with his students generated. But, when so
many of that generation were dispersed at the outbreak of war in 1914 and
above all after the death of Reinach, the relationships of a number of the best
of Husserl's students to Husserl were damaged. They continued to acknowledge their debt to Husserl with respect and affection and to continue their
philosophical dialogue both with him and with some at least of their fellow
students, but they took their own distinctive way: so it was with Ingarden,
with Lipps, with Conrad-Martius, and with Stein herself. Each had to decide
both how to define their own philosophical stance in relation to Husserl's
and with whom to continue further their philosophical conversation. And
this differentiated them sharply from those other students of Husserl who
continued in their commitment to his project of transcendental phenomenology.

What the dissenters had in common was their rejection of what they took
to be Husserl's turn away from realism and towards idealism. Indeed Ingarden in his account of how Husserl was led to become a transcendental idealist (*On the Motives Which Led Husserl to Transcendental Idealism*, tr. A. Han-
nibalson, The Hague: Martinus Nijhoff, 1975) begins by considering the
possibility that Husserl in fact never was a realist, but that a realist interpretation of his early work had been projected onto it by some of his Göttingen
students under the influence of Reinach, who was himself influenced by the

realism of the Munich phenomenologists. Ingarden then proceeds to argue that Husserl's accounts of truth and of being in the *Logical Investigations* had in fact committed him to realist positions, although he concedes that Husserl's formulations are in some respects unclear.

The core of Ingarden's disagreement with the later Husserl was neatly captured by Herbert Spiegelberg: "What was at issue was the question whether ontology or phenomenology, namely the transcendental phenomenology of the process of constitution, had to come first. Ingarden was of the opinion that an analysis and evaluation of the constitutive processes involved in our knowledge of things presupposed as a 'guiding thread' the prior possession of a clarified notion of those things, while Husserl maintained that a clarified notion of the things could only be obtained on the basis of a prior understanding of the process of constitution" (*The Phenomenological Movement*, p. 225; see also footnote 78 where Spiegelberg gives the evidence for this interpretation of the disagreement). On this central issue, Lipps, Conrad-Martius and Stein were all in agreement with Ingarden. But beyond this point they took very different paths. Lipps undertook a series of remarkable piecemeal phenomenological investigations, each marked by his distinctive gift for close and accurate observation of phenomena, and issuing in accounts of language use, of logic, and of the relationship of the prelinguistic to the linguistic in which he steers a course, as he himself put it, "between pragmatism and *Existenz* philosophy," understanding the abstract as secondary to the concrete and particular and intentional relations to objects as always embedded in preintentional natural and social relationships. For him, unlike Ingarden, the reality '*an sich*' which we ascribe to things has to be understood primarily in the light of our practical encounters with those things.

Conrad-Martius by contrast had her own systematic view of the relationship of phenomenology to ontology, one that rivals Ingarden's in penetration and richness, but that makes the real itself an object of our phenomenological enquiry. The world presents itself to us as real and among the tasks of the phenomenologist is that of discovering what is essentially and necessarily true of the real. So she is led to advance an account of being and of beings that is at odds in important ways with Ingarden's ontology.

Yet it was not only that Ingarden, Lipps and Conrad-Martius took different philosophical directions. They, like other members of that philosophical generation, were dispersed geographically and socially. Ingarden returned to Poland. Lipps recovered from his war wound, completed his second dissertation, habilitated at Göttingen and later taught there. Conrad-Martius was for long periods isolated at Bergzabern. And in 1919 Stein returned to Breslau, living once more in the family home, giving tutorials and classes in phenomenology in her home, and teaching ethics part-time in the Breslau schools.

This diversity in philosophical directions and this geographical and social dispersal together fractured the phenomenological movement, at least as

Reinach had understood it. It was no longer anything like the same way or to anything like the same extent a cooperative enterprise. There had instead emerged a set of competing phenomenologies. And Stein, too, therefore, had to redefine her relationship, both philosophical and personal, not only to Husserl, but also to those of his students to whom she had been closest. The question of where she might now find communal relationships through which she could develop further her distinctive philosophical and other potentialities and to which she could contribute what she had in her to give had become urgent. What in the treatises were formulated as abstract and general questions about human capacity, individuality and community as such were thrust upon her as immediate particular and concrete questions about her own condition. Had she pursued these questions at Breslau in 1919 and 1920 with no more than the resources provided on the one hand by her own life-experience up to 1918 and on the other by the phenomenological insights and understanding that she had developed up to this point, it is not clear that she would have known how to proceed.

In fact however this was a period of radical self-transformation in which her story as recounted so far becomes no more than a prologue to what was to come next, an indispensable prologue certainly, but one whose importance lies precisely in what Stein was able to achieve later after the remaking of her self. In the second treatise, after having described the importance of the inner life, Stein emphasizes how little any of us is able to do by our own efforts to change that aspect of our lives. "If a change enters into this sphere, then it is not the occurrence of a 'development,' but rather is to be regarded as an 'otherworldly' (*jenseitige*) power, that is, a power situated outside of the person and outside of all the natural connections in which she is entangled" (p. 233).

The possibility of such an encounter with just such a power was something that Stein had not entertained before 1918. And her statement of her belief in such a possibility in 1919 is therefore something that cries out for explanation. That explanation is provided by the train of events that contributed to her conversion to Catholic Christianity.

15

Three Conversions

To tell the story of key events in Stein's life from 1918 to 1922 as the story of a conversion requires us first to understand what a conversion is. And at once an influential misconception of conversion has to be gotten out of the way, a misconception shared by some defenders of religious belief and some of its hostile critics. It is that to be converted to some particular form of belief in the God of the great theistic religions is necessarily to move beyond reason and perhaps against reason. The beliefs that we take for granted in our everyday lives and the beliefs that we acquire from the observations and theorizing of natural scientists are, if they are justified, supported by sound reasoning. If they are unjustified, they are corrigible by such reasoning. Belief in the God of theism by contrast, so it is suggested, can neither be justified nor refuted by reasoning. So to move from unbelief to belief is to move beyond reason. The word 'faith' is appropriated from theology to provide a name for beliefs that cannot by their very nature be justified by reasoning and one common metaphor for describing the movement from unbelief, thus understood, to belief is that of 'a leap of faith'. When this phrase is used by those hostile to theistic beliefs, the suggestion is that the convert has left behind what is taken to be the solid ground of reasoning. When it is used by friends of theistic belief, the suggestion is that reason has limitations that faith enables the convert to transcend.

Yet this common view of conversion obscures key aspects of some conversions. First, conversion is not necessarily conversion to some form of theistic belief. It may be conversion *from* theistic belief or conversion to some secular *Weltanschauung* that requires both intellectual and moral commitment. Secondly, many conversions, including many theistic conversions, are understood by those who undergo them as not taking them beyond reason,

but rather as enhancing their rational powers. They now perceive and understand something that previously they were unable to perceive and understand, both about themselves and about the world. So they are in a position to answer to such questions as: What new light has been cast on my past
life? What power was it that transformed me? And what new direction must
my life take, given that I now perceive and understand as I do? The claim
made by such converts is, to put matters in Augustine's terms, that, because
they now believe, they now are able to understand certain things. Of course,
many converts must be mistaken in making this claim, if only because converts from atheism to theism and from theism to atheism, from Judaism to
Christianity and from Christianity to Judaism, from Catholicism to Protestantism and from Protestantism to Catholicism, cannot—to put it mildly—all
be right. Nonetheless the claim made by converts is an important one.

For it is a claim that only from a particular standpoint and only in the company of certain others can some things be perceived and understood as they
are, and that only a certain kind of transformation of the self, which it was
not in the convert's own power to bring about, has enabled her or him to attain that standpoint. And this is a type of claim that itself provides a subject-
matter for rational enquiry. But in order to pursue that enquiry we need to
consider more than one type of conversion. So I preface my account of
Stein's conversion by recounting the conversion narratives of three of her
contemporaries, beginning with Reinach's story.

Reinach as a phenomenologist had always recognized the importance of
the question: What must be changed in me, if I am to perceive and to understand things as they are? Husserl in *Ideen* had emphasized the need for
an *epoché*, a putting on one side of whatever habits of mind, attitudes and
beliefs belong to the natural standpoint, our standpoint as plain prephilosophical persons, in order to focus attention on what is presented in and to
consciousness. Conrad-Martius was to argue that Husserl's account of the
epoché was inadequate. But both recognized that phenomenology requires
new habits of mind and to that degree a remaking of the self.

Stein had insisted that we can only understand the apprehension of value,
if we are able to distinguish those cases in which there is a recognition of objective values from those in which there is a blindness to those values, a failure in moral perception. But this distinction can surely be made only by
those who themselves have learned how to recognize both the reality of
such values and the blindness of some individuals to them. And for this, as
Stein made clear, one must have become a certain kind of person with developed capacities for both recognition of and response to values and, that
is to say, a person with moral and aesthetic habits of a certain kind.

'Phenomenology' is not then the name of a set of methods which anyone
with sufficient intellectual acuteness can apply. It requires of its practitioners
a disciplined and difficult openness to a wide range of different types of ex-

perience, a refusal to set a priori limits to the possibilities of experience, and whatever intellectual and moral attitudes and habits are necessary, if one is to possess such openness. What then is to be said about the possibilities of specifically religious experiences? What then of claims to have experienced the presence of God?

The phenomenologist best known for providing answers to these questions was Max Scheler, who had been strongly influenced by Rudolf Otto's *The Idea of the Holy*. But Scheler was not alone in constructing a phenomenology of religion. Gerda Walter, a student of Pfänder as well as of Husserl, who while at Freiburg had attended a class taught by Stein, in 1923 published not only an essay on the ontology of social communities in the sixth volume of the *Jahrbuch*—against which Alfred Schutz later leveled the same accusations that he leveled against Stein's work—but also a study of religious experience, *Phänomenologie der Mystik*. And Reinach at the very end of his life had become intensely interested in the question of what is distinctive in both our experience of and our conception of God.

While a soldier he continued to read the few books that he had with him: a New Testament, Augustine's *Confessions*, Thomas à Kempis, some of Simmel's essays. His writing consisted only of letters to his wife, entries in a notebook and a short draft of the opening paragraphs of the book that he hoped one day to write, *Das Absolute*. At the beginning of that draft, Reinach contrasted our attitudes to other human beings and our attitudes to God. "No gratitude and no trust in a human being is possible that cannot be conceived as yet greater. By contrast the trust and the gratitude that we experience with regard to God, the love and the goodness that we ascribe to him can be no greater" (*Sämtliche Werke* I, p. 606).

What Reinach is elucidating here is the relationship between the nature of the attributes that we ascribe to God and the nature of the attitudes that we take to God. Just as the goodness that we ascribe to God is without limit, so the trust that we place in God is without limit. This is a conceptual claim. If I trust someone somewhat or even a very great deal then necessarily the one in whom I am trusting is not God. But of course, even if my trust is such as to presuppose the existence of God, it does not follow that there is such a being. Whence then Reinach's confidence, his certainty, that there is?

Reinach had not always believed in God. In his earlier philosophical career he had considered some concepts of God more adequate than others—as concepts. But at an early stage in his military service he had experiences such that he found himself unable to withhold trust in God, as being, not as concept. His wife, Anna, had preceded him in this and he wrote to her about his life at the front: "The first weeks were terrible; then God's peace came to me too, and now all is well." A year or so later he wrote to her about his plans for further philosophical work: "I should like to start from the inner experience of God, the experience of being sheltered in Him, and shall be content to show that 'objective science' cannot gainsay it. I should like to expound the full meaning of this experience, to show how far it can claim objectivity, to demonstrate why it is a genuine cognition, though of its own kind; and, finally, to draw the conclusions. . . . To do such work with humility is most important today, far more important than to fight this war. For what purpose has this horror if it does not lead human beings closer to God?" (quoted in John M. Oesterreicher, *Walls Are Crumbling*, New York: Devin-Adair, 1952, pp. 122–23). Reinach's notes and the opening passages of *Das Absolute*—less than three thousand words—are all that we have of this project.

In Reinach's notes, Simmel is assigned the role of stating the case against religious truth. On May 13, 1916, Reinach takes note of Simmel's view that the states of affairs envisaged by religion are nothing other than exaggerations of empirical states of affairs and that the 'object' of religious belief is the product of religious experience. "It is not religion that creates religiosity, but religiosity religion." And a day later he quotes Simmel's observation that the peace, the trust, and the exaltation that religion brings derive not from transcendent powers, but from the soul itself. Reinach's comment on Simmel on the same day is that the analogies that Simmel draws between the social and the religious—seeing in the religious no more than a disguised form of the social—shows that he "has not grasped the essence of religion." And this is presumably what Reinach would have hoped to demonstrate in *Das Absolute*. But he did not live to do this.

Reinach seems even before this last period to have taken it for granted that, if there is a true religion, it is Christianity. The only alternatives that he considers are Christianity and unbelief and this suggests that, as with Stein, his Jewish childhood had left him with almost no sense at all of the distinctive claims that Judaism makes upon Jews. But what he wrote in his notes about Jesus also suggests an idiosyncratic reading of the gospels. Reinach was perhaps at this stage a committed, but not an instructed, Christian.

He was able to joke about his own possible coming death, talking of Stein and others who were now close friends to Anna and to himself that they would belong to "the mourners of the first rank" at his funeral. And he had excellent reason to foresee his death. In the third battle of Ypres, towards the close of which Reinach was killed, the German dead numbered 83,000 (the British between 62,000 and 65,000). Reinach was a good soldier—an artillery officer—who received the Iron Cross, and the probability of survival for junior officers was very low. This must have been in his mind when earlier in 1916, while on leave, he and Anna were baptized by a Lutheran pastor.

Just before the Reinachs were baptized, Reinach expressed a doubt as to whether they were doing the right thing. He feared that his desire to be baptized by a Lutheran pastor was the result of his not yet being "ready for the Catholic Church." To which Anna Reinach replied: "You are not precluding anything. Once we are in communion with Christ, we shall see where He will lead us." In November 1917, Reinach died in action. Within a few years Anna, Reinach's sister Pauline, who was a close friend of Stein's, and Reinach's brother and sister-in-law were all received into the Catholic Church.

Reinach's own philosophical and theological commitments in this final period of his life are then at least threefold. First, against Simmel he asserts that there is a distinctive type of experience in which what is presented to consciousness as object is nothing other than God, a presentation that excludes doubt. As with any other distinctive type of experience it has essential characteristics that differentiate it. It is not reducible to nor explicable in terms of the objects of the psychological or social attitudes and acts of human beings. It can have no naturalistic explanation, since it is an experience of that which transcends all natural characteristics. Its object is, as no natural being is, unqualifiedly great. To look for a justification for belief in such a being of the kind that we are able to advance for our other beliefs is not to have understood this uniqueness both of God and of the experience of His presence: "the direction towards God is worlds apart from strivings for knowledge" (May 2, 1916). To ask for such a justification of belief in God is to show that one has not understood what is at issue.

What is perhaps surprising in these claims is the lack of references to Augustine's *Confessions*, a book that Reinach had known well for a long time. In his notes he quotes Augustine only once, much less than he quotes, for example, Schleiermacher. Yet in the *Confessions* there is much that is relevant to Reinach's preoccupations. In Book VII, Augustine briefly describes a sequence of experiences through which his mind had ascended from judgments about physical beauty to a contemplation of the timelessness of unchanging truth, and then further to a momentary contemplation of God Himself as unchanging, a contemplation that could not be more than momentary, because of Augustine's lack of spiritual strength, but which remained as a memory and as a focus of desire (VII, 23). And elsewhere in the *Confessions* Augustine identifies precisely the path that must be taken, in order to be directed towards God, and the habits that may obstruct one's progress. This is surely the kind of setting into which Reinach's phenomenological insights concerning the experience of God need to be integrated. And Reinach's apparent failure to see this need leaves the account that he does give us of awareness of God curiously bare. But that was perhaps the effect of trying to write under the conditions of trench warfare.

A second commitment concerns human attitudes towards God. Reinach, as I noted earlier argues that corresponding to the object of distinctively religious experiences is the responsive attitude towards that object that it elicits from us, an attitude that is as distinctive as its object. It is an attitude of unqualified trust and unqualified gratitude. This gratitude is not gratitude "for something" (May 21, 1916), for this or that particular good or deliverance from evil. It is gratitude for God's giving one whatever one is given, just as trust in God is not contingent on this or that happening to one. So that—this is my comment, not Reinach's—it remains gratitude and trust even in the killing fields of the Third Battle of Ypres.

Thirdly, Reinach takes it that God is apprehended uniquely in the person and teaching of Jesus. "Absolute gratitude, dependence, love, reverence, trust. These also with regard to Jesus. The beauty encountered in and the 'praise' of his teaching have an absolute character" (June 16, 1916). Jesus therefore presents himself to us as different from all other human beings (May 18, 1916). There is no such thing as a life or a history of Jesus, as there are for everyone else, since the concept of development has no application to Jesus. This does suggest that Reinach had an imperfect grasp of the Christian doctrine of the human nature of Jesus. But that he is defending a peculiarly Christian construal of the experience of God is clear.

Reinach's account of religious experience is therefore put to the question both by rival accounts that agree with his in their understanding of what it is for God to be present, but deny that an exclusively Christian interpretation of this experience is to be accepted, and also by rival accounts that agree with his in holding that there is a distinctively religious experience, but deny that what such experience affords is knowledge that God exists. And we have just such rival accounts advanced by two of Reinach's contemporaries, each of whom himself underwent a conversion experience. I refer to Franz Rosenzweig's conversion to Judaism in 1913 and Georg Lukács's conversion to Bolshevism in 1918. Lukács was two years younger than Reinach, Rosenzweig one year younger than Lukács, and all three had had the same kind of education, within an academic culture in which each had learned to reject the Neo-Kantianism that continued to dominate the academic scene up to 1914. Moreover, all three were sons of Jewish families.

Of the three, Rosenzweig was the only one who returned to the belief and practice of his ancestors. The Judaism of his early upbringing had been purged of anything that might hinder Jewish assimilation to German culture, but it was still an observant Judaism and one with which, somehow or other, Rosenzweig had to come to terms. But for more than a decade those terms were the terms of rejection.

Philosophically, Rosenzweig's heroes were at first Goethe and Kant. From them he turned to Hegel and, as a philosophically minded historian, a student of Meinecke, he wrote a doctoral dissertation on Hegel's theory of the state, which he submitted in 1912. But he was already reevaluating Hegel's thought, when, in the summer of 1913, he encountered Eugen Rosenstock, then a teacher of medieval constitutional law at Leipzig. Rosenstock, a devout Lutheran, had thought his way through what a Christian acknowledgment of the claims of divine revelation entailed, and from his extended conversations with Rosenstock, Rosenzweig acquired three convictions. The first was that he had to reckon with at least the possibility and very possibly the fact of divine revelation, of an encounter with God by reference to whom everything else is to be measured. When he asked Rosenstock what he meant by revelation, Rosenstock's aphoristic reply was "Revelation is orientation," the discovery of the one fixed point in the universe (Letter to Rudolf Ehrenberg in Franz Rosenzweig, *Philosophical and Theological Writings*, tr. and ed. Paul W. Franks and Michael L. Morgan, Indianapolis: Hackett, 2000, p. 49).

A second conviction that Rosenzweig owed at least in part to Rosenstock—he may well have been influenced by the tradition of rabbinical argument, as Marianne Sawicki has pointed out to me—concerned the insight that truth emerges in dialogue and that the thinking characteristic of dialogue differs importantly from the dominant conception of thinking in the German philosophical tradition. Later Rosenzweig was to express this insight by saying,

In actual conversation, something happens. I do not know in advance what the other will say to me because I myself do not even know what I am going to say; perhaps not even whether I am going to say anything at all. . . . The [traditionally conceived] thinker knows exactly his thoughts in advance; that he 'expresses' them is a concession to the deficiency of our, as he calls it, communicative medium, which does not consist in the fact that we need language, but rather that we need time. To need time means being able to anticipate nothing, having to wait for everything, being dependent on the other for one's own. All that is completely unthinkable to the thinking thinker, while it corresponds uniquely to the language thinker.

Although this was written very much later—in 1925 in *The New Thinking* (p. 136)—it captures very well the shared standpoint of Rosenstock and Rosenzweig from their first meeting onwards. And at once it becomes plain that there must have been within Rosenzweig a tension between his role as an academic thinker, engaged in completing his dissertation on Hegel and turning it into a book, and his new conception of himself as a language thinker, committed to defining through dialogue with others his relationship to the claims of revelation. One step towards the resolution of this tension was taken by a transformation in his view of Hegel.

Hegel, as Rosenzweig had now come to view him, had indeed in some sense brought philosophy to its completion. For Hegel had produced a system within which the inheritance of pagan, that is, of Greek thought had been integrated with elements of Christian theology, so that every aspect of human history had been reduced to expressions of a single principle, that of the self-development of the Idea. Hegel's system takes our philosophical inheritance from the ancient pre-Christian world as far as it can be taken and its end-product is a final statement of the theses of philosophical idealism. What Hegel's system thus understood omits and conceals is threefold. It has no place for the particularity of the thinker as one who is more and other than his thought. The monologues of the self-development of thought prevent any acknowledgment of the dialogical existence of thinkers. And it also has no place for the reality of a God who speaks in revelation. Lacking both of these, it lacks too an adequate conception of the world as a place where encounters between thinkers and encounters between God and human beings occur as contingent historical happenings. So Rosenzweig's acknowledgment of Hegel's achievement was accompanied by what he took to be compelling grounds for rejecting Hegel's stance.

It was not that there was no further work for philosophy to do. Within philosophy there had already been those who understood how to move beyond Hegel and this in a variety of ways. The first was Schelling. In the summer of 1914 Rosenzweig had come across a manuscript in Hegel's handwriting outlining a program for German idealism. It was in fact, so Rosenzweig deduced, not by Hegel, but by Schelling. And he found in Schelling, particularly in the late Schelling, ways of doing philosophy which enabled him to make a new beginning in his own thinking. Others who now became important were Schopenhauer, Kierkegaard and Nietzsche, the latter two because in their writings the question of the relationship of the thinker to revelation is so sharply posed, by Kierkegaard as one who can only recognize revelation in the form of the Paradox, by Nietzsche as one for whom a passionate rejection of and scorn for revelation is a precondition for truthful utterance.

Yet philosophy at this point is of secondary importance to Rosenzweig. What is primary is the question of his own self-definition, of his own orientation to God who reveals himself. And at first, in the light of his conversations with Rosenstock, Rosenzweig seems to have taken it for granted that he now has to redefine himself as a Christian. Much earlier he had thought about the possibility of an individual Jew making his own particular way in matters of religion, taking what he needed from Jewish and from Christian sources. Understood thus "the baptism of Jews loses some of its stigma of desertion" (entry in his notebook, May 25, 1906). And now he understands Rosenstock's post-Hegelian Christianity, with its Christocentric understanding of history, as a way opening up before him. For it was Christianity that had engaged in the long struggle with paganism and it was Christianity that would now have to raise once more the issue of revelation in the peculiar context of the twentieth-century world. Judaism had been no more than a bystander in the struggle with paganism. What place could there be for it now?

The answer that Rosenzweig finally gave to this question was not at all the answer that he had at first expected to give. From July 1913 to early October he intended to become a Christian, but had resolved to enter the Christian church—he would have become, like Rosenstock, a Lutheran—as a Jew and so in these months he lived as an observant Jew, attending first the services for Rosh Hashanah and then the services for Yom Kippur in a Berlin synagogue. Yom Kippur in 1913 fell on October 11. On that day, Rosenzweig entered the synagogue as a would-be Christian and left it as one recommitted before God to Judaism. What happened to him in that synagogue?

About this Rosenzweig never spoke or wrote. Nahum Glatzer called it "the secret ground of his new life" ("Franz Rosenzweig's Conversion" in *Essays in Jewish Thought*, Tuscaloosa: University of Alabama Press, 1978, p. 235). Yet it is clear that what happened in that synagogue on October was what happened on that day in that and every other synagogue. In the Kol Nidre service in preparation for Yom Kippur, devout Jews seek forgiveness for wrongs done to other human beings. On Yom Kippur, they stand before God just as they will do on the day of their death, asking forgiveness for wrongs done to God. The liturgies for Yom Kippur rehearse moments of atonement in Jewish history and the rites celebrated at those moments. The worshippers relive those moments and rites before God, until they become able finally to proclaim that "The Lord is God: this God of love, He alone is God." What the liturgies of Yom Kippur tell Jews and what they must have told Rosenzweig was that only by acknowledging unconditionally their need for atonement are they able to recognize—so far as human beings can—Who and What the God who reveals himself is.

On October 23, Rosenzweig wrote to his mother that "You will have learned from this letter that I have found the way back for which, for almost three months, I had struggled in vain." And eight days later he wrote to Rudolf Ehrenberg about his previous decision to become a Christian that "I have arrived at the point of taking back my resolution. It seems to me no longer necessary and, therefore, in my case, no longer possible. So I am remaining a Jew" (*Briefe*, pp. 22–23).

Rosenzweig had of course to undertake a radical revision of his views of the relationship between Christianity and Judaism. The contrast that he came in time to draw was one which emphasized the difference between Jewish inwardness and withdrawal from history and Christianity's externalization of a self turned towards the world. Each has its characteristic dangers.

But in truth our dangers represent no danger at all for us in the final analysis. For here it turns out that the Jew simply cannot descend into his own interior without at the same time ascending to the Highest. This is, in fact, the profound difference between Jewish and Christian men: the Christian is by nature or at least by birth—a pagan; the Jew, however, is a Jew. Thus the way of the Christian must be a way of self-externalization, of self-renunciation; he must always take leave of himself, must forfeit himself in order to become a Christian. The life of the Jew, on the other hand, must precisely not lead him out of himself, he must rather live his way ever deeper into himself. (*The Star of Redemption*, tr. from the Second Edition of 1930 by William W. Hallo, Notre Dame, IN: Notre Dame Press, 1985, pp. 407–8)

Here Rosenzweig suggests that implicitly or explicitly he had recognized at the time of his conversion that by becoming a Christian he would have left himself behind. Instead he had recovered that about to be lost self, preserved for him in Jewish obedience to the Torah. "For in the law everything of this world that is comprised in it, all created existence is already given life and soul directly as content of the world to come" (p. 406). Rosenzweig in his conversion had not become a Jew, he had acknowledged that he already was one. He had not turned away from what he was. He had turned back to what he was.

What we do not know is how far he articulated this to himself in the days, weeks, and months after October 11. What we do know is that one month later he attended a lecture by Hermann Cohen at the *Lehranstalt für Wissenschaft des Judentums* in Berlin and was at once impressed. Cohen had retired from his chair at Marburg in 1912 and devoted himself to a restatement of what he took to be at the heart of Judaism. He was of course still a Neo-Kantian and, when Rosenzweig reread Kant in 1916, it was almost certainly the result of Cohen's influence. But what impressed Rosenzweig most were the human qualities that Cohen brought to his philosophical and theological activity: "he is nonetheless the first full-blown professor of philosophy I have seen whom, without mockery, I would call a philosopher" (*Judaism despite Christianity: The "Letters on Christianity and Judaism" between Eugen Rosenstock-Huessy and Franz Rosenzweig*, ed. Eugen Rosenstock-Huessy, New York: Schocken Books, 1971, p. 97).

It was then with Cohen that he began his systematic study of Judaism. Cohen in his lectures emphasized the irreconcilable differences that divide Jews from Christians. Christians fail to acknowledge the unity of God and they have fallen victim to their inheritance from Greek culture, as, among Jews, did Philo. But rabbinic Judaism, faithful to the Torah, resisted this and with it any assimilation to pagan thought. It was Cohen who provided Rosenzweig with an alternative intellectual vision to Rosenstock's. Yet on two major issues he was to depart curiously far from Cohen. In *The Star of Redemption*, that extraordinary restatement of Judaism and of the relationship between Judaism and Christianity, Rosenzweig certainly acknowledged the deep incompatibility of the Jewish doctrine of God and the Christian doctrines of the Trinity and the Incarnation. Yet he could also write: "Before God, then, Jew and Christian both labor at the same task. He cannot dispense with either. He has set enmity between the two for all time, and withal has most intimately bound each to each. . . . The truth, the whole truth, thus belongs neither to them nor to us . . . we both have but a part of the whole truth" (pp. 415–16).

By not merely dismissing Christian doctrines as Cohen had done, but understanding them as expressive of a way towards God complementary to the Jewish way, Rosenzweig places an added onus of justification upon any individual who, having been a Jew, becomes a Christian. The question that he poses is that of how such a one can understand the relationship of Judaism to Christianity in terms that do justice to Rosenzweig's account, terms that preclude any mere denial of Jewish claims, let alone the sterile hatreds of anti-Semitism. And this is an existential and not only a philosophical question.

For a second matter on which Rosenzweig departs from Cohen concerns the part that philosophy can play in our thinking. After the publication of *The Star of Redemption* in 1921, Rosenzweig at the invitation of a publisher wrote a short book, *Das Büchlein vom gesunden und kranken Menschenverstand* (*The Little Book of Healthy Common Sense and Sick Reasoning*), which he then circulated among friends, but decided not to publish (tr. and ed. by N. Glatzer as *Understanding the Sick and the Healthy: A View of World, Man and God*, Cambridge, MA: Harvard University Press, 1999). In it, the view he takes of philosophy is very close to that taken at one period by Wittgenstein, that philosophy is the cure of a disease of which it is itself a symptom. "To speak of the world is to speak of a world which is ours and God's. . . . This is the ultimate secret of the world. Or rather, this would be its secret, if there were anything secret. But common sense blurts out this secret every day" (p. 74). The mistake of philosophers, especially idealist philosophers, has been to suppose that there is a more profound truth waiting to be discovered. But this philosophical attitude is a symptom of a sickness from which we need to recover, if we are to recognize the realities of ourselves, the world and God that we confront in our everyday existence.

Reinach did not survive to read Rosenzweig. Had he done so, he would have been peculiarly challenged by these two aspects of Rosenzweig's thought. For concerning the relationship of Judaism to Christianity, Reinach would have had to respond to Rosenzweig's assertion of the continuing dependence of Christianity upon Judaism: "Whether Christ is more than an idea no Christian can know it. But that Israel is more than an idea, that he knows, that he sees. For we live" (p. 415). And for Reinach this would have been the question of how far he could disown his own Jewish identity and inheritance without also making it impossible for him to be a Christian. But what he might have said about this we do not know.

Moreover, Reinach would have been put to the question by Rosenzweig, not only as a Christian, but also as a philosopher. For it was Reinach's declared ambition to demonstrate that the "inner experience of God" is "a genuine cognition" and this was just the kind of philosophical enterprise for which Rosenzweig saw no place. Yet of course once again we do not know how Reinach would have responded. What we can do however is later on to raise these same two questions about Stein. But before we do so, it will be worth considering a third example of a conversion, that of Lukács.

Lukács's conversion was to the Marxism of Lenin as represented by the Hungarian Communist leader, Bela Kun. It took place in December 1918, when he joined the Hungarian Communist Party. But that act is intelligible only as the outcome of Lukács's life and thought during the previous ten years. Gyorgy—later Germanized to Georg—Lukács's family was Jewish, but unlike those of Stein, Reinach and Rosenzweig no longer identified themselves as Jews. And Lukács seems to have been an atheist, even as an adolescent. He studied first in Budapest and then in Berlin, where he attended Simmel's lectures. He had already become a left-wing social democrat, but at this stage his radical politics was subordinated to his larger aspirations. What he aspired to become was a theorist of culture or rather a theorist of his own culture, the culture in which he participated in Budapest as drama critic, as founding member of an avant-garde theatre group, and as author of the essays collected and published first in Hungarian in 1910, and then in German in 1911 as *Die Seele und die Formen*.

Those essays have as a unifying theme the contrast between the formlessness of life and the forms by which it is represented by poets and dramatists. "Life is an anarchy of light and dark: nothing is ever completely fulfilled in life, nothing ever quite ends. . . . Everything flows, everything merges into another thing, and the mixture is uncontrolled and impure. . . ." (*Soul and Form*, tr. A. Bostock, Cambridge, MA: MIT Press, 1974, p. 153). By contrast, "Drama alone creates—'gives form to'—real human beings, but just because of this it must, of necessity, deprive them of living existence" (p. 156). Human beings more generally, in this view of Lukács's, represent the world to themselves through the imposition of forms upon what would otherwise be formless. They do so through the work of the imagination, but also through that of the understanding and in their practical lives. And one task of the theorist of culture is to distinguish those forms that are specific to particular cultures from those that belong to human life as such. Those setting themselves such a task in central Europe in the first decade of the twentieth century were bound to become aware that to their questions there were a set of Neo-Kantian answers, indeed more than one set of Neo-Kantian answers.

The Neo-Kantian answers that spoke directly to Lukács's aesthetic and historical concerns were those formulated by Rickert, whose most able pupil, Emil Lask, was teaching at Heidelberg, as was Max Weber, whose conception of sociological method was strongly influenced by Rickert. It is therefore unsurprising that in 1912 Lukács, who had failed to secure an academic position in Hungary, almost certainly because of anti-Semitism, chose Heidelberg as the place where he could best confront both the practical problem of his own future and the philosophical problems of carrying further lines of thought that had begun to emerge in *Die Seele und die Formen*. And he was fortunate in so doing. If Emil Lask had not been killed at the front in 1915—his obituary in *Kant-Studien* was written by Lukács—he would, I believe, have been one of the great names in twentieth-century philosophy. And certain elements of his thought have been influential, even though not recognized as his. Rickert, who directed Heidegger's *Habilitationsschrift*, emphasized the extent of Heidegger's dependence on Lask and Lask was a continuing influence on Heidegger (see Theodore Kisiel, *The Genesis of Heidegger's Being and Time*, Berkeley and Los Angeles: University of California Press, 1993, especially pp. 28–29).

Part of what Lukács learned from Lask, Lask had learned from Husserl. (For an excellent discussion of central aspects of Lask's relationship to Husserl, see Steven Galt Crowell, "Husserl, Lask and the Idea of Transcendental Logic" in *Edmund Husserl and the Phenomenological Tradition*, ed. Robert Sokolowski, Washington, DC: Catholic University of America Press, 1988.) In a letter to Husserl in 1911, Lask had told Husserl that for him intentionality, understood as Husserl understood it, had taken the place of any notion of consciousness-in-general (Edmund Husserl, *Briefwechsel* Bd. V, ed. E. Schuhmann and K. Schuhmann, pp. 33–34), a notion characteristic of Neo-Kantian thought. What, in Lask's view, as in Husserl's, attention to the mind's intentional objects reveals are relationships between the givenness of experience and the concepts and categories through which it is ordered, relationships that cannot be accommodated within any conventional Kantian or Neo-Kantian scheme. But Lask's account of how these are to be understood differs from Husserl's.

On Lask's account, at the most basic level of experience we apprehend a given which is mediated by categories, but at this level we are unaware of the categorical features of experience, of that "pretheoretical something" which by reason of our immediate absorption in our experience has not yet come into view. For it to come into view we have, as it were, to stand back, so as to be able to recognize that even this elementary categorial intuition is presupposed in our acts of judgments about the things that we encounter in experience. In acts of judgment we abstract from the objects of experience aspects and features of those objects, so that the subject matter of our judgment is never the object of experience itself, but only those aspects and features detached from it in thought that are amenable to our conceptualization of them. The forms of judgment do not correspond to the forms of experience and the objects of judgment are to some degree conceptual artifacts.

The object of scientific knowledge is therefore not nature as it is, let alone nature as we encounter it in lived experience, but an abstract conceptualized substitute for nature as it is, one that enables us to theorize and to control. And philosophers whose task it is to understand the relationships between theory and lived experience are themselves one more set of theorists, among whose tasks it is to investigate the relationship between their own philosophical theorizing and their own lived experience and practical activity.

For Lukács, Lask therefore raised questions about the place of philosophical enquiry in a life such as his. In what ways might philosophy illuminate his situation? In what ways might it by its abstractions obscure from view the nature of the realities that he encountered? Might it be possible to transform theory so that it no longer distanced theorists from their lived experience? Might it not perhaps be the case that the forms that artists and others impose on reality distort and disguise the nature of those realities? Lukács's further development of this line of questioning was strongly influenced by his reactions to Weber's sociological understanding of the contemporary world.

According to Weber, what was salient about the culture of modernity was the large and increasing extent to which its values were those of instrumental rationality. Certain ends are taken as given and rationality is taken to consist in calculation as to the most efficient means to achieve those ends. Instrumentality rationality is socially embodied in the bureaucratic structures both of private corporations and of governments. And the public social world increasingly becomes one in which there is no place for any other values, in which the domination of nature and the remaking of society through the exercise of technical intelligence provide the taken for granted ends to be achieved by bureaucratic and technological means. Within such a culture little place is left for what Weber called 'sacred values', for that which had given to life in premodern cultures a magical or enchanted quality. The world of modernity is a disenchanted world in which only in certain limited areas of the private lives of individuals does there remain any place for values that escape disenchantment, whether values surviving from traditional religion or, increasingly for those educated into modernity, the values of art. Lukács had already envisaged the modern artist as someone at odds with the social order that she or he inhabited. But Weber enabled him to identify what it was in the nature of modernity that generated conflicts between the artist and the social order.

Weber had spoken of the disenchantment of modernity. Lukács spoke of it as abandoned by God, an abandonment that "manifests itself in the incommensurability of soul and work, of interiority and adventure" (*The Theory of the Novel*, tr. A. Bostock, Cambridge, MA: MIT Press, 1971, p. 97; the essays that compose this book were written by Lukács in 1914–1915). But as a result of his reflections on Lask's work, he raised questions about the characteristics of modernity that Weber had not raised. Is it possible that Weber's account of the modes of thought and practice of modernity is not an account of how things are, but only of how the inhabitants of modernity take them to be? Are they perhaps imprisoned within and dominated by a set of abstract conceptions of how things must be which prevent them seeing alternative possibilities? Is it possible to become someone who can enable others to identify its limitations and to move beyond it? And what would I, Lukács, have to become in order to become someone who is able to do this? How may I discover a Utopianism that is realizable in the practice of everyday life and not just in the form of artistic creation?

So Lukács already in 1914–1915 judged it necessary to provide a better account than Weber's of the nature of modernity and a better account than Lask's of the place of theoretical understanding in a human life. In 1914 Lukács had quarreled bitterly with both Max and Marianne Weber over their support for the declaration of war and in October 1915 he returned to Budapest, where as someone unfit for active duty he served in a military hospital and then as a censor of the mail, later dividing his time between Heidelberg and Budapest.

Two authors became of paramount importance for Lukács in this period: Kierkegaard and, more especially, Dostoievski. About Kierkegaard he had already written, both in one of the essays in *Die Seele und die Formen* and in a 1912 essay on poverty of spirit, an essay in which he had also discussed Dostoievski. He now embarked on a study of Kierkegaard as a critic of Hegel at the same time as he began work on what was to be a major piece of writing on Dostoievski. Neither work was to be completed. And Lukács seems to have taken pains later on not only to ensure that they remained unread, but to conceal, so far as he could, the extent of and the nature of his preoccupation with these authors. For part of what he came to think that he had learned from Kierkegaard and Dostoievski was the necessity of abandoning their standpoint. There was of course always something strange about his devotion to them. For both of them the defining question of both their lives and their writings was: How are we related to God? Yet Lukács by contrast was an atheist, albeit one who asserted that God was absent or dead rather than that He did not exist. His wife, Ljena Andrejevna Grabenko, asked him in a letter in July 1914: "If God is dead, why is He needed: how and why is salvation perceived to come only in His presence?" (quoted in Lee Congdon, *The Young Lukács*, Chapel Hill: University of North Carolina Press, 1983, p. 101; I am deeply indebted to Lee Congdon's work on Lukács). What then was the answer to Ljena's question?

Lukács would have responded by saying that, just because Kierkgaard and Dostoievski affirmed the existence of God with such integrity and seriousness, they posed the questions: What would it be to live without God? What would it be to choose, as Kierkegaard understood choice, but to do so without the possibility of faith in God? What would it be to live as one of Dostoievski's characters, but in the knowledge that God never intervenes? Rosenzweig emphasized how demanding it is to believe in God. Lukács in this period was concerned to show how demanding it is not to believe in God, how difficult it is to be an atheist with seriousness and integrity. So just as Rosenzweig distinguished his position from that of the conventional believers of the day, so Lukács distinguished his position from that of the conventional unbelievers of his day, such as Max Weber.

What is it about conventional unbelief that Lukács took to be inadequate? It seems to have been twofold. First, conventional unbelief, in abandoning belief in God has also abandoned belief in evil. And Lukács at this stage took evil with great seriousness. So he saw the outbreak of war in 1914 as confirmation of Fichte's thesis that the present age is an "age of absolute sinfulness," the third of four stages through which the idea of freedom has been and will be realized in successively more adequate forms. What Fichte took to be characteristics of "the present age," that is, of *his* present, 1806, when he published *The Characteristics of the Present Age*, Lukács took to be characteristics of *his* present, and of those characteristics Lukács focused not only on the age's "absolute sinfulness," but on the fact that it is a precursor of two succeeding ages, through which enlightened freedom will be realized. The problem is: how to break out of the present age into the enlightened freedom of the future?

Here we encounter a second respect in which Lukács's atheism differed from conventional unbelief. The counterpart to his recognition of the reality of evil is his sense of urgent need for deliverance and redemption. We have to break free from the social and conceptual forms that imprison us within the present age. But how to do this? From Kierkegaard Lukács learned to entertain the thought that what faith in God—for which Lukács substitutes faith in a Utopian future—may require of us is "a teleological suspension of the absolute"; that is, a willingness to perform acts which are normally taken to be unqualifiedly prohibited, as Abraham was by faith willing to kill Isaac, an act of murder, even if commanded by God. From Dostoievski, Lukács learned to entertain the closely related thought that it may be part of saintliness to be willing to sin out of compassion, as Sonja sins in *Crime and Punishment*. To these influences was added that of the Russian anarchist and terrorist, Boris Savinkov, who argued that a human being of moral integrity may have to sacrifice that integrity by violating the moral law. To fail to sin may be to sin. Under the influence of Savinkov, Lukács distinguished an ethics of duties, of rules that are unqualified and exceptionless, and an ethics of the soul's imperative, an ethics which may on occasion enjoin one to do what is forbidden by the ethics of duties and so to sacrifice one's moral integrity for the sake of effective action in the service of good. The action thus enjoined does not thereby cease to be a violation of what is morally required. It is as just such a violation that it is required.

This strange and paradoxical view emerged not only from Lukács's reading, but from extended debates with a group of more or less like-minded intellectuals. But unsurprisingly, as that group was confronted with concrete political choices, disagreements began to emerge. They had been united in opposition to the war and had welcomed the replacement of Hapsburg rule in October 1918 by a democratic republic led by Count Mihály Károlyi. But, when his government prepared to resign in protest against the harshness of the peace settlement imposed by the Western powers, they divided over whom to support.

Lukács was initially among those who rejected the Bolshevism of the nascent Hungarian Communist Party. He feared that their conception of the dictatorship of the proletariat would lead not to a democratic, classless society, but to a new form of oppressive domination. And he believed that the Bolsheviks' willingness to use terror and violence as a means might of itself prevent them from achieving the ends at which they aimed. The only justification for doing what is evil is that good will issue from that evil and the Bolsheviks' belief that good would in fact issue from their acts of violence and terror was no more than unreasoning faith in a metaphysical assumption. The question raised by Bolshevism is: "can the good be achieved by evil means, and freedom by tyranny; can there be a new world if the means to its realization are only technically different from the rightly abhorred and abjured means of the old order?" ("Bolshevism as an Ethical Problem" in *The Lukács Reader*, ed. A. Kadarkay, Oxford: Blackwell, 1995).

These were Lukács's views as expressed in a contribution to the journal *Szabadgondolat* late in 1918. But in the short interval between the submission of his article and its appearance in print Lukács reversed himself and joined the Communist Party, a deliberate act of faith—the terms in which Lukács had posed his problem precluded it from being anything else—and not at all the conclusion of a chain of reasoning. Indeed as Lukács had approached the question of Bolshevism he had confronted himself with a recognizably Kierkegaardian 'Either-Or', a choice so fundamental that it cannot be supported by reasons, since it is a choice that determines what is henceforward going to count as a reason for the one who makes the choice. (Here I follow not only Lee Congdon, but also Lukács's contemporary, Ervin Sinkó, who in his novel *Optimisták* introduced Lukács as a character, naming him Vértes. When Vértes is asked how one acquires the necessary faith in communism, he advises his questioner to read Kierkegaard: Lee Congdon, op. cit., p. 143.)

No one was more surprised by Lukács's conversion than those communists in Budapest who already knew him and there were those who opposed his admission to the Communist Party, believing and being fully justified in believing that no one could without gross inconsistency take up the attitudes to the world of a Kierkegaard or of a character in one of Dostoievski's novels and also be a Marxist. But their scruples were overruled by the party leadership who wished to exploit Lukács's prestige among the intelligentsia. And Lukács almost immediately became active in the events that led to the Hungarian Soviet Revolution of 1919, active in the revolution itself as one of the People's Commissars for Education, and then, after the military defeat of the revolution, active in the day-to-day politics of the leadership in exile. So that it was only somewhat later that Lukács was forced to rethink his position.

When he did so, it was with a brilliance and an inventiveness that enabled him later on to conceal from others and, I have no doubt, increasingly from

himself, the path that he had in fact taken. In the series of essays written between 1919 and 1922 that were collected in *History and Class Consciousness*,
Lukács not only rediscovered key elements in Marxism that had been lost sight
of in the Marxism of the Second International, but was able to present the
Marxism that he had rediscovered as the key to the resolution of the problems
posed by German idealist philosophy. Those problems can be shown, so
Lukács argued, to be insoluble at the theoretical level at which they had been
posed from Kant through Fichte and Hegel to the Neo-Kantians. They can be
resolved however by adopting the standpoint of proletarian activity, the standpoint of a theory unified with a particular kind of practice. To become a Marxist is through participation in such practice to move beyond the limitations of
pre-Marxist philosophy and so to become able to identify those limitations.
And Lukács understands himself as someone who has achieved this new
standpoint. Where in 1918 and in early 1919 he had still spoken in Kierkegaardian terms, so that his choice of Marxism was represented as an act of arbitrary,
nonrational faith, now he presents his Marxism as the rational solution of his
earlier philosophical difficulties. His new standpoint excluded what he was in
the future going to characterize as Kierkegaardian irrationalism.

What then was the moment of Lukács's conversion? It was the moment at
which he not only for the first time saw and felt himself as morally self-
indulgent in his condemnation of Bolshevism, as sacrificing the future possibility of a humane society to his selfish regard for his own moral integrity,
but also understood himself as impaled on a moral and philosophical contradiction, which could be resolved only by joining the Communist Party and
affirming its doctrines. How far was it the case then, or soon after, that he understood the resolution of this contradiction as exemplifying the solution that
Marxism offered to the contradictions of German idealist philosophy and
that communism offered to the contradictions of bourgeois society is far
from clear. But that his conversion—although he would never from his later
vantage point have used that word—had enabled him to perceive and to understand aspects of himself and of the social order which his bourgeois educational attitudes had hitherto obscured he never doubted.

If we consider Lukács's conversion together with those of Reinach and
Rosenzweig, we will of course be struck immediately by how different each
of their stories is. Yet it is perhaps by comparing them that we can best bring
out what is distinctive in each narrative. Three questions are pertinent. First,
what is the difference between how each of them understands himself after
the moment of conversion and how each previously understood himself?
Secondly, what change is there in the philosophical positions taken by each
as a result of his conversion? And thirdly, what is it in the experience of each
that makes them either theist or atheist in their interpretation of their experience? Yet if those are the questions that we ought to ask about Reinach,
Rosenzweig and Lukács, then they must also be questions that we should ask

about Stein. And, if, in order to get answers to those questions, we need to compare and contrast the narrative accounts of the conversions of Reinach, Rosenzweig and Lukács, then we will presumably enrich our answers by comparing and contrasting these three narratives with an account of Stein's conversion. And so to the events that constituted that conversion I now turn. There is however one problem in writing about those events that I should note immediately. The evidence that we have is of a number of different kinds, some of it from accounts that were written many years later, some from accounts that conflict with other accounts, some perhaps colored by the attitudes of those who provided it. I have constructed the best overall narrative that I can, but a better historian might well do better.

16

Stein's Conversion

The narrative of Stein's conversion, like the narrative of her philosophical development, turns out to be continuous with that of Reinach's. It begins early in 1918, around the time when she resigned from her position as Husserl's assistant. She had been sent a transcript of the notes on the philosophy of religion that Reinach wrote while at the front and says of them in a letter to Fritz Kaufmann that they are "very beautiful things. A few pages of exposition are so beautiful that they might be printed as a fragment. I must see what Frau Reinach thinks about that" (*Self-Portrait in Letters 1916–42*, Letter no. 21).

She soon had an opportunity to do so, traveling to Göttingen in time to spend Easter there. During the month of April she discussed with Anna Reinach and others what should be done about publishing Reinach's papers and celebrating his philosophical achievement. Should there be a volume of commemorative essays? Should there be a collected edition of his works? How should this be prepared? The admirable end-product of these discussions, in which not only Anna Reinach, but also Hedwig Conrad-Martius and Jean Hering, played a key part, was the publication of Reinach's *Gesammelte Schriften* by Max Niemeyer Verlag in Halle in 1921 (the most recent edition is *Sämtliche Werke*, ed. Karl Schuhmann and Barry Smith, Munich: Philosophia Verlag, 2 vols., 1989).

What was for Stein the most striking aspect of her visit was the calm demeanor and inner peace of Anna Reinach. Stein, like others who out of their own grief had come to console her for her husband's death, found themselves instead consoled by her. She evidenced a power in her life that had transformed her grief. Very much later Stein was to say of that visit that "It was my first encounter with the cross and the divine power that it bestows on those who carry it. For the first time I was seeing with my very eyes the church, born from its Redeemer's sufferings, triumphant over the sting of death. That was the moment my unbelief collapsed. . . ." (quoted in Waltraud Herbstrith, *Edith Stein: A Biography*, tr. B. Bonowitz, O.C.D., Second Edition, San Francisco: Ignatius Press, 1992, p. 23). This is of course a retrospective, theologically informed description. How precisely Stein characterized her experience at the time we do not know, although there are some inferences that it is safe to make. But it certainly involved the kind of empathetic perception and understanding to which she had earlier devoted so much philosophical attention. She saw, felt and understood what it was to which Anna Reinach was responding. And that can only have been, given what Stein does say, Jesus presenting himself to her, as to Anna Reinach, as both human and divine, as someone to be trusted unconditionally, as someone whose gift is an inner peace that comes only as a gift, as something that cannot be willed or otherwise contrived and that has no psychological explanation in purely natural terms.

What further philosophical account of the relevant experiences Stein would have given at this stage we do not know. But the question was certainly on her mind. In a letter to Roman Ingarden in June she tells how she had visited Husserl in the hope of discussing Ingarden's work with him, but "on the doorstep I met the little Heidegger, so the three of us took a long walk—very nice—and talked about the philosophy of religion" (*Briefe an Roman Ingarden, 1917–1938*, Freiburg: Herder 1991, p. 36, quoted in T. F. O'Meara, O.P., *Erich Przywara, S.J.: His Theology and His World*, Notre Dame, IN: University of Notre Dame Press, 2002, p. 120). Stein had first met Heidegger two years earlier and had liked him immediately. And Heidegger too was partly preoccupied with religious questions at that time. Early in 1919 he was to write to Engelbert Krebs—Krebs had been a seminarian along with Heidegger and was now a priest and a teacher of theology at Freiburg—that "Epistemological insights, applied to the theory of historical knowledge, have made the *system* of Catholicism problematic and unacceptable to me—but not Christianity *per se* or metaphysics, the latter albeit in a new sense" (quoted in Rüdiger Safranski, *Martin Heidegger: Between Good and Evil*, Cambridge, MA: 1998, p. 107). Krebs had performed the marriage ceremony for Heidegger and his Protestant wife, Elfride Petri, who had promised that they would bring up their children as Catholics. This letter was to inform Krebs that they now intended to break that promise. Two months later, writing to Rudolf Otto, Husserl described Heidegger as an "undogmatic Protestant" (op. cit., p. 108).

Heidegger's path was thus in an opposite direction to Stein's. While she was moving closer to the Catholic Church, he was moving steadily away from it. But at this period neither could have predicted their future development and Stein certainly did not as yet recognize the direction of her own thought. In the two treatises, both written during 1919, there are only a few explicit references to theological questions and the only work of theology referred to is *Der christliche Glaube* by Theodor Haering (1848–1928), a Protestant follower of Ritschl and a professor of theology at Tübingen. But two passages are of some importance.

In the section of the first treatise on the adoption and denial of attitudes, Stein considers a set of cases where someone, confronted by what is evident, refuses to acknowledge it and successfully neutralizes it, so that it does not inform their attitudes. One example that she uses is that of the mother who resists acknowledging that her son has died in the war. But another is that of the convinced atheist who has an experience that makes God's existence evident. "He cannot escape from the belief, but . . . he does not allow it to become operative in himself and he staunchly sticks with his 'scientific worldview.' . . ." (p. 50). What Stein is envisaging here surely is an alternative attitude that she might have taken up, but did not.

The second passage is one in which Stein has just described those types of cases in which we experience an increase in the inflow of life-power, new vigor and new energy, but she notes that this occurs only when some measure of life-power is already present—yet with one exception. "There is a state of resting in God, of complete relaxation of all mental (*geistige*) activity, in which you make no plans at all, reach no decision, much less take action, but rather leave everything that is future to the divine will 'consigning yourself entirely to fate.'" Stein goes on to say that, compared with the cessation of activity that results from lack of life-power, resting in God is something new and unique, a feeling of being safe, of being relieved from anxiety and responsibility, to which, if I surrender, new life impels me to new activity, and this without voluntary exertion in my part. "The sole prerequisite for such a mental (*geistige*) rebirth seems to be a certain receptivity" (*Philosophy of Psychology and the Humanities*, pp. 84–85).

Is Stein describing her own successive states of mind from February to April, 1918? The experience that had left her exhausted was that of contending with Husserl and of struggling with herself over whether or not she should resign her position as Husserl's assistant. And the state of resting in God was one that she enjoyed after her encounter with Anna Reinach's devout grief. Marianne Sawicki, noting the phrase "surrendering yourself entirely to Fate" (*"dem Schicksal überlässt"*), has suggested that Stein is here using a Stoic conception of the divine and has pointed out, "This need not be a religious stance in the Jewish or Christian sense of the term" (footnote 115, p. 84). But what Stein says in this passage is close to what we know of Anna and Adolf Reinach's experiences, the experience that Adolf Reinach described as "being sheltered in God," and Reinach also spoke of the receptivity needed. Sawicki's comment is nonetheless to the point. Stein's use of the word 'fate' does suggest that she was not as yet able to characterize her experience in any theologically precise way. She therefore faced the question:

towards what theological position did her own experience—however it was to be characterized—point? And to answer this question she must have engaged in discussion with her closest friends, especially Anna Reinach and Hedwig Conrad-Martius, but what she read was also important.

Her most important reading was the New Testament. But she also read Kierkegaard's *Practice in Christianity* (ed. and tr. H. V. Hong and E. Hong, Princeton, NJ: Princeton University Press, 1991), published under the pseudonym "Anti-Climacus" in 1850. Kierkegaard called it "the most perfect and truest things that I have written" (quoted in the "Historical Introduction" by the editors, p. xviii), but she did not become a follower of Kierkegaard. Why not? It may perhaps have been the one-sidedness of Kierkegaard's portrayal of what it is to be a Christian, his almost exclusive emphasis on the suffering that is involved in the Christian life (see *Practice in Christianity*, No. III, pp. 186–99) without adequate reference to its hope and its consolation. Yet the experience of the Reinachs and of Stein was of an extraordinary inner peace. Or it may perhaps have been the lack of specificity in Kierkegaard's account and its consequent failure to address particular questions about what is required of a Christian that Stein was beginning to ask in this period. But, even if it was either or both of these, Stein as a philosopher most surely had found unacceptable Kierkegaard's characterization of what it is in Jesus Christ that offends human beings who encounter him.

"The contradiction in which the possibility of the offense lies is to be an individual human being, a lowly human being—and then to act in the character of being God" (p. 97), something, so Kierkegaard asserts, that only comes fully home to those who understand themselves as, or as if they are, contemporaries of Jesus. What is the contradiction of which Kierkegaard speaks? It is a contradiction which belongs to a sign.

"In Scripture," says Kierkegaard, "the God-man is called a sign of contradiction" (p. 125) and he has already said, "A sign of contradiction . . . is a sign that contains a contradiction in its composition" (p. 125). Yet he has also said that "the contradictory parts must not annul each other in such a way that the sign comes to mean nothing or in such a way that it becomes the opposite of a sign" (p. 125). Kierkegaard clearly wants to assert that, when Jesus presents himself as both human and divine, he presents himself in contradictory terms. Yet, if these terms are genuinely contradictory, they cancel each other out, they, in Kierkegaard's own words, annul each other, just as if Jesus had said "I am God and I am not God" or "I am human and I am not human." And, if the terms in which Jesus presents himself do not annul each other, then there is no contradiction. So it is Kierkegaard who has entangled himself in contradiction.

Worse still, it is not true that in Scripture the God-man is called a sign of contradiction. The relevant passage is in Luke's Gospel where Simeon says to Mary about Jesus "Behold, this [child] is destined for the fall and rise of many in Israel and for *sēmeion antilegomenon*" (ch. 2, v. 34). The translation in the *New American Bible* is "for a sign that will be contradicted" and the phrase could equally well be translated as "for a sign that will be disputed." And that is to say that there is no suggestion of there being a contradiction in the composition of the sign. Kierkegaard has projected his own view onto the Scripture.

For any follower of Husserl, Kierkegaard's assertions about contradiction would have been unacceptable. In the first of the *Logical Investigations*, Husserl, while insisting that the expressions used in formulating a contradiction are not thereby deprived of sense, took them to be meaningless in another way, that they suffer from "the *a priori* impossibility of a fulfilling sense" (p. 294). To assert a contradiction is to deprive one's assertion of the possibility of truth. And Stein, like Reinach, a close follower of Husserl on all matters of logic, would certainly have responded negatively to Kierkegaard's view of contradiction. Whether, as someone able to read Greek, she also responded to his mistranslation we do not know.

The reading that was to be most fruitful for Stein was in the works of St. Teresa of Avila, beginning with her autobiography. How she first came to read the autobiography is a story that has often been told. In the summer of 1921 she was staying with her friends, Hedwig Conrad-Martius and her husband, at Bergzabern. Conrad-Martius later wrote of that period that "we [herself and Stein] were both in the middle of a religious crisis. We stuck very close to each other like people walking along a narrow ridge, waiting for the divine summons to come at any moment. It did come, but ended up in taking us in two different directions" (*Briefe an Hedwig Conrad-Martius*, Munich: Kösel Verlag, 1960, p. 72, quoted in Waltraud Herbstrith, *Edith Stein: A Biography*, San Francisco: Harper & Row, p. 30).

One evening Stein was left alone in the house, took down Teresa's autobiography from the shelf, began reading and was unable to stop until she had come to the end of the book, deciding as she did so that she had no alternative but to enter the Catholic Church. Four features of Teresa's account of her life are worth noting. First, she understands the experience of God's presence as something that in those who undergo it has a history, the history of a life of prayer. We grow or fail to grow in our apprehension of God and we have to identify our limitations at each stage of that growth and be instructed as to how to move beyond them. The life of prayer is a life of learning. Secondly, she identifies the obstacles and difficulties that arise at different stages and the conflicts through which we have to move to overcome them, especially the obstacles, difficulties and conflicts that arise initially from our strong attachments to so much in ourselves and in our worldly environments that prevents us from acknowledging God's presence.

Thirdly, she rejects a false spirituality. We are human beings with bodies, not angels, and it is as such that we pray. And it is the human nature of Jesus through which we come to apprehend his divine nature. God discloses himself through that embodied human nature to our embodied humanity. Fourthly, Teresa is always open to the possibilities of delusion and illusion. But what those possibilities are is also something that has to be learned. We do not bring with us from our previous life an adequate grasp of the criteria of illusion, a set of rules which would prevent us from being deceived. What Teresa requires of us is what Stein would have recognized as a version of the discipline of phenomenological attention to what is given to us in our experience, so that we can distinguish it from what we bring to that experience from our natural and worldly prejudices.

Consider especially in this light the experience of the absence of God which characterizes some crucial stages in the life of prayer. To have been first aware of the presence of God and then later to find that presence withdrawn is of course a terrible and difficult moment. But those familiar with phenomenological accounts of absence will have understood its possibility as inseparable from the possibility of presence. To experience the absence of something or someone is not just very different from, but incompatible with, treating that something or someone as nonexistent.

What Stein decided immediately in responding to Teresa's autobiography was to follow the path that Teresa had described; that is, the Carmelite path. And, because a Carmelite life is possible only within the Catholic Church, her decision was from the outset both to become a Catholic and to become a Carmelite. She was surprised some months later to learn that she could not at once, as a sequel to her baptism, be admitted into a religious order. And she also had to recognize that, because of the impact of her conversion on her family, she would have to move slowly. The immediate sequel to her reading of Teresa was to buy a catechism and a missal, to study them, to go regularly to mass, and to ask the parish priest at Bergzabern to baptize her. She needed a much shorter period of instruction than most converts and on January 1, 1922, she was baptized. Her godmother was Hedwig Conrad-Martius, who was by then a convinced Lutheran.

Kierkegaard and Teresa were not her only reading in this period. Przywara remembered her telling him that "while still an atheist she found in the bookstore she frequented a copy of the *Spiritual Exercises*" of St. Ignatius. "It interested her first only as a study of psychology, but she quickly realized that it was not something to read but to do." And Przywara further reports that it was after making the retreat of thirty days that she converted to the Catholic faith ("Die Frage Edith Stein" in *In und Gegen* 72, quoted in T. F. O'Meara, O.P., op. cit., p. 121). How we are to reconcile this report with all the other accounts of the stages of Stein's conversion is not clear and Przywara may have misunderstood what he was told. But that she read Ignatius in this period, first as an atheist and then as a believer, does not seem to be in doubt. And after her return to Breslau, on the advice of the Catholic university chaplain, she began to read Aquinas, probably, since we have no earlier reference to such reading, for the first time.

Her return to Breslau from Bergzabern made it important that she should make her conversion known to her family. Her mother, on being told, responded not with anger, but with intense grief. Stein had never before seen her mother weep. Her siblings were not so much grieved as shocked and puzzled. Much later Stein wrote of her mother's attitude that "she declines anything that is beyond her Jewish faith. . . . She particularly rejects conversions. Everyone ought to live and die in the faith in which they were born. She imagines atrocious things about Catholicism. . . ." (Letter no. 158 written on October 17, 1933, to Gertrude Lefort in *Self-Portrait in Letters, 1916–1942*). Stein continued to accompany her mother to the synagogue whenever she was living at home, as she had done previously, while an atheist, and it is important that the liturgies of the synagogue only became meaningful to her—for the first time since childhood—after her baptism. Stein was converted to the Catholic faith not from Judaism, but from atheism (the baptismal register at Bergzabern is in gross error on this point).

How then should we think of her conversion as compared with those of Reinach, Rosenzweig and Lukács? Where Reinach is concerned, she was, up to a certain point at least, following in a direction to which he and Anna Reinach had pointed. Her first experiences of the presence of God seem to have been very like theirs. And she seems to have no quarrel with what Reinach had written about those experiences. But of course we do not know how Reinach would have proceeded, if he had survived the war. So I put that comparison in one side and ask how we should think of Stein's conversion narrative in relation to the narratives of Rosenzweig and Lukács and to do so pose once more the three questions that I formulated at the end of chapter 15. First then, what difference did their conversion make to how each of these three understood her or himself?

With Rosenzweig, the answer is plainly that his conversion was for him the acknowledgment of an identity that had always been his, but which he had for a time been unable to acknowledge. His conversion was not a moment of discontinuity in his life, but rather the discovery of a continuity. It was not that he had been a Jew, had then become or envisaged becoming a Christian, and finally once again become a Jew, but that he had always been a Jew and now had learned what it is to be a Jew. To have this or that particular identity is to have a well-defined relationship to one or more communities. So Rosenzweig's rediscovery of his Jewish identity opening up the question of his relationship to various forms of community. And the enquiries which had led to that rediscovery were continued not only through his participation in the worship of the Jewish synagogue, but in his participation in Hermann Cohen's class, and finally in the *Freies Jüdisches Lehrhaus* in Frankfurt, which he headed from August 1920.

The change in Lukács's understanding of himself was of a very different order. His conversion to Bolshevism was experienced as a moment of radical discontinuity, in which he took himself to have found a new identity and to have discarded whatever in his past as a bourgeois intellectual was discordant with that identity. He had not of course done so, as he himself realized when he looked back on that moment from a number of different later vantage points. Very much later in 1967 he wrote of his ideas in 1918 and after as involving a "disharmonious dualism" in which his increasing comprehension of Marxism warred with his "purely idealistic ethical preoccupations," as he made the transition from one class—the bourgeoisie—to "the class directly opposed to it"—the proletariat (Preface to the 1967 edition of *History and Class Consciousness*, tr. R. Livingstone, London: Merlin Press, 1971, p. x).

So the transformation in his class-identification was still to be completed by the transformation of his consciousness, of his various modes of thinking, feeling, willing and imagining. And this transformation took place through continuing enquiry and debate with other members of the community with which he now identified himself, that of the Communist Party, enquiry and debate generated by reflection upon their shared past and future activity as members of the vanguard party of the proletarian revolution. Yet a condition for this continuing transformation was a rupture, a decisive break in Lukács's life.

Stein's conversion involved neither the discovering of an underlying continuity as with Rosenzweig nor the kind of discontinuity that Lukács experienced. It was on the one hand a transformation of every aspect of her life. Everything had to be reevaluated in the light of and subordinated to the love and worship of God, as understood in Catholic theological terms, so that her life involved both a new direction and a new ordering of goods. Yet on the other hand everything that had been of importance in her adult life up to this point was to find some place in her new life, although—to varying extents— a different place from that which they had enjoyed before her conversion. So it was with her relationships to her mother and other family members, to her friends, most of them, but not all drawn from the phenomenologists who had studied together at Göttingen, and to Husserl himself, and so it was with her other commitments, including her liberal democratic political commitments. What then about her commitment to philosophy, up till then the central passion of her life? This is a question that has a complex answer and for the moment I put it on one side, moving instead to a closely related question, the second of the questions that I posed about the conversions of Rosenzweig and of Lukács as well as of Stein: What change was there in each of their philosophical positions?

Rosenzweig, as I noted earlier, was led to a rejection of past philosophy and especially of idealism. But philosophy still had, in his new view, a necessary function. The mistakes of past philosophers were mistakes in thinking. But from thinking we need to turn back to experience. "Expe.ience, no matter how deeply it may penetrate, discovers only the human in man, only worldliness in the world, only divinity in God. And only in God divinity, only in the world worldliness and only in man the human. *Finis philosophiae?* If it were, then so much the worse for philosophy!" ("The New Thinking," intended as an introduction to *The Star of Redemption* for Jewish readers, *Philosophical and Theological Writings*, ed. P. W. Franks and M. L. Morgan, pp. 116–17). But this is a point where "experiential philosophy can begin" and what Rosenzweig had achieved in the first volume of *The Star of Redemption* was to show "that none of the three great concepts of philosophical thinking [humanity, the world, God] can be reduced to another" (p. 117). Beyond this the new thinking opens up new problems, including that of the 'I-Thou' relationship about which Martin Buber had lectured at the *Lehrhaus*. So the appeal to experience puts an end to one kind of philosophy, but generates another. And, had Rosenzweig been able to continue his work, this new understanding of philosophy would have been central to it.

Lukács, like Rosenzweig, takes a new philosophical turning at the time of his conversion. And, although his philosophical history was very different from Rosenzweig's, there are also significant similarities. Both understand the moment of their conversion as one in which they had made a decisive break with idealism. Both announce the end of what they took to be the German philosophical tradition. And both do so, because they are able, so they believe, from their new standpoint for the first time to perceive and understand realities as they are, no longer disguised by a set of intervening conceptual distortions. Why then did Lukács believe that from the standpoint of the proletariat things can be seen as they are?

It is because from that standpoint and only from that standpoint, in practice as well as in theory, we can free ourselves from those conceptual mythologies which always point to "the failure to understand a fundamental condition of human existence" (op. cit., p. 18). Among these mythologies are the antinomies with which Kant and others had grappled, especially those that concern the relationship of subject to object. The life of the proletariat is a form of revolutionary practice within which the social conditions that generate those antinomies have been or are about to be abolished. And in *History and Class Consciousness*, Lukács spelled out what he took to be Marx's account both of the relevant social conditions and of how the philosophical antinomies are to be resolved.

Whatever else *History and Class Consciousness* is, it is a brilliant interpretation of Marx, one later partially confirmed by the subsequent discovery of manuscripts written by Marx during his stay in Paris in 1844, but unknown at the time that Lukács was writing. But to treat Lukács's book only as an interpretation of Marx is to underrate its originality. Lukács had made of Marxism

what the Marxism of the Second International was not, something to be reck-
oned with philosophically, even by those who rejected its claims.

Stein by contrast deferred any rethinking of her philosophical views. She
had completed both her essay on political philosophy and the two treatises
on the philosophy of psychology and the humanities before she became a
Catholic. And she did not do any further philosophical writing for several
years. She moved to Speyer, where she became an instructor at the Teachers
College of the Dominican sisters of St. Magdalena's convent. She lived with
the sisters in the convent, said the Divine Office with them, devoted herself
to the teaching of German literature to the future teachers who were her students, and, outside the convent, to the needs of the poor of Speyer (see
chapter 6 of Waltraud Herbstrith, op. cit.). "I do not take myself too seriously
as a teacher," she wrote to Fritz Kaufmann in 1925, "and still have to smile
when I have to put it down anywhere as my profession. But that does not
hinder me from taking my responsibilities seriously, and so, in spirit and
soul, I am deeply absorbed by them" (*Self Portrait in Letters, 1916–1912*,
Letter no. 38a). She took herself to have abandoned philosophical activity,
although she had in fact only deferred its resumption.

What she did not do is as significant as what she did. Adolf Reinach's immediate response to the experiences which had been the occasion of his
conversion was to start making notes for a philosophical account of those
experiences. The focus of his philosophical interests had changed, but the
impulse to respond philosophically was as strong as ever—not so with Stein.
Moreover she did not immediately turn to reading Catholic philosophical authors. A number of Husserl's students had preceded her in converting to the
Catholic faith—the most notable was Dietrich von Hildebrand, by then
teaching at Munich—but, although later on her interest in them and their
work was rekindled, she did not at this time seem to take any interest in how
they understood the relationship between their philosophy and their faith.

It was not of course that she did not retain strong philosophical commitments. When later on she resumed her philosophical work, it became evident that she had never set aside her most basic phenomenological convictions. And she had remained a realist, continuing to reject that in Husserl's
work which she, like Ingarden, took to be a return to idealism. Both philosophically and politically she was committed to a denial of some central
Marxist theses. But these commitments and rejections became tacit. She no
longer made explicit philosophical statements. Why not?

There are, I suggest, two explanations, one that she herself gave at the
time and one that she did not give, but which in retrospect assumes a certain
importance. Her own reason she expressed in a letter to a Dominican sister
in 1928: "Immediately before, and for a good while after my conversion, I
was of the opinion that to lead a religious life meant one had to give up all
that was secular and to live totally immersed in thoughts of the Divine. But

gradually I realized that something else is asked of us in this world and that, even in the contemplative life, one may not sever the connection with the world" (op. cit., Letter no. 45).

Given this, why look for any other reason? Perhaps because for anyone who had been as engaged with philosophical enquiry as Stein had been, it must have been difficult not to have philosophical thoughts, even if she believed strongly that the impulse to have them should be suppressed. But in Stein's case there were two aspects of her engagement with philosophy which would have made it both prudent and easier to defer any continuation of her philosophical enquiries. First, she had perhaps by then gone as far with what purely phenomenological enquiry can afford as it is possible to do. I do not mean by this that there was not more phenomenological work to be done in many of those areas to which she had given her attention, but rather that the limitations inherent in phenomenology as a method of philosophical enquiry had begun to show up in her work. It was becoming clear that her phenomenological enquiries, that any phenomenological enquiries, needed to be complemented and perhaps corrected by work done from some alternative philosophical standpoint.

Secondly, in part perhaps because of this, but in part for other reasons, she could not have known as yet what to say philosophically about her new experiences and commitments. They could not be adequately accommodated within the scheme of concepts through which she had hitherto understood the world, herself, and the existence or nonexistence of God. Yet she did not at this time have any alternative way of thinking about them. So that even if she had wanted to open up new philosophical enquiries, as Reinach, Rosenzweig and Lukács had all done, she would have had to fall silent. And this is to her credit. Falling silent is generally not something that philosophers are good at and perhaps it should be done more often.

I turn then to the third question that I posed: what is it in the experience of each of them that makes them either theist or atheist in the interpretation of their experience? Rosenzweig wrote in *The Star of Redemption*, "Man is no more capable of proof than are the world and God. If knowledge tries to prove one of these three, then it necessarily loses itself in the Nothing" (p. 63). And later he wrote about truth that "It is not some concept for elucidating God's essence. . . . To the contrary, God is himself the clear light which elucidates the truth" (p. 388).

We do not, that is, begin with some adequate grasp of the concepts of knowledge and of truth and in the light of these pass judgment on whether or not we know something of God or whether or not it is true that God exists, but rather it is from our encounters with God—and with the world and with human beings—that we learn what it is to have knowledge and what truth is. So Rosenzweig is not committed to defending some inference from the world or human nature to God. And the experiences in which God confronts us are ones in which he confronts us directly. "The true prophet is not like the master of the great plagiarism who lets God speak. Rather he has only to open his mouth and God already speaks" (p. 178). What makes Rosenzweig a theist is that he takes himself to have heard God speak in the voices of others.

For the atheist nothing could count as hearing God speak. In the atheist's view, theistic believers project onto something that they hear or see or otherwise experience what they take to be some revelatory mark of the divine. In a theistic view, atheists prescind from their experience and erase from what is presented to them that in it which would otherwise have left them unable to refuse to acknowledge God's presence. So, where Rosenzweig argued that the conceptual mythology of idealism prevented those who were in its grasp from recognizing what was plainly presented to them as the realities of God, the world and human beings, Lukács argued that the conceptual mythology of idealism was the latest historical stage in a sequence of illusions which had concealed the deceptive character and the social function of theistic belief and practice.

Both Lukács and Rosenzweig saw themselves as having been victims of an illusion that they had now unmasked, although they were in radical disagreement about what it was that that illusion had obscured. Lukács later in life believed that even after his movement to a Marxist position he had still been to an important extent the victim of an "abstract and idealistic conception of praxis" (op. cit., p. xix) and had failed to grasp the truth of "the materialist view of nature that brings about the really radical separation of the bourgeois and socialist outlooks" (p. xvii), with the result that *History and Class Consciousness* was deeply infected with error that survived from his past outlook.

Rosenzweig likewise stigmatized his past philosophical allegiance as abstract and idealist. And, like Lukács, he identified Hegel as the source of some of his central errors. In both cases the movement out of illusion required a change of fundamental philosophical standpoint. It is here that the great difference of both from Stein appears. She was given no reason by her conversion to move away from any of the fundamental philosophical positions that she had adopted. Of her phenomenological colleagues, some—including Husserl—believed in God, some did not. And, unlike both Rosenzweig and Lukács, she did not think of her previous philosophical commitments as obstacles that had stood between her and what she now took to be truth. She did understand from very early on that her new religious and theological commitments themselves posed crucial philosophical questions. But these were not for the moment questions for her.

I emphasized earlier how in the stage of Stein's life that preceded her conversion, two questions had been central and urgent: Of what communities should I make myself a part? And together with whom, in dialogue with whom, should I carry forward my thinking and my personal formation? It was these questions that were answered for Stein by her conversion, so that it was in the contexts provided by a range of Catholic communities and associations that Stein now thought her own way forward. That did not preclude continuing in reflective conversation with members of her family, with older friends, and more particularly with her philosophical colleagues.

Their responses to her conversion varied. Ingarden was sympathetic, anxious only that she should not be lost to philosophy. With Husserl, her good relations, reestablished very soon after she had resigned as his assistant, continued remarkably unchanged. Lipps had been for some time absent and silent, although he must have disapproved. Conrad-Martius was of course her now devoutly Lutheran godmother. Only Fritz Kaufmann, himself a Jew, broke off all relations with her. She and he had been very close. She had written regularly to him while he was serving in the German army and had, in letters, told him the whole story of the fiasco over her attempted *Habilitation*. She had plainly not expected the strength of his reaction and it was very painful to her. She and he had earlier had a falling out over the conflicts that had arisen within Husserl's circle, especially between Husserl and Lipps, and Kaufmann had accused her of arrogance and of failing him as a friend (op. cit., Letters 32 and 32a). So that when she wrote to him once more in 1925, after five years in which they had not corresponded, let alone met face to face, she must have been surprised, as well as extraordinarily pleased, when he replied with warmth and friendship, a friendship that continued to be close until 1936, when Kaufmann, in order to escape the Nazi persecution, left Germany first for England and then for the United States, where his wife and children succeeded in joining him.

17

Philosophy Deferred

In the letter to Fritz Kaufmann which I quoted earlier (*Self Portrait in Letters, 1916–1962*, Letter no. 38a), Stein recounts how, after two years of teaching, "I wanted to get at something bigger, namely a critical examination of St. Thomas. I did make a start with the study of the *Quaestiones Disputatae*, but so far the necessary continuity has not been established." And in the letter to Sister Callista Kopf, O.P., from which I also quoted (Letter no. 45), she wrote, "that it is possible to worship God by doing scholarly research is something I learned, actually, only when I was busy with St. Thomas." It was about this time that she met the Jesuit, Erich Przywara, who first enlisted her services as translator into German of Newman and, only a very little later, as translator of Aquinas's *Quaestiones Disputatae de Veritate*. It was in doing this work that she first came to terms with Aquinas's thought. By the way she organized the text as well as by her own comments, she produced what is at once a translation and a commentary, Aquinas rendered into a modern German philosophical idiom, Aquinas made as accessible as possible to phenomenological readers. To this the response of some Thomists was that Aquinas read phenomenologically is no longer Aquinas. And among them was at least one who had given her some assistance with the work.

This was the Cologne Dominican, Laurentius Siemer, who accused her of a quite inadequate knowledge of Aquinas and of consequent failures in translation. "No one knows better than I how little versed I am in Thomism," wrote Stein in reply. (See Maria Adele Herrmann, *Die Speyerer Jahre von Edith Stein*, Speyer: Pilger, 1990, p. 111, and op. cit., Letter no. 184. The translation was not completed until 1929—Stein continued throughout this period with her full-time teaching duties—and was published in two volumes in 1931 with a preface by the German Thomist historian, Martin Grabmann, who situated her

work in relation to the variety of modern Thomisms, each responding to its encounters with some type of modern philosophy. She received Siemer's letter
in 1934, when she was already a Carmelite.)

What had offended Siemer was the extent to which Stein's interpretation
of Aquinas was a reading or misreading of Aquinas's text in phenomenological terms. But Stein had also and at the same time embarked on a corrective
reinterpretation of phenomenology in Thomistic terms. What Thomism clarified for her in a new way was what Thomists have taken to be—and I believe rightly—the necessary incompleteness and one-sidedness of the phenomenological enterprise. Her new grasp of this incompleteness and
one-sidedness carried further insights that had already informed some of her
earlier work and, as I noticed earlier, she was far from alone among the phenomenologists of her generation in recognizing it. But as to what was
needed to remedy this incompleteness and one-sidedness there was considerable disagreement.

Conrad-Martius was and remained the closest to Stein in her views. Stein
had already drawn on her thoughts about the nature of human, animal and
plant souls in the second of the two treatises and, like Stein, Conrad-Martius
found herself compelled by her investigations to raise questions that took her
beyond phenomenology. But it was Ingarden who was to pursue these questions most systematically and in the greatest depth. Because, in Ingarden's
view, what is presented to us in consciousness depends on what kinds of objects there are and can be, we have to begin by understanding what it is to
be something, what it is to be a kind, and what it is to be possible or actual.
And, apart from his work on aesthetics, the development of an ontology
which was prior to and independent of phenomenology—unlike Husserl's
ontology—was Ingarden's major preoccupation throughout his long philosophical career.

Both Conrad-Martius and Ingarden drew on both Aristotle and the
scholastics, but neither of them confronted what became Stein's task, that of
bringing to bear on one and the same set of problems the very different resources of the phenomenological and the Thomistic traditions. And it is important that Stein's primary focus was on the problems, problems which for
the most part she had already identified during her years of philosophical apprenticeship between 1913 and 1922. We can distinguish at least four problem areas within which Stein was to pursue enquiry, when she resumed her
philosophical activities after 1925, each one of them, although to varying degrees, already defined for her by her earlier philosophical work or her life-
experiences or both.

The first of these problem areas is that in which questions about the limits
and limitations of the phenomenological enterprise arise. The 1929 volume
of the *Jahrbuch für Philosophie und phänomenologische Forschung* was
published as a *Festschrift* for Husserl, in celebration of his seventieth birth-

day. Heidegger edited the *Festschrift*, which included Stein's "An Attempt to contrast Husserl's phenomenology and the philosophy of St. Thomas Aquinas." She had originally submitted her essay in the form of an imaginary dialogue between Husserl and Aquinas, but Heidegger found this form unacceptable and asked her to rewrite it (both versions are in *Knowledge and Faith*, tr. W. Redmond, Washington, DC: ICS Publications, 2000). In it Stein took up a position which was not only critical of Husserl, but which affronted Ingarden. For she argued that faith affords a kind of knowledge that can be brought to bear on philosophical questions. And she noted at once that "if the modern philosopher positively insists from the outset that philosophy of religion should be regarded as a matter of reason and not faith, it would naturally appeal to him even less that faith should have a say in other areas of philosophy" (op. cit., p. 15). And indeed it was Ingarden's deeply regretful view that, insofar as Stein argued from premises derived from her Catholic faith, she became a religious thinker and ceased to be a philosopher ("Über die philosophischen Forschungen Edith Steins," *Freiburger Zeitschrift für Philosophie und Theologie*, 26, 1979, p. 468). So just what was Stein's claim and did it justify Ingarden's verdict?

Stein was concerned with a particular, if large philosophical problem, that of how to determine the limits of reason, or rather of natural reason. By natural reason Stein means reason uninformed by faith, and she speaks of reason informed by faith as supernatural reason. She noted that Kant had set himself the task of marking the limits of reason, but that he had taken as self-evident that reason—or what she calls natural reason—must determine its own limits. And this appeared to her a paradoxical claim. "One might ask whether, to be able to solve the problem, reason would need some Archimedean fulcrum outside itself—and how it could get out there" (op. cit., p. 16). That is, if natural reason is able to demarcate its own boundaries and to say what lies within and what outside its territory, it must be able to view itself and its limitations from outside, that is, it must somehow or other transcend limits that, so it is claiming, cannot be transcended.

It follows that, if natural reason has limits and it is possible to determine what they are, this must be determined from some standpoint beyond natural reason. And so far at least, whether justified or not, Stein's argument—which, rightly or wrongly, she takes to be Thomistic—is as strictly philosophical as Husserl or Ingarden could want. It is with the next step, that of saying what that standpoint beyond natural reason is, that her view comes into conflict with theirs.

What in Stein's view faith-informed reason possesses, but natural reason lacks, is a certain kind of finality and certainty. Husserl had aimed at achieving complete finality and certainty by a method that would "eliminate all possible sources of error. It did away with fallacies in reasoning by renouncing all conclusions reached through mediate thinking and by allowing use of

immediately evident states of affairs only." She then notes Husserl's successive attempts at achieving such certainty and finality, at attaining "a knowledge that would be absolutely one with its object and hence safe from all
doubt," and concludes that "It is surely clear by now that from St. Thomas's
point of view this goal is unattainable" (p. 23).

Husserl's mistake was to suppose that human beings are capable of a kind
of knowledge possessed only by God: "for him being and knowing are one,
but for us they are separate" (p. 24). Natural reason can never provide the
certainty that belongs to divine knowledge. And not only this: the way of
natural reason "is endless, and this implies that it can never reach its goal but
only approach it step by step. Another consequence is that all human philosophy is bound to be fragmentary," unlike the fullness of truth that belongs
to divine knowledge (pp. 11–12).

How do we come to be aware of this contrast between the fragmentary
and incomplete character of the natural human understanding and God's
knowledge? We will only grasp it adequately when we attain the goal of our
life's journey in heaven, but "Something of what our mind will then see—
what it needs in order to avoid straying from its goal—has been imparted to
it through revelation" (p. 13). And it is because such truths of revelation can
only be apprehended by faith that we have to rely on premises provided by
faith in order to establish the contrast between Husserl's aspirations and
what is actually possible for natural human reason.

This is how Stein presents her argument and by so doing she certainly invited Ingarden's accusation. Moreover she takes her position to be that of
Aquinas, which it was not. Yet it is worth noting that Stein could have made
her case without arguing from premises provided by faith. Consider an argument advanced by Maritain against Descartes. Maritain's thesis is that what
Descartes presents to us as characteristics of the human mind are in fact characteristics of an angelic intelligence and he concludes that Descartes has misunderstood human intelligence. Yet no one has to believe that there are angels, either to understand Maritain's point or to be convinced by it. All that
Maritain needs for his argument is a conception of angelic intelligence that is
fully accessible to natural human reason and all that Stein requires for her argument is a similar conception of God's knowledge, a conception of the
characteristics that God's mind and knowledge would have to have, *if* he existed. Her argument, as I have interpreted it, does not require as a premise
that God exists.

This interpretation of Stein's argument is not of course sufficient to ap-
pease Ingarden. For Stein insisted, "If faith makes accessible truths unattainable by any other means, philosophy . . . cannot forego them without renouncing its universal claim to truth" (p. 17) and she made it clear that she
did believe that faith makes accessible truths to which we cannot attain by
any other means. Faith's principal contribution to the *Weltanschauung* of

scholastic philosophers is "largely knowledge of facts" (p. 35), facts that have to be taken into account by a metaphysician, such as Aquinas, in providing "the broadest possible picture of *this* world" (p. 34), the actual world that we inhabit.

Husserl had argued that phenomenology has a subject matter that is peculiarly its own and that the natural sciences have quite another. Stein by contrast takes it that the enquiries of phenomenology, like the enquiries of the Thomist, are complemented by the findings of the natural sciences, each contributing to philosophy's overall descriptive task, a task that proceeds through stages towards a goal that will never be finally achieved, so that philosophy can never be fully systematic, but is always in some respects a fragmented and untidy set of enquiries. And Stein came to understand her own philosophical vocation within this overall perspective as that of contributing to the formulation and solution of particular problems. So she was to put behind her the kind of large general reflections about the nature of philosophy in which she engaged in her essay for Husserl's *Festschrift*.

Her work in a second area of continuing philosophical interest had as its starting-point the account of the structure of the individual personality that she had given in the two treatises. She reflected further on mind, body, soul and their relationship, both in *Finite and Eternal Being* (translated from *Endliches und Ewiges Sein: Versuch eines Aufstiegs zum Sinn des Seins*, published as the second volume of *Edith Steins Werke*, Freiburg im Breisgau: Verlag Herder, 1986, by Kurt F. Reinhardt, Washington, DC: ICS Publications, 2002) and in *The Science of the Cross* (translated from *Kreuzeswissenschaft: Studie über Joannes a Cruce*, published as the first volume of *Edith Steins Werke*, Freiburg im Breisgau: Verlag Herder, 1983, by Josephine Koeppel, O.C.D., Washington, DC: ICS Publications, 2002). *Finite and Eternal Being* was developed out of *Potenz und Akt*, which she wrote in 1931, when she was considering the possibility of once again submitting a *Habilitationsschrift*, this time at Freiburg. It was completed in 1937. *The Science of the Cross* was completed just before she was arrested and sent to her death in 1942.

In both books she renews the enquiries of the two treatises by drawing upon a much richer set of conceptual and other resources. In *Finite and Eternal Being*, she makes use of Aristotelian and Thomistic concepts. In *The Science of the Cross*, she provides a phenomenological commentary on the reports by John of the Cross of the stages that the soul experiences in its progress towards union with God, but since the vocabulary used by John of the Cross is itself informed by scholastic concepts, some of the issues raised in *Finite and Eternal Being* recur in *The Science of the Cross*. What would be instructive—and not just for the study of Edith Stein's thought—would be a systematic comparison of what is said on these matters in the two treatises with what is said in the later writings.

For example, in the first of the two treatises, on psychic causality, Stein discussed experiences of weariness and dullness and their relationship to the ebb and flow of life-power, of energy, in order to identify both the causal relationships that hold between different elements in the stream of an individual consciousness and the impact of causal factors external to consciousness. In doing so she distinguished the 'I' that is internal to any experience, the 'I' that makes of any feeling or willing or desiring an 'I feel' or 'I will' or 'I want' from the 'I' that is *Das Psychische* (p. 23; Marianne Sawicki, who translates *'Das Psychische'* as 'That which is sentient' notes how at this point she is distinguishing her position from Husserl's). But in *Finite and Eternal Being* she advances the discussion of the ego and its relationship to experience by providing it with a quite new context, one in which all experience is ascribed to a subject whose unity of body and soul is characterized in terms of Aristotelian and Thomistic concepts of form and matter. It is not that Stein is now able to resolve problems that she had identified earlier, but rather that her statement of those problems has itself become both more complex and more focused.

Where *The Science of the Cross* is concerned, the contrast with the two treatises is of a different order. In the second treatise, Stein had said that sensory pain and pleasure may wholly engross the 'I''s attention, yet do not invade its depths (p. 163). She does not develop this suggestive remark further, but in *The Science of the Cross* she presents John of the Cross's account of how those who have freed themselves from desire for and attachment to temporal goods discover a new kind of pleasure in them, a pleasure that is not available to those who are greedy for those goods. And this implies not necessarily a different, but certainly a more complex relationship between pleasure and pain on the one hand and what occurs in the depth of the soul with respect to the ordering of our desires on the other. If we juxtapose these two short passages from very different periods in Stein's thought, over twenty years apart, what we become aware of is that sixty years later we still do not have an adequate phenomenology of pleasures, pains and desires in all their variety and of the different roles and functions that these may have at different stages in someone's progress towards the achievement of her or his final good. Such a phenomenology would not only be valuable for its own sake, but any attempt to provide it would involve carrying further just those conceptual enquiries into the relationship of body, soul, mind, will, memory and the passions with which Stein was concerned in *Finite and Eternal Being*.

So far I have ascribed to Stein a twofold agenda deriving from her philosophical work before 1922: first, to develop a conception of philosophy's methods and goals that can accommodate both what needs to be learned from Husserl's phenomenology and what needs to be learned from Aquinas; and, secondly, to understand how the different parts and aspects of the individual human being relate to one another. This latter enquiry she could not pursue without attending to a third question, one which had become increasingly urgent for her ever since her work on empathy. It is the question of what it is that constitutes the unity of a human being, what it is that makes an individual *this* particular individual and no one else. In the second treatise she had raised the question of the sources of individuality, of the distinctive flavor and style of the particular qualities that particular individuals exhibit. And this question is reopened in *Finite and Eternal Being*. Here she made constructive use of work on the relationship between particularity and essence by Jean Hering, a fellow student in her Göttingen days, whose dissertation (*Bemerkungen über das Wesen, die Wesenheit und die Idee*) had been published by Husserl in the *Jahrbuch* for 1921. But she now also attempted to answer the question of what constitutes the particularity of individual human beings.

A fourth area of enquiry can be approached through Stein's concerns about death and dying. What she had to say philosophically about death is contained in an appendix to *Finite and Eternal Being* in which she discusses Heidegger's philosophical positions, as these had been elaborated in works published between 1927 and 1929, especially in *Sein und Zeit*. This appendix was omitted by the editors when *Endliches und Ewiges Sein* was finally published in 1950 as the second volume of the collected works, but it was later published separately in the sixth volume. (It remains untranslated in English, but an excellent summary is in "Edith Stein and Martin Heidegger" by John Nota, S.J., in *Carmelite Studies*, Vol. IV, Washington, DC: ICS Publications, 1987.) Part of the interest of 'his appendix is in the background that it provides for Stein's discussions of Heidegger in a number of extended footnotes in *Finite and Eternal Being*. But it has an independent interest, not least for its critical evaluation of what Heidegger says about death and dying.

It is important that Stein, as a military nurse, had recurrent experience of what it is to be with someone when they are dying. And it is unsurprising that her disagreements with Heidegger over death and dying derive in part from her criticism of Heidegger's account of what it is to be with others. With her own future death Stein had come to terms in the course of becoming a Catholic and a Carmelite. She had been brought up in a household where death was a forbidden topic of conversation (see the report of her conversations with Father Günther Schulemann in Walstraud Herbstrith, *Edith Stein*, p. 40). But she seems to have looked forward to it without anxiety, including in her *Testament* a sentence commonly used by Carmelite sisters "I joyfully accept in advance the death God has appointed for me" and joking to another Carmelite that her death would give their sisters in Cologne good reason to say a Te Deum (op. cit., pp. 77 and 95). Yet, if her own death became unproblematic for Stein, how could death and dying become matter for a set of philosophical problems? They did so only because her conceptions of what it is to confront one's own death and of what it is to be with another as that other dies were both radically at odds with Heidegger's understanding of death in *Sein und Zeit*. After the publication of *Sein und Zeit* in 1927, Heidegger had become the most important philosophical presence in Germany. No philosopher, at least no German philosopher, could from then on avoid defining her or his positions in relation to Heidegger's, as Stein herself did, both in the footnotes to the text of *Finite and Eternal Being* and in the appendix.

"The dying of Others is not something which we experience in a genuine sense," wrote Heidegger in *Sein und Zeit* (tr. as *Being and Time* by John Macquarrie and Edward Robinson, New York: Harper & Row, 1962, 239, p. 282). Why not? Because "Dying is something that every Dasein itself must take upon itself" and the only dying that I can take upon myself is my own. "By its very essence death is in every case mine" (240, p. 223). In anticipating my own death I recognize Dasein for what it is and I can either yield to the fear and anxiety aroused by the prospect of my death or confront my coming death with resoluteness and authenticity.

Stein has two sets of criticisms of Heidegger's account. First, she believes that Heidegger is not open to the possibility of being with others in such a way as to be with them, to share with them, in their anticipation of their death. Here issues about what empathetic understanding of others can achieve, the very issues that Stein had examined in her doctored dissertation, are clearly relevant. But Stein also takes it that my anticipation of my own death can be and perhaps characteristically is informed by my experience of the death of others. We learn what it is to anticipate our own deaths from those others whose anticipation of their deaths we have in some significant way shared. If this is so, it is not just Heidegger's account of death and dying, but also his analyses of *Mitsein* and *Dasein* that are put in question, since these are presupposed by his account of death and dying.

Secondly Stein argues that Heidegger does not distinguish adequately two very different kinds of *Angst* elicited by the prospect of death. There is, says Heidegger, that in the face of which we are anxious and that about which we are anxious, but in the anticipation of my own death they are one and the same, in both cases that nothingness which I confront as I anticipate my own death (342–43, p. 393). Stein suggests that in fact there are two different objects of our anxiety and fear, and not just one. We are afraid *of* nothingness as a possibility, but we are also afraid *for* the loss of our being. The human being is such that he "desires to receive the ever new gift of Being. . . . Whatever gives him fullness, he does not want to leave, and he would like to *be* without end. . . ." ("Anhang," *Edith Steins Werke* VI, p. 110). It is just because it pleases us to be that we fear not to be, an aspect of *Dasein* to which Heidegger does not do justice, even although he does recognize that "care summons *Dasein* towards its ownmost potentiality-for-Being" (*Being and Time*, tr. J. Macquarrie and E. Robinson, New York: Harper & Row, 1962, p. 365).

Stein had a further quarrel with Heidegger's conception of *Dasein*. She follows Aquinas in holding that, if one has understood adequately what it is for any particular finite being, including oneself, to be, one will have understood that particular being as a dependent being. Finite being can only be adequately understood as a gift that we have received and the same is true of those aspects of our finite being that make us free and self-determined. This conception of our lives as gifts is as central to Stein's understanding of *Dasein* as it is alien to Heidegger's.

Stein thus added to her concern with the nature of philosophy's methods and goals, her attempt to map the interrelationships of various aspects of body, mind and *psyche*, and her enquiries into the unity and individuality of the human being, a concern with the nature of *Dasein*. And in an important way these were not distinct and separable preoccupations, but rather aspects of a single enterprise, one with both philosophical and theological dimensions, whose defining questions are: How is the finitude, the temporality and the particularity of human existence to be understood? And can it be understood except by its contrast with and its relationship to infinite and eternal being?

It was by her answers to these questions that Stein was to set herself against Heidegger. And a comparison with Heidegger is very much to the point in at least two respects. First, the trajectory of her career and the trajectory of Heidegger's career could not stand in sharper contrast. Heidegger begins as a Catholic and a Thomist, but moves to a rejection of all theologies. Stein, when she first begins her philosophical studies, is inimical to theology, but becomes a Catholic and, if not a Thomist, a student of Aquinas. Heidegger and Stein both aspire to move beyond Husserl, but they do so in incompatible ways, so that while Heidegger's rejection of traditional ontology is even more radical than Husserl's, Stein hopes to reconcile phenomenology and Thomistic ontology.

Heidegger puts behind him all the relationships that he had formed in Husserl's circle, and in the future enters into relationships only with those who are prepared to acknowledge his superiority. Stein continues to learn from her contemporaries and especially from Conrad-Martius and from Ingarden. (Would that Heidegger had been prepared to learn from Ingarden, especially his great treatise on ontology! It is one of the philosophical tragedies of Heidegger's life that he never learned to speak or read Polish.) Continuing friendships played a part in Stein's life that they never played in Heidegger's. And Heidegger deprived himself of just those philosophical and moral resources that would have enabled him to recognize the unqualified evil of National Socialism, while Stein at an early stage had identified signs and precursors of that evil.

It goes without saying that Heidegger is an incomparably greater philosopher than Stein. But the history of philosophy is punctuated by the interventions of genuinely great philosophers who have redirected and misdirected philosophical enquiry. And if, as I take to be the case, Heidegger was one of these, then the question of what it would be to set out from Husserl's starting-point in the *Logical Investigations*, to criticize and to reject some of the central theses of *Ideen*, and to open up a philosophical path forward which is other than and alternative to Heidegger's becomes of some philosophical importance.

It was, I believe, Reinach who first and best understood what needed to be done next, if one made one's starting-point the *Logical Investigations*. And it has been one of the two aims of this book to exhibit the continuity of Stein's thought with Reinach's. A second aim has been to explain why, in order to go beyond Reinach, Stein needed to go beyond phenomenology. It was a providential accident that she encountered the thought of Aquinas when she did and so became able to open up just those questions that needed to be asked about the relationship of Thomistic philosophy to phenomenology. And here it is Stein's questions that I am praising rather than her answers. The answers are characteristically of great interest, but they leave a lot of room for disagreement and very often they provoke further questions. Stein's writings, both early and late, are not so much an invitation to agreement as they are an invitation to rethink in her company the issues with which she was concerned. And, since she generally and characteristically identified those issues that were and are philosophically crucial, this makes her a significantly more important thinker than she has often been taken to be.

That importance of course attaches more and more obviously to her later writings, to those writings that I have not discussed in this book. But in the reading of Stein, as in the reading of any philosopher, it is necessary to understand where she begins and why she begins where she does. So that, although this book does not take us beyond Stein's beginnings, it may nonetheless provide something of an introduction not only to her philosophical writings before her conversion, but also to those later works to which her early writings were a prologue.

Index

Metaphysische Gespräche (Conrad-
Martius), 125
Meyer, Toni, 68, 69
Mill, John Stuart, 77–78
Mind, 40
mind-body relationship, 61
Mitsein, 184
modal necessity, 51
Mommsen, Theodor, 12
Moskiewicz, George, 14
motivated inclinations, 115–16
motivations, 113–14
Müller, G., 16, 74
Münsterberg, Hugo, 117

Nalanda, 4
Natorp, Paul, 36, 41, 48, 100
natural necessity, 58
natural reason, 179–80
nature, disclosure of, 47
Nazi Germany: destruction of Jüdisch-
Theologisches Seminar by, 12;
expulsion of Jewish professionals by,
13; regime of, 5
necessity, modal and material, 51
negative judgment, 18
Nelson, Leonard, 36, 63–64
Neo-Kantianism, 19, 22, 27, 33–37, 40, 41,
47, 48, 63, 131, 132, 148, 152, 154, 160
Neopositivism, 37
Neumann, Friedrich, 16
New American Bible, 167
Newman, Cardinal, 177
The New Thinking (Rosenzweig), 149
Newton, Isaac, 31, 34–35
Newtonian mechanics, 31, 48
Nietzsche, Friedrich, 150

object of, 25–26
objects: categorical, 52; as goods, 137;
intentionality of, 46, 52; presentation
of, 46–47
"On Individual and Community" (Stein),
95
*On the Doctrine of the Content and
Object of Presentations*
(Twardowski), 23

ontology, 62, 140, 178, 185
Otto, Rudolf, 145, 164

Paradox, 150
Pedagogical Group, 14
perceptions, 47; first-person, 81, 82;
third-person, 81, 82
perceptual objects, 102
Petri, Elfride, 164
Pfänder, Alexander, 17, 134
Phaedo (Socrates), 72
Phänomenologie der Mystik (Walter),
145
*The Phenomenological Movement: A
Historical Introduction*
(Spiegelberg), 15
phenomenology, 6, 18, 41; concepts of,
47; focus of, 20–21; on linguistic
expressions, 44–45; practice of,
80–81, 117, 141, 144–45; standpoint
of, 45, 46–47, 60; theory of, 19–20; as
way of seeing, 20–21
Philo, 152
Philosophical Society, 18
philosophy: *Agrégation* in, 2;
contemporary discipline of, 2–3; of
everyday activities, 3, 4;
Habilitationsschrift of, 2, 17, 51;
theoretical and practical views of, 2;
as transforming or disruptive, 4;
views on state of affairs, 53–54
The Philosophy of Arithmetic (Husserl),
17
Plato, 3, 72
Platonism, 43
Polish philosophy, 23
polite society, 130
Potenz und Akt (Stein), 181
Practice in Christianity (Kierkegaard),
166–67
presentation, of an object, 46–47
Principia (Newton), 31
prolegomena, 41
promising, act of, 58, 59; acts/states of,
55–56; claim in, 55; obligation and,
55; as philosophical commonplace,
55; as social act, 56

About the Author

Alasdair MacIntyre is research professor of philosophy at the University of Notre Dame. He previously taught at a number of British and American universities, most recently at Duke University. He is the author of *A Short History of Ethics*, *After Virtue*, and *Dependent Rational Animals*.

Made in the USA
Middletown, DE
19 December 2023

46219942R00116